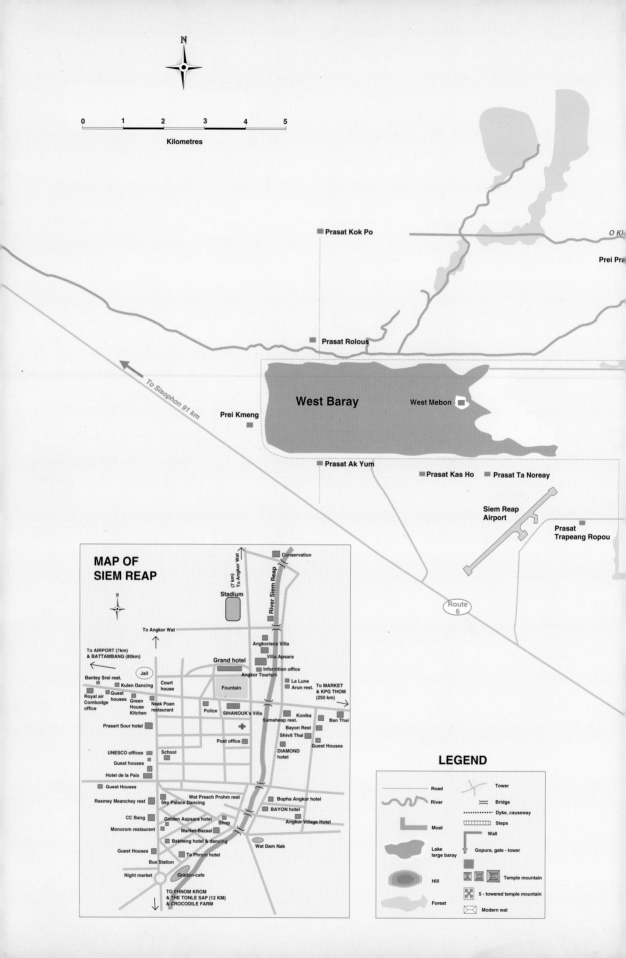

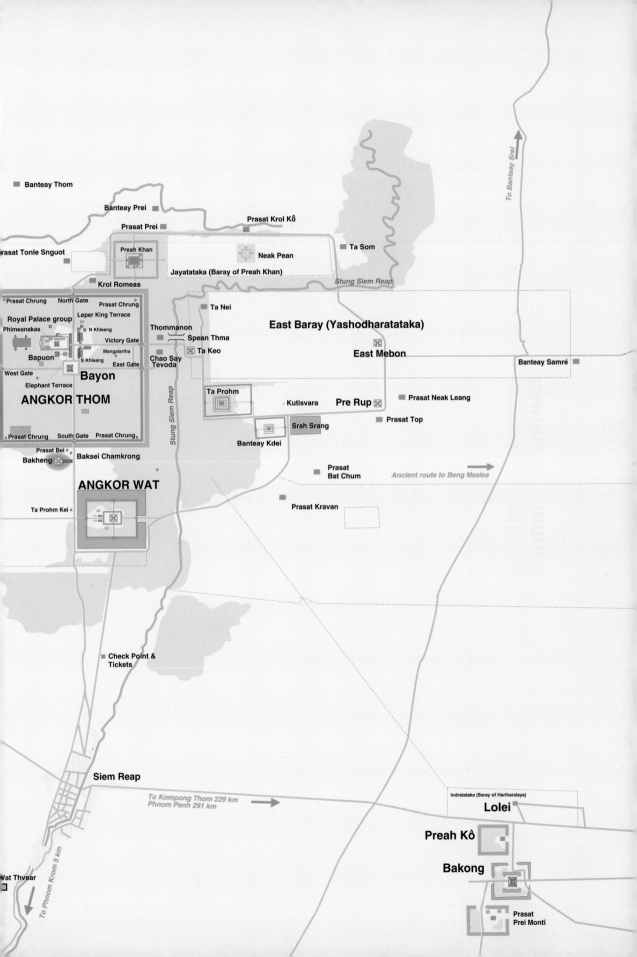

Banteay Thom

Banteay Prei

Prasat Prei

Prasat Krol Kô

Prasat Tonle Snguot

Preah Khan

Neak Pean

Ta Som

Krol Romeas

Jayatataka (Baray of Preah Khan)

Stung Siem Reap

Ta Nei

Prasat Chrung   North Gate   Prasat Chrung

Royal Palace group   Leper King Terrace

Phimeanakas   N Khleang

Thommanon

East Baray (Yashodharatataka)

Spean Thma

Ta Keo

Victory Gate

Mangalartha

East Mebon

Bapuon   S Khleang

Chao Say   East Gate   Tevoda

Banteay Samré

West Gate   Bayon

Elephant Terrace

ANGKOR THOM

Stung Siem Reap

Ta Prohm

Prasat Neak Leang

Kutisvara   Pre Rup

Prasat Chrung   South Gate   Prasat Chrung

Prasat Top

Srah Srang

Prasat Bei

Banteay Kdei

Bakheng   Baksei Chamkrong

ANGKOR WAT

Prasat
Bat Chum

Ancient route to Beng Mealea

Ta Prohm Kei

Prasat Kravan

Check Point &
Tickets

Siem Reap

Indratataka (Baray of Hariharalaya)

To Kompong Thom 229 km
Phnom Penh 291 km

Lolei

Preah Kô

To Banteay Srei

Bakong

Wat Thvear

To Phnom Krom 5 km

Prasat
Prei Monti

ANCIENT ANGKOR

ANCIENT

ANGKOR

MICHAEL FREEMAN

CLAUDE JACQUES

WEATHERHILL

First published and distributed in USA
and Canada in 1999 by Weatherhill Inc.
41 Monroe Turnpike, Trumbull, CT 06611

British Library Cataloguing-in-
Publication Data.
A catalogue record for this book is
available from the British Library.

ISBN 0 8348 0426 3

Editor and Publisher Narisa
Chakrabongse
Design Bradbury and Williams
Production Supervision Paisarn
Piemmettawat

Printed and bound in Thailand by
Amarin Printing and Publishing Public
Co. Ltd

Previous pages: Angkor Wat at sunrise

Contents

INTRODUCTION

We have both published large illustrated books on Angkor, separately and together, the latest being our joint effort *Angkor: Cities and Temples*. As a result of this collaboration, we decided to work together on a smaller book, one which would work as a guide, light enough to carry and organised in a way useful to the visitor, but also beautifully produced and illustrated as a book in its own right.

Angkor is visitable today largely because of the efforts of the archaeologists from the Ecole Française d'Extreme Orient. From 1908 there have been an illustrious line of *conservateurs*, beginning with Jean Commaille, and it was he who wrote the first guide to Angkor in 1912. This became something of a tradition, and guidebooks by successive *conservateurs* Henri Marchal, Henri Parmentier and Maurice Glaize followed.

These were all classics in their day, but the last edition of the last of these by Maurice Glaize was published nearly four decades ago. Two strong arguments convinced us that the time is right for a modern guide. After a hiatus of two decades caused by the dreadful events of the Vietnam War and its aftermath, significant research has been carried out, with important new information as a result. The excavations around the royal enclosure at the heart of Angkor Thom are just one example.

Furthermore, modern printing technology has made it possible and affordable to use colour photographs throughout the text, something that in the past was out of the question. Quite apart from its size, Angkor contains sites of unusual complexity, some of them further confused by the tropical forest setting. Simply locating, let alone interpreting, certain bas-relief panels takes some effort, and if any of the world's major monuments calls for visual assistance, it is here.

What we have tried to do, then, is to incorporate the latest knowledge and research, to present the material step by step through the temple complexes, and to give as many visual references as necessary to help in the description of these rich and sometimes labyrinthine sites. There will inevitably be revisions, for while Angkor appears so monumental to the visitor, the archaeological work surrounding it is on-going, and as excavation and historical research reveals new information, we will incorporate this in future editions.

Michael Freeman and Claude Jacques, 1999

HISTORY

Traditionally, the history of Angkor as we know it from inscriptions and the existing temples begins in the ninth century, when the young king Jayavarman II declared himself the supreme sovereign and established his capital first near present-day Roluos, and a little later in the Kulen Mountains. Up to that point, Khmer history had been that of small independent states occasionally consolidating into larger empires, but never for long. It took a conqueror to establish the beginnings of one of Southeast Asia's most powerful empires.

The Angkor region, bordering the Great Lake with its valuable supply of water, fish, and fertile soil, has been settled since neolithic times, as is known from stone tools and ceramics found there, and from the identification of circular habitation sites from aerial photographs. For the whole Khmer country, there is more descriptive evidence from the accounts of the Chinese, who began to trade and explore the commercial opportunities of mainland Southeast Asia in the early centuries of the Christian era. The picture is one of small town-states, moated, fortified and frequently in conflict with each other. The Chinese called the principal country with which they traded

Suryavarman II on top of his elephant from the Great Procession relief, Angkor Wat

Funan; it had a strategic importance in controlling the sea routes around the Mekong delta and the Gulf of Thailand. In particular it controlled the narrow Isthmus of Kra – the neck of the Malay Peninsula – which connected eastern Asia with India. Indeed, it was trade with India that gave the Khmers their primary cultural contacts, and introduced them to Hinduism and Buddhism. Khmer religious beliefs, iconography, art and architecture all stemmed directly from India, and this had a profound influence on the development of its civilisation.

The 6th century sees the first historical evidence from local inscriptions. At around this time, the Chinese accounts begin to write of a kingdom called 'Chenla' in the interior, but this is a Chinese rather than a Khmer name. In the second half of the century there is a record of a city called Bhavapura, with its king, Bhavavarman I extending his rule from near the present-day site of Kompong Thom to at least as far as Battambang in the west. He was succeeded by his brother, who ruled as Mahendravarman, who in turn was succeeded by his son, Isanavarman I. These three kings progressively conquered the Khmer part of Funan, while the western part was taken by other peoples, in

particular the Mons of the kingdom of Dvaravati to the W of Bangkok. Isnavarman I was responsible for the temple at Sambor Prei Kuk, establishing the first of the pre-Angkorean styles of architecture. Under Isanavarman's son, Bhavavarman II, who took the throne in 628, the empire disintegrated back into small states, and it took until 654 for Jayavarman I, a grandson of Isanavarman I, from one of these princedoms, to reconquer much of the territory. There is evidence that he ruled from Aninditapura, close to Angkor. On his death, the empire again collapsed, and his successors, including his daughter Jayadevi, the only ancient Khmer queen, controlled only the small kingdom of Aninditapura. The country remained this way until the end of the 8th century, when Jayavarman II became king in 790.

Jayavarman II's conquests, first of Vyadhapura (SE of Cambodia), then Sambhupura (present-day Sambor), then N as far as Wat Phu, and finally of Aninditapura, established his power. He settled first at Hariharalaya, an ancient capital in the region of what is now Roluos, but then, trying to go further NW, experienced an unknown setback which resulted in him relocating to the Kulen Plateau, some 30 km NE of Angkor. Here he pronounced himself 'world emperor' in 802, but it was many years before he was strong enough to move his capital back to Hariharalaya on the shores of the Great Lake, where he died in 835.

His son Jayavarman III succeeded him on his death. He seems to have built the laterite pyramid of Bankong, which his succesor, Indravarman I, had clad in standstone. The date of his death is unknown, but most probably his successor took the throne with violence. This king remodelled his capital, building in his palace the

Cham warships on the Tonlé Sap,
probably during the last battle
sometime before 1181, when they were
defeated.

Preah Kô temple, dedicated in 880 and improving Bakong. He also
began the *baray* of Indratataka, which his son Yasovarman I completed
after he came to power in 889. This accession was a bloody one,
involving a struggle with the crown prince, his brother, and destruction
of the palace. Therefore he decided to move his capital to Angkor.

In his ambitious plan, he selected the hill of Bakheng as the centre of
the new city of Yasodharapura, and as the site of his state temple, first
levelling the top. Surrounding the hill, the earth banks of the city limits
were 4 km on each side, and traces remain today on the S and W. In
addition, Yasovarman built the East Baray, a great reservoir more than
7 km long and almost 2 km wide. Earlier in 893, he had built the Lolei
temple in the middle of the Indratatak and the temples of Phnom
Krom and Phnom Bok were possible built by him. He died in 910. His
two sons, Harshavarman I and Isanavarman II, continued the dynasty,
but on the death of the latter, around 928, the capital abruptly moved
to Koh Ker, some 100 kilometres to the NE.

The background to this is obscure, but there was a change in the
royal succession, and the throne went to Jayavarman IV for at least
seven years. He probably owed allegiance to the Angkor kings, and it

is not known how he took the throne. Nevertheless, the scale of the
brick temple of Prasat Thom that he had built at Koh Ker shows that
he was rich and powerful. Having started a considerable building
programme there, he clearly decided to continue and make it his
capital. Many smaller temples were added, and a *baray*, all in the short
space of 20 years until the capital reverted to Angkor. The state temple
was a seven-storey sandstone pyramid, 35m high.

On his death, Jayavarman IV was succeeded, briefly, by his son
Harshavarman II, although an inscription makes it clear that this was
not the father's choice. Moreover, the succession was contested, and
after a reign of only three years, Harshavarman met what was probably
a violent end. He was succeeded, in 944, by his cousin Rajendravarman, king of the old kingdom of Bhavapura. He had, in fact, helped
Harshavarman II in his bid for power and, after the latter's death,
decided to seize power for himself.

Rajendravarman took the capital back to Angkor, but not to the city
that Yasovarman had created around the Bakheng. Instead, he placed
his state temple and palace some kilometres to the E, on the S bank of
the great East Baray. Pre Rup (961) was the state temple, and another
major construction was the 'island' temple of East Mebon (953) in the
middle of the *baray*. These temples were overseen by his chief architect
Kavindrarimathana, who built for himself Bat Chum and Srah Srang.
Other constructions in the same general area include Kutisvara. At the
same time, Rajendravarman strengthened his grip by declaring former
'kingdoms' under his rule to be 'provinces'. He also expanded his
empire, reconquering the lands ruled by Yasovarman I, and even
sending an expeditionary force to fight the Chams in the coastal areas
of what is now central Vietnam. Violent rivalry between the Khmers
and the Chams had been continuing for some time.

After Rajendravarman's death in 968, his son Jayavarman V
succeeded to the throne, moving the capital slighty to the W to a more
defensible location. Calling it Jayendranagari, he had a new state
temple built at its centre – Ta Keo. At this time, his priest and mentor
Yajñavaraha built the exquisite small temple of Banteay Srei, which
was dedicated in the last year of Rajendravarman's life. Jayavarman V's
reign, which lasted three decades, began with armed struggle to quell
rebellions, but eventually settled down to be relatively peaceful.

Jayavarman was succeeded by Udayadityavarman I, who ruled for
only a few months, after which there was a nine-year war between
Jayaviravarman and Suryavarman I, both pretending to have been
consecrated in 1002. The war ended around 1010 with the final victory
of Suryavarman I. This king built the Royal Palace at Angkor Thom
and, most probably, a new reservoir, the West Baray, measuring 8km x
2km and still in use.

He was succeeded by his son, Udayadityavarman II (1050-1066),
who built the Bapuon, a spectacular temple-mountain, and the West
Mebon in the middle of the West Baray. His younger brother
Harshavarman III (1066-about 1080) was the last of this dynasty; the
throne then changed hands to a line of kings who came from the
Khorat Plateau in present-day Thailand. After two reigns (Jayavarman
VI and Dharanindravarman, both brothers), a grandnephew seized
power – Suryavarman II, builder of Angkor Wat and commander of

KHMER RULERS
CHRONOLOGY OF KINGS AT ANGKOR

King	Temples begun	Temples rebuilt or added to
Jayavarman II	790-835	Rong Chen on Phnom Kulen, earlier shrine on the site of Kutisvara
Jayavarman III	835-877	Prei Monti, Trapeang Phong, Bakong
Indravarman I	877-c.886	Preah Kô, sandstone cladding of Bakong, Indratataka *baray*
Yasovarman I	889-c.915	Lolei, Bakheng, Prasat Bei, Thma Bay Kaek, earlier shrine on the site of Phimeanakas, Phnom Krom, Phnom Bok, East Baray
Harshavarman I	c.915 -923	Baksei Chamkrong, Prasat Kravan
Isanavarman II	923-c.928	
Jayavarman IV	c.928-c.941	Koh Ker site
Harshavarman II	C.941-944	
Rajendravarman	944-968	Pre Rup, East Mebon, Bat Chum, Kutisvara, Banteay Srei, earlier temple on the site of Banteay Kdei, Srah Srang, Baksei Chamkrong
Jayavarman V	968-c.1000	Ta Keo
Udayadityavarman I	1001-1002	
Jayaviravarman	1002-1010	North Khleang, continuation of Ta Keo
Suryavarman I	1002-1049	South Khleang, Preah Vihear in the Dangrek Mountains, Phimeanakas and the Royal Palace, Suryaparvata at Phnom Chisor, Preah Khan at Kompong Svay, West Baray, Wat Phu
Udayadityavarman II	1050-1066	Bapuon, West Mebon
Harshavarman III	1066/7-1080	
Jayavarman VI	1080-c.1107	Phimai in present-day Thailand
Dharanindravarman I	1107-1112	
Suryavarman II	1113-c.1150	Angkor Wat, Thommanon, Chao Say Tevoda, Banteay Samré, Phnom Rung in present-day Thailand, Beng Mealea,
Yasovarman II	c.1150-1165	Beng Mealea, Chao Say Tevoda, Banteay Samré, Bakong
Tribhuvanadityavarman	c.1165-1177	
Jayavarman VII	1181-c.1220	Ta Prohm, Preah Khan, Jayatataka baray, Neak Pean, Ta Som, Ta Nei, Banteay Chhmar in NW Cambodia, Angkor Thom, Prasats Chrung, Bayon, Elephant Terrace, Ta Prohm Kel, Hospital Chapel, Krol Kô, Srah Srang, Royal Palace
Indravarman II	c.1220-1243	Prasats Suor PratTa Prohm, Banteay Kdei, Ta Som, Ta Nei
Jayavarman VIII	c.1243-1295	Mangalartha, Preah Palilay?Bayon, Ta Prohm, Preah Khan, Prasats Chrung, Angkor Wat, Bapuon, Chao Say Tevoda, Banteay Samré, Beng Mealea, Terrace of the Leper King, Elephant Terrace, Preah Pithu, Royal Palace
Srindravarman	1295-1307	Ta Prohm, Preah Pithu, Preah Palilay
Srindrajayavarman	1307-1327	
Jayavarman Paramesvara	1327-	

many military campaigns to expand the empire. His rule, from 1112 to about 1150, marks the peak of Angkor's power and influence. Thereafter, there were increasing revolts in the provinces. There were both alliances and conflicts between some Khmer and Cham princes, rendering the political situation very confused. In 1165 the throne was taken by a usurper, Tribhuvanadityavarman, who was killed 12 years later when a Cham and Khmer group mounted a surprise naval attack from the Great Lake and took Angkor.

Jayavarman VII

This might have been the end of the city, had it not been for the return of a prince, later crowned as Jayavarman VII. After four years of fighting, he succeeded in driving out the Chams, beginning his reign in 1181 as the last great king of Angkor. A fervent Buddhist, unlike his predecessors who worshipped Hindu gods, Jayavarman VII crammed into his 30-year rule the largest building programme ever undertaken. His new city is the surviving Angkor Thom, centred on the Bayon. He was also responsible for Ta Prohm, Banteay Kdei and Preah Khan, among others, not to mention hundreds of temples, hospitals and other buildings across the empire.

This hurried, almost frenzied, building activity is generally considered as the last; but it is difficult to evaluate the part played by Indravarman II in the programme. Moreover, Jayavarman VIII, responsible for the destruction of so much Buddhist imagery, tried to restore and improve some important Hindu temples – Angkor Wat, Bapuon and the central plaza of Angkor Thom. Nothing else has survived at Angkor from later than the early 13th century, partly of course because many of the structures were perishable. After the rise of Theravada Buddhism only wooden temples were made and thus it is difficult to evaluate the wealth of Angkor at this time. The empire continued to prosper – a Chinese emissary, Zhou Daguan, left an intriguing account of the city and its riches in the years 1296-7. After this time, there was increased fighting with the newly-emerged Siamese kingdom. However, other factors may have been more important in its decline. One was the importance of trade for which Phnom Penh and Ayutthaya, the capital of the Siamese state, were much better suited. In the fifteenth century, new rulers emerged on the Mekong River, where modern Phnom Penh now stands. Nevertheless, the kingdom at Angkor endured until the end of the sixteenth century.

RELIGION

Why was it so easy for the indigenous people to adopt the gods the Indians had brought with them to Southeast Asia? It may well be imagined that the prosperity of the Indians with their methods was ascribed to divine protection, and that the Khmers and the Chams accordingly began to establish them in their temples. Moreover these foreign gods could readily find a place beside the local deities, as they had already done in India, within what was doubtless a very similar cosmology. Thus particular devotion was accorded to the gods Siva and Vishnu, and also to the Buddha. Siva, however, is the dominant figure, as he was long considered by the kings as supreme protector of their empire. It is thus to him that most of the temples are dedicated, and he in turn had to ensure the prosperity of the kingdom.

The proliferation of sects which flourished in India does not feature in the land of the Khmers, however. As in other domains, the Khmers were the assiduous pupils of their first masters, and do not seem to have sought to delve deeper into doctrines which perhaps remained somewhat alien to them, nor indeed to dispute them by proposing new ones. It is for this reason that only one or two sects of each of the Sivaite or Vishnuite 'religions' are known. Similarly it is probable that Buddhism, of which much less is known, was not broken down into

Garuda *at the centre of a lintel, Preah Kô*

numerous sects, although besides
Mahayana Buddhism of (the 'great
vehicle') which was more
widespread, or at least more visible
now, there is some early evidence
for the existence of simpler
followers of 'primitive' Buddhism.

The temples as seen today give
only a sketchy idea of the total
number of shrines which
bejewelled the land of the Khmers,
many of which must have
disappeared over the centuries.
They are in durable materials, and,
as such, they imply considerable
wealth on the part of their builders.
They were far from being the only
Hindu shrines in the Khmer
countryside, as others were built by
the less wealthy in perishable
materials. The inscriptions reveal
that sometimes there were years of
delay before enough funds were
availabe for a stone or laterite
shrine for a divinity, and doubtless,
some never saw the light of day
because the means were lacking.

*Siva's dance of destruction,
Banteay Srei*

The Khmers did not abandoned their indigenous deities, the masters
of the land and its abundance, human heroes who became guardian
spirits, and of course the protecting ancestors of each lineage. Evil
spirits also roamed the land, bringing sickness or death. All these
numerous and diverse divinities were worshipped, although obviously
with less complex rituals than those of the Indian gods, and similarly
their shrines would generally have been much simpler and built of
perishable materials, as are those which house them nowadays. They
were nevertheless of considerable importance in Khmer eyes and
probably evoked much more dread than the Indian gods, who were
naturally more remote, if only because of their ability to inflict
immediate retribution when they were annoyed. These divinities were
thus probably the subject of more regular attention, but not a single
shrine survives, nor even a description of their rituals – unless, of
course, it has gone unrecognised. While there are occasional allusions
to some of these divinities in the inscriptions they are as it were
accidental, since none of the texts is specifically intended for them.
This is why so little is known of the foremost local deity, the 'king of
the gods' who were the masters of the land, the renowned *Devaraja*,
'the god who is king', who was the counterpart of the Khmer 'king of
kings'. Much ink has flowed on the subject of this divinity, in inverse
proportion to the scanty and succinct references which exist in the
actual documents.

At the end of the twelfth century some short inscriptions occur
which give the names of the gods who inhabited the cellae of the

temple complexes at the time. Often, these inscriptions have been erased and replaced with others, which shows the mobility of the images. Occasionally they give the name of the donor of the statue, or that of the person on whom it was modelled. This type of information can also be found on the base of some of the bronze statues, and in rare cases the date of a statue's enshrining in a temple is also given.

Over the Khmer Empire as a whole, Hinduism dominated until the end of the 12th century, when it gave way to Mahayana Buddhism, although not for long. Both came from India, and although the exact means are in doubt, it is likely that Indian traders were the first to introduce their religion to Cambodia. Hinduism over the centuries had changed its focus, with different gods in ascendancy, but by the time it reached the Khmers there were two principal cults – that of Vishnu and that of Siva. One or other would be the Supreme god, while both these two gods were also part of the Hindu Trinity (the third was Brahma) which commanded a pantheon of lesser gods and had *inter alia* a complex relationship. They were connected in many of the same myths, acted partly in concert, partly in rivalry.

THE HINDU PANTHEON
Vishnu
In the Hindue Trinity, Vishnu is the Protector, the god who preserves universal order and fights to restore harmony. He is represented as a four-armed man, holding four attributes, or symbols: a conch shell, for sounding his victory over chaos, a discus, the invincible weapon given to him by Indra, a mace, symbol of his power, and, in Cambodia, a small ball, representing the Earth. His consort is Lakshmi, goddess of wealth and good fortune. Because he takes a particular interest in human affairs, he must often take on an earthly form to intervene. These various forms of Vishnu are known as *avatars*, and traditionally there are 10, known as Dashavatara, the Ten Incarnations, each taken on during one of Vishnu's descents to earth:

1st: As Matsya, in the form of a fish, to save mankind from the great flood at the beginning of creation.

2nd: As Kurma, a turtle, to support the Churning of the Sea of Milk in one creation myth.

3rd: As Varaha, a boar, to save the earth goddess Bhumi dragged to the bottom of the sea by the demon Hiranyaksha.

4th: As Narasimha, half-man, half-lion, he kills a tyrant king who believes himself to be immortal and who dares to forbid the worship of Vishnu.

5th: As Vamana, a dwarf, he confounds the demon king Bali who has acquired great power, and who condescendingly offers the god as much land as he can cover in three steps. Vamana transforms himself into a giant and takes

Opposite: Indra on his three-headed elephant Airavata, Banteay Srei

Vishnu as Kurma, the turtle supporting the Churning of the Sea of Milk, Angkor Wat

possession of heaven, earth and underworld.

6th: As Parashurama, a warrior who avenges the death of his father and restores the importance of the *brahmins.*

7th: As Rama, he defeats the forces of evil under the demon Ravana.

8th: As Krishna, he rights wrongs and brings happiness to the world.

9th: As Buddha, he helps direct mankind towards the right path of living. This *avatar* was invented as a means of putting Buddhism in a subordinate position.

10th: As Kalki, either riding a horse or as a horse, the future *avatar,* who will appear at the end of the present era, the Kali Yuga.

According to local and regional traditions, Vishnu can also take other forms. However, the two most famous of these *avatars* are Rama, eponymous hero of the epic the *Ramayana,* and Krishna. Both of them are ideal heroes, both physically and morally, and their exploits have always been enormously popular among Hindus. More than this, they are a rich source of incident for the many narrative reliefs that appear at Angkor on lintels, pediments and gallery walls.

Life of Krishna

In a number of stories, Krishna's exploits demonstrate his divinity and his love for mankind. In one, the demon Kamsa, though once killed by Vishnu, had returned to Earth. Vishnu plucked two hairs from his head, one fair and one dark, and these became two half-brothers, Krishna and Balarama. Kamsa learns of their presence on Earth, and for protection they are forced to spend their childhood disguised as cowherds. In one scene, Krishna uses his supernatural powers to shelter the cattle he tends from a storm unleashed by the sky god Indra, by holding aloft Mount Govardhana. In other episodes he battles the forces of evil: tearing apart the *naga* Kaliya, fighting various animals sent to kill him including the bull Arishta, the horse Kesin, the elephant Kuvalayapida and the lion Simha, and ultimately killing Kamsa. In the *Mahabharata,* Krishna is the charioteer and adviser to Arjuna, helping the Pandavas to defeat their foes the Kauravas.

Krishna killing King Kamsa in his palace, Banteay Srei

The Ramayana

This is the best loved and most widely told of all Hindu legends, and is an epic of the triumph of good over evil, which remains very popular in Southeast Asia.

Siva

Siva contrasts with Vishnu in a number of ways. In the Hindu Trinity, his main cosmological role is as the Destroyer – he brings each *kalpa,* or world cycle, to an end with his dance of destruction. However, Siva's force is by no means just a negative one. As in modern physics, Hindu cosmology envisaged the universe has having a cyclical nature. The end of each *kalpa* brought about by Siva's dance is also the beginning of the next. Rebirth follows destruction. In the cosmological sense, Siva's powers are more fundamental than Vishnu's.

The Khmers worshipped Siva primarily in the form of a *linga* – a pillar, usually in stone, derived from a phallus and

A makara *spews out a multi-headed* naga, *Banteay Srei*

A nine-headed naga *in the hidden reliefs of the Terrace of the Leper King*

representing the essence of the god. The *linga*, mounted in a pedestal representing an equally abstract *yoni*, or female organ, occupied the shrine of a temple, and, as for any statue, was the focus of rituals conducted by the priests. The other forms in which Siva was represented were as the 10-armed god dancing the universe to destruction, just mentioned, as the supreme yogi, or ascetic, and riding with his consort Uma on his steed, the bull Nandi.

The third member of the Trinity, Brahma, despite his designation as the Creator, was less commonly represented in Cambodia. He is worshipped in temples where three shrines were used for the Trinity, one in each, such as at Phnom Krom where he occupies the S shrine. In reliefs he is shown emerging from the lotus that grows out of

20

Vishnu Reclining, with Brahma emerging from the lotus flower that grows from Vishnu's navel, Banteay Samré

Vishnu's navel as he sleeps. Brahma is recognisable by his four heads, each facing a cardinal direction.

Other, lesser gods make appearances. The most commonly met with is Indra, important as king of the gods, in a manner corresponding to the king of men. He is also the god of the sky and rain, as such bringing prosperity. As the chief of the guardians of the cardinal points, he is associated with the E and is frequently seen on the E lintels. Like all Hindu gods he has a steed, or *vahana*. In Indra's case, this is the elephant Airavata, normally shown with three heads. Other gods include Ganesha (Siva's elephant-headed son), Agni (the Vedic god of fire), Kubera (guardian of the N), Surya (Vedic god of the sun), Varuna (god of seas and rivers and guardian of the W) and Yama (god of Death and guardian of the S).

Buddhism

Buddhism was the other important religion. Its two principal forms are Mahayana ('Greater Vehicle') and Theravada (also known as Hinayana – 'Lesser Vehicle', a term not surprisingly considered derogatory by its followers). The Buddhism practised throughout Southeast Asia today is Theravada – 'the sayings of elders', following the pure precepts of the Buddha – but at the time of the Khmer Empire, official Buddhist worship was exclusively Mahayanist.

Mahayana Buddhism seems to have played a more important role in what is now Thailand than in Cambodia – or at least, it was important over a longer period. At Angkor, it made its major appearance at the end of the 12th century with the accession of Jayavarman VII, but on

Dikpalas, the guardians of direction:–

East:	Indra, on the three-headed elephant Airavata, God of the Sky
Southeast:	Agni, on a rhinoceros (or a ram), God of Fire
South:	Yama, on a buffalo or a bull, God of Judgement and Hell
Southwest:	Nirriti, on the shoulders of a *yaksha*, Goddess of Death and Corruption
West:	Varuna, on a *hamsa*, God of the Ocean
Northwest:	Vayu, on a horse, God of the Wind
North:	Kubera, on throne, God of Wealth
Northeast:	Isana on? (although Isana is Siva, his role as a *dikpala* is specific and must not be confused with Siva in general)

Planetary deities:-

Sun:	Surya on a horse-drawn chariot
Moon:	Chandra on a pedestal
Mars:	Angaraka (Mangala)
Mercury:	Buddha
Jupiter:	Brhaspati (Guru)
Venus:	Sukra
Saturn:	Sani
Eclipses:	Rahu emerging from clouds

the Khorat Plateau it was established much earlier. The temple of Phimai. in particular, was a centre of Buddhist worship. After the 7th century, Tantric thought began to infiltrate both Buddhism and Hinduism, and makes an important appearance at Phimai. Tantra is 'the doctrine and ritual of the left hand', in which the female force, or *shakti*, plays a dominant role in the universe. This esoteric belief involved many magical and mystical rituals, and female divinities played an increasing part. Vajrayana Buddhism was a development of Tantric thought, and had elaborate iconography. One of the characteristics of Mahayana Buddhism is the number of bodhisattvas. Literally 'Buddhas-to-be', these were beings who had voluntarily halted their progress on the path to Buddha-hood, stopping just short of Enlightenment in order to be able to assist mankind.

The Buddha calling the Earth to witness, Preah Palilay

KHMER TEMPLES

The main evidence for Khmer architecture, and ultimately for Khmer civilisation, however, remains the religious buildings, considerable in number and extremely varied in size. They were destined for the immortal gods, and as they were built of the durable materials of brick, laterite and sandstone, many have survived to the present day. They were usually surrounded by enclosures to protect them from evil powers, but confusion has often arisen as to which is a temple enclosure and which is that of the town of which the temple was a part.

Characteristics of Khmer architecture

To gain a proper understanding of what a Khmer temple was, it should first be recalled that it was not a meeting place for the faithful but the palace of a god, who was enshrined there to allow him to bestow his beneficence, in particular on the founder and his familiars. There was thus the need to build the finest possible residence for him, to be sure, although as he was there in the form of a statue there was little need for a large space. One of the largest is the central shrine of Angkor Wat and its cella has internal dimensions of 4.6 metres by 4.7; the pedestal of the statue being approximately the width of the door, would have been 1.6 metres square. So a great temple would not be a vast palace for a single god but a grouping of multiple shrines with a main divinity at the centre. Preah Khan temple, for example, was originally conceived to house more than 400 deities, and many others were to be added subsequently. The shrines could be linked or surrounded by galleries, which usually had doors and themselves housed certain divinities. In any case they were in no way intended to provide passage for great processions as has too often been asserted;

Brick sanctuary towers, Preah Kô

such processions would have been greatly impeded, or rendered impossible by the doors and their disproportionately large thresholds. Some are not even accessible on foot, for example Ta Keo where it seems there was not even provision for doorways. As the residence of a god, or gods, the sacred territory in which the temple is sited is an image of the universe, where the gods sit on Mount Meru, the centre of the world, surrounded by the primordial ocean. This is the image which the sacred compound of a state temple in the Khmer country offers us, in which the *prasat*, the sanctuary tower, usually represents Mount Meru and can be flanked by four further *prasats*; the various enclosures being the mountains surrounding it, and the moat being the ocean.

The sandstone temple-mountain of Ta Keo

This world image was to impose a rigorous order of construction on Khmer architecture, from the simplest buildings to the most complex monumental groups. The characteristic applies of course to the temple as originally conceived. In reality, as might be expected as long as a temple remained an active place of worship, the Khmers added smaller or greater numbers of extra shrines to the original coherent group – especially from the reign of Jayavarman VII onwards. This is particularly evident at Preah Khan, and the practice can result in an impression of chaos to the modern eye. It is not too difficult, however, to ascertain the original layout.

From Sambor Prei Kuk at the beginning of the seventh century to Angkor Wat in the twelfth century, the temples are designed in enclosures of quadrangular shape which centre on the main shrine, or on the central group of shrines, and are laid out according to a precise method. Geometrical rules, which probably varied according to the type of shrine, determine the siting and dimensions of each subsidiary group in relation to the centre of the temple and its sanctuary. But in the absence of written documents, there is no alternative but to retrace the original design *a posteriori*.

The order is marked too by the hierarchy of the elements of the overall plan. The central *prasat* is dominant, at least through its height, although not always its overall area, and the other elements are distributed around it according to their size and volume, so as to grant

Sanctuary (with ogival tower in the style of Angkor Wat) connected to an antarala *and* mandapa*, Banteay Samré*

'Flat' temple with concentric galleries and corner towers in the Bayon style, Banteay Kdei

its full significance as the exact centre of the temple. The primacy of the central shrine is also emphasised by its elevation on a terrace of variable height, or in the case of the state temples, on a stepped pyramid. Hierarchical considerations also dictated the type and positioning of the decorative work. It is more profuse and richer on the central shrine which it sometimes covers entirely, and diminishes progressively in scope as it recedes from the centre. The most obvious example is Banteay Srei , where the three main shrines are richly decorated over their whole surface, with *dvarapala* carved on the central tower and *devata* on the north and south towers, whilst the preceding hall, linked by a screen or newel, is adorned with a patchwork of small squares in alternate patterns. The 'libraries' feature fine decoration on their main E and W faces, and have pediments which count among the most beautiful in Khmer art, but their sides are undecorated. The decoration becomes less profuse as it reaches the gate-lodges and ancillary buildings, up to the entry pavilion to the so-called fourth enclosure. An alternative explanation might be possible, namely that the original intention was to cover the whole temple with decorative carvings, beginning traditionally with the central shrine, and moving progressively outwards. Counter-examples would however be easy to adduce, and the reality is that, for one reason or another, not a single Khmer temple was actually 'completed'.

There are other conventions governing the design of Khmer monuments. In the case of the sanctuary towers, the superstructure features several storeys progressively reducing in height, superposed on the central mass, and representing the successive concentric levels of Mount Meru, the abode of the gods. In the 'temple mountain' design, however, the pyramid is itself an image of Mount Meru, through the ascending concentric universes of its superstructure, echoing those of the sanctuary towers. The elements which form the towers and the levels of the pyramid diminish progressively in size, producing the effect of "vertical soaring: a genuine optical illusion, a trick of perspective, which enhances the actual height".

These steadily diminishing proportions are also present in the miniature buildings nestling in the corners of each scaled-down level of the pyramid, like elements of an acroterium. An outstanding example, illustrating reduction in both scale and imagery can be seen in the northern group of monuments at Sambor Prei Kuk. On the east side of the central shrine's south face, there is a 'flying palace' – a kind of picture of a facade sculpted in brick. Every detail is present: the frame, the colonnettes, the lintel with its *makaras*, the pilasters and the pediment. The sculpted panel is about two metres high. At the top of this carved picture, in the tympanum of the pediment, is a miniature of the same 'flying palace', also sculpted in brick. The temple thus 'decorates itself' in its own likeness.

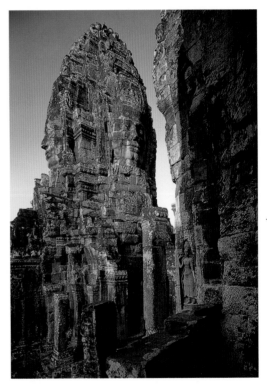

The inscriptions often mention the date, and sometimes the precise moment, at which a statue was 'brought to life' (the text speaks of 'opening a statue's eyes'), which was the crucial instant in the life of the temple. There was no solemn ceremony for the inauguration of a temple on its completion (which would have been difficult to determine exactly), nor one for laying the first stone. We know, however, that the Indian *Shastras* which laid down the rules of architecture, emphasised the extreme importance of the initial ceremonies for a building, and this is well attested by the presence of various 'foundation offerings' deposited beneath the actual foundations of the shrine, and also beneath the pedestals of the statues (which is why they have all been overturned by thieves), or even at the summit of the towers. The offerings were deposited in a square flagstone with various cavities, some of which were marked by letters and covered with a lid. In these cavities, precious stones, thin gold leaves, or even strands of hair or nail-clippings from the donor's body, were placed.

Face-tower, Bayon

One final point is that the deity was not always a statue at the centre of the shrine, especially in the case of Siva who, as supreme god, was most often represented by the *linga*, or phallus. Inserted in its pedestal, the *linga* in Khmer sculpture comprises three sections, and is a symbol of the Brahman trinity. Only the cylindrical top third was visible, sometimes ending in an ovoid shape, and representing Siva. The middle section was octagonal and represented Vishnu, while the bottom third was square and symbolised Brahma. Both were hidden within the pedestal. As with the statues in the round, the pedestal was surmounted by a square stone slab with a central hole and a spout to allow the lustral water to run off and be collected by the faithful. When a *linga* is the central feature, this slab is called a *yoni*, a 'womb', which is a symbol of fertility and, by extension, prosperity.

BUILDING TECHNIQUES

Used in different proportions across the centuries, brick, sandstone and laterite were the three materials used by Khmer builders in their temples. Domestic structures and even palaces were in wood and, as such, have not survived. The earliest temples were in brick, because it was the easiest to use, while stone, which demanded more manpower and greater skills, made a gradual appearance, beginning with secondary use as door frames and only later being used for basic construction. Laterite, easy to work but always rough in its finished appearance, was throughout a favourite choice for foundations and other massive elements. Of the three, sandstone was the most expensive and would be used in its entirety only for the important temples, except, of course, where there was a good local source.

Brick

Khmer bricks varied in size with the largest and oldest being about 30 x 15x 7cm. Long experience enabled

the builders to use them to great effect, both structurally and in appearance. They were bonded with a vegetable compound rather than mortar, and the result was great strength and an almost invisible join. The facade was sometimes directly carved, as displayed at its best at Prasat Kravan. More normally, however, decoration was in stucco, as at Preah Kô and Lolei, both at Roluos. Often on the bricks there is only a sketch of what has to be applied in stucco.

Sandstone

The stone used exclusively by Khmer builders was sandstone, and at Angkor the source was the Kulen Mountains. Its weight and the distances over which it needed to be hauled added to the structural problems that the architects had to face. These included finding designs for structures that would not collapse under their own considerable weight, and it was not until the end of the 10th century at Angkor that the Khmers had the confidence to build more or less exclusively in stone – the first large sandstone temple was Ta Keo. Khmer temples not being places of congregation, there was no real need for vaulting or creating large interior spaces, as was happening in European cathedrals at the time. One of the problems with sandstone,

derived from its geological structure, was that when used for upright supports (in other words against the way it was laid down) it had a tendency to flake. For their purposes the device known as corbelling was sufficient and simple to execute with no need for scaffolding. Each higher stone course projects a little over the one below, until the sides finally meet at the top. Gravity prevents collapse as the two sides of the gallery roof press in on each other.

One of the great advantages of sandstone was the fine detail of

Above: Sandstone was sometimes used in imitation of traditional materials, such as tiles, as on the south 'library' of Ta Som.

One of the earliest all-stone temples was Ta Keo, although the carving was not completed

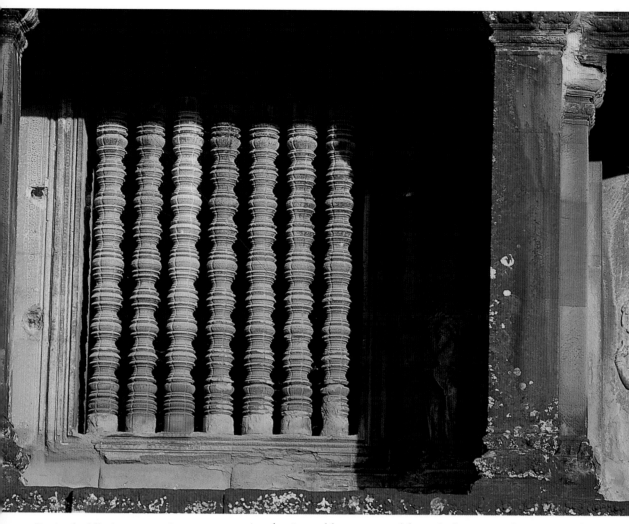

Despite the difficulty, stone windows commonly featured lathe-turned balusters, as at Angkor Wat

carving that it would support, and from the beginning door surrounds and lintels were elaborately carved. The evolving decorative styles on these elements provides a fascinating and useful method of dating Khmer temples. This decorative use of sandstone reached its apogee at Angkor Wat, with its nearly 2,000 square metres of bas-relief panels, not to mention *apsaras*, lintels, pediments and friezes.

Laterite

When cut out from the ground, this iron-rich clay, widely found in Southeast Asia, is relatively soft and easy to dress into blocks. However, after it has been exposed to the air and sun it becomes very hard indeed, making it ideal for any hidden parts of a building. Foundations and the core of buildings faced in stone or brick were often of laterite. On the other hand, its deeply pitted surface after drying makes it unsuitable for finishing, and any decorative work has to be applied, like stucco. Laterite was used in this way more extensively in the Khmer provinces, particularly in what is now Thailand, than at Angkor itself.

Wood

Wood was used for palaces, houses and monks' dwellings. It was also used in temples for certain roofs, ceilings and temporary structures such as pavilions. At Angkor small pieces of a wooden ceiling to the Heaven and Hells have been found. Exterior wooden roofs would have been tiled with pottery tiles and remains of these have been found. Recently lead tiles have also been discovered. Interestingly, Zhou Daguan noted that the royal palace was roofed with lead.

Although wooden structures have virtually disappeared we can gain a good idea of Khmer techniques from observing stone doorways and false doors and balusters carved in imitation of wood. In particular the joints of doors and windows are those of the wood carver, not the stone mason.

Painting

It is often not appreciated today that the surfaces of Khmer temples were painted. Traces of paint have been found at Preah Khan, Neak Pean and Angkor Wat. Although in the latter case, the painting could have been added later or reapplied in renovation work.

Below left: Corbelling, seen here at the W gopura of Ta Prohm, was structurally unsound

Because of its crude appearance, laterite was normally used structurally rather than for finished walls. It is quite clear that these laterite blocks would have been coated with stucco, probably before being painted. Banteay Srei

ARCHITECTURAL STYLES

Style	Dates	Ruler	Where found in Angkor	Chief Characteristics
PRE-ANGKOREAN				
Sambor Prei Kuk	c.610-c.650	Isanavarman I, Bhavavarman II		Round, plain colonettes with capitals that include a bulb.
Prei Kmeng	c.635-c.700	Jayavarman I		Masterpieces of sculpture, but architecture scarce. Colonettes larger, more heavily decorated. General decline of standards.
Kompong Preah	c.700-c.800	Various	Ak Yum	More decorative rings on colonettes, which remain cylindrical. Continuing brick construction.
TRANSITIONAL				
Kulen	c.825-c.875	Jayavarman II		Continuation of pre-Angkorean, but a period of innovation and borrowing, such as from Cham temples. towers mainly square, and relatively high. Mainly brick, with laterite walls, and stone door surrounds. Square and octagonal colonettes begin to appear.
ANGKOREAN				
Preah Kô	877-c.886	Indravarman I Jayavarman III	Preah Kô, Bakong, Lolei	Simple plan: one or more square brick towers on a single base. First appearance of concentric enclosures and of *gopuras* and 'libraries'. Decorative 'flying palaces' replaced by *dvarapalas* and *devatas* in niches. First major temple-mountain at Bakong.
Bakheng	889-923	Yasovarman I, Harshavarman I	Bakheng, Phnom Krom, Phnom Bok, Baksei Chamkrong (trans.)	Development of the temple-mountain. More use of stone, particularly for major temples, and more decorative stone carving
Koh Ker	c.921-944	Jayavarman IV		Scale of buildings diminishes to-wards centre. Brick still main material., but sandstone also used
Pre Rup	944-968	Rajendravarman II	Pre Rup, East Mebon, Bat Chum, Kutisvara	Transitional between Koh Ker and Banteay Srei. Long halls partly enclose sanctuary. The last great monuments in plastered brick, increasing use of sandstone.

Style	Dates	Ruler	Where found in Angkor	Chief Characteristics
Banteay Srei	967-1000	Jayavarman V	Banteay Srei	Ornate, superposed pediments, sweeping gable ends, rich and deep carving. Plastered brick replaced by stone and laterite. Appearance of scenes in pediments. Voluptuous *devatas* with gentle expressions
Khleang	968-1010	Jayavarman V	Ta Keo, The Khleangs, Phimeanakas, Royal Palace.	First use of galleries. Cruciform *gopuras*. Octagonal colonettes. Restrained decorative carving
Bapuon	1050-1080	Udayadityavarman II	Bapuon, West Mebon	A return to rich carving: floral motifs, but also lintels with scenes. *Nagas* without head-dress. Bas-reliefs appear at Bapuon temple, carved with lively scenes enclosed in small panels, often in narrative sequence.
Angkor Wat	c.1080-1175	Jayavarman VI, Suryavarman II, Yasovarman II	Angkor Wat, Banteay Samré, Thommanon, Chao Say Tevoda, some of Preah Pithu (and Phimai and Phnom Rung in the N; Beng Mealea to the E)	The high classical style of Khmer architecture. Fully developed conical towers with curved profile. Galleries wider and with half galleries on one side. Concentric enclosures connected by axial galleries. Nagas with head-dress; naga balustrades raised off the ground. Invention of cross-shaped terrace. Richly carved lintels and other decorations. Bas-reliefs. Apsaras.
Bayon	1181-1243	Jayavarman VII, Indravarman II	Ta Prohm, Preah Khan, Jayatataka *baray*, Neak Pean, Ta Som, Ta Nei, Angkor Thom, Prasats Chrung, Bayon, Elephant Terrace, Ta Prohm Kel, Hospital Chapel, Krol Kô, Prasats Suor Prat (and Banteay Chhmar in the NW)	The last great style. Hurried construction, often in laterite not stone; carving less elegant. Complex plans, huge temples. In Cambodia, face-towers, and historical narrative bas-reliefs. Three periods: 1. large, complex temples on a single level; 2. face-towers and avenues of giants carrying *nagas*; 3. decline of building standards, *devatas* acquire Angkor Wat-style diadem.
Post Bayon	1243-15th C	Jayavarman VIII and others	Terrace of the Leper King, Preah Pithu, Preah Palilay (modifications to temples)	Invention of cross-shaped terrace, causeways on columns, low or high.

LINTEL STYLES

Style	Dates	Ruler	Where found in Angkor	Chief Characteristics
PRE-ANGKOREAN **Sambor Prei Kuk**	c.610-c.650	Isanavarman I, Bhavavarman II		Inward-facing *makaras* with tapering bodies. Four arches joined by three medallions, the central one carved with Indra. Small figure on each *makara*. A variation is with figures replacing the *makaras*, and a scene with figures below the arch.
Prei Kmeng	c.635-c.700	Jayavarman I		Continuation of Sambor Prei Kuk, but *makaras* disappear, being replaced by incurving ends and figures. Arches more rectilinear. Large figures sometimes at each end. A variation is a central scene below the arch, usually Vishnu Reclining.
Kompong Preah	c.650-c.800	Various		High quality carving. Arches replaced by a garland of vegetation (like a wreath) more or less segmented. Medallions disappear, central one sometimes replaced by a knot of leaves. Leafy pendants spray out above and below garland.
TRANSITIONAL **Kulen**	c.825-c.875	Jayavarman II		Great diversity, with influences from Champa and Java, including the *kala* and outward-facing *makaras*.
ANGKOREAN **Preah Kô**	877-c.886	Indravarman I	Preah Kô, Bakong, Lolei	Some of the most beautiful of all Khmer lintels, rich, well-carved and imaginative. *Kala* in centre, issuing garland on either side. Distinct loops of vegetation curl down from garland. Outward-facing *makaras* sometimes appear at the ends. Vishnu on *Garuda* common.
Bakheng	889-923	Yasovarman I, Harshavarman I	Bakheng, Phnom Krom, Phnom Bok, Baksei Chamkrong (trans.), Prasat Kravan (trans.), Prasat Bei (trans.), Thma Bay Kaek	Continuation of Preah Kô, but less fanciful, and tiny figures disappear. Loops of vegetation below the *naga* form tight, circular coils. Garland begins to dip in the centre.
Koh Ker	c.921-944	Jayavarman IV	mainly at Koh Ker	Centre occupied by a prominent scene, taking up almost the entire height of the lintel. Usually no lower border. Dress of figures shows a curved line to the *sampot* tucked in below waist.

LINTEL STYLES · 33

The Preah Kô style is often regarded as the apogee of Khmer lintels, with finely detailed, imaginative carving. The outward-facing makaras, and horsemen emerging from the central garland, are typical.

At Banteay Srei, lintels developed to their most complex form, rich in detail and deeply carved

LINTEL STYLES

Style	Dates	Ruler	Where found in Angkor	Chief Characteristics
Pre Rup	944-968	Rajendravarman	Pre Rup, East Mebon	Tendency to copy earlier styles, especially Preah Ko and Bakheng. Central figures. Re-appearance of lower border.
Banteay Srei	967-1000	Jayavarman V	Banteay Srei	Increase in complexity and detail. Garland sometimes makes pronounced loop on either side, with *kala* at top of each loop. Central figure.
Khleang	968-1010	Jayavarman V Jayaviravarman Suryavarman I	Ta Keo, the Khleangs, Phimeanakas, Royal Palace	Less ornate than those of Banteay Srei. Central *kala* with triangular tongue, its hands holding the garland, which is bent at the centre. *Kala* sometimes surmounted by a divinity. Loops of garland on either side divided by floral stalk and pendant. Vigorous treatment of vegetation.
Bapuon	1050-1080	Udayadityavarman II	Bapuon, West Mebon	The central *kala* surmounted by divinity, usually riding a steed, or a Vishnuite scene, typically from the life of Krishna. Loops of garland no longer cut. Another type is a scene with many figures and little vegetation.
Angkor Wat	c.1080-11775	Jayavarman VI, Suryavarman II, Yasovarman II	Angkor Wat, Banteay Samré, Thommanon, Chao Say Tevoda, (and Phimai and Phnom Rung in the N; Beng Mealea to the E)	Centred, framed and linked by garlands. A second type is a narrative scene filled with figures. When nagas appear, they are crowned. When there is vegetation, its curls are tight and prominent. Dress mirrors that of *devatas* and *apsaras* in bas-reliefs. No empty spaces.
Bayon	1181-1243	Jayavarman VII, Indravarman II	Ta Prohm, Preah Khan, Jayatataka baray, Neak Pean, Ta Som, Ta Nei, Angkor Thom, Prasats Chrung, Bayon, Elephant Terrace, Terrace of the Leper King, Ta Prohm Kel, Hospital Chapel, Krol Kô, Prasats Suor Prat (and Banteay Chhmar in the NW)	Most figures disappear: usually only a *kala* at the bottom of the lintel surmounted by small figure. Mainly Buddhist motifs. In the middle of the period the garland is cut into four parts, while later a series of whorls of foliage replace the four divisions.

The later style of the Bayon featured Buddhist motifs like this reclining Buddha, over a central kala *head at Preah Palilay.*

DAILY LIFE

All the visible buildings at Angkor are religious monuments; the only remains of any royal dwellings in the Royal Palace are a few scattered tiles and the foundations of some wooden constructions. However, the Elephant Terrace was the base of the royal reception hall and the Leper King Terrace the base of another unknown royal building. The lower parts of big wooden columns from the 10th century have been recently discovered in the Royal Palace area, leading to the hope of further discoveries. Of ordinary Khmer houses of the period, no trace remains, and yet there is ample evidence of cities and towns in the layout of the larger temples. You need only look to your left and right as you walk along the main causeway of Angkor Wat to see the traces of city streets on a grid pattern. Again, driving through the South Gate of Angkor Thom on the way to the Bayon, the forest on either side was a living city.

"They also keep beside them a bowl of tin or earthenware filled with water for rinsing their hands, since only their fingers are used in eating rice, which is sticky and could not be got rid of without this water."

"In Cambodia it is the women who take charge of trade . . . Market is held every day from six o'clock until noon. There are no shops in which merchants live; instead, they display goods on a matting spread upon the ground."

The record of daily life at Angkor available to us is very limited. The inscriptions were largely concerned with matters of religion and state, and yet there are some important inventories that give some idea of local produce and populations. That not all the land belonged to the king is obvious from the mention of donations of rice fields to temples, and if there were large landowners capable of making such donations, there may well have been small holdings as well. Moreover, the 'slaves' listed in temple records could not have been real slaves in the modern meaning of the word, for the simple reason that slaves could not defile the sacred precincts, let alone be named in religious inscriptions. They

"Generally speaking, the women, like the men, wear only a strip of cloth, bound round the waist, showing bare breasts of milky whiteness." Clearly, Zhou Daguan would be referring to the breasts of upper class women, as the skin of Khmer women living in the villages and working in the fields would have had much darker

"The wearing of fabrics patterned with recurring groups of flowers is permitted to high officers and princes."

were more likely to have been 'slaves of god'. There were, however, certainly real slaves, as described in the text mentioned below: *"Wild men from the hills can be bught to serve as slaves. Families of wealth may own more than one hundred; those of lesser means content themselves with ten or twenty; only the very poor have none."*

Perhaps the clearest mirror that we have of daily life in those distant times is the celebrated account of the Chinese emissary Zhou Daguan (Chou Ta-Kuan), who lived at Angkor for a year from 1296 to 1297. The Chinese had a strong commercial interest in knowing the customs of far-away countries, and Zhou Daguan was particularly diligent in describing this exotic society. He wrote his *Notes on the Customs of Cambodia* after his return to China, sometime before 1312.

To this account we can add the demotic bas-reliefs carved on the outer gallery walls of the Bayon at the turn of the 13th century. This was the one occasion on which the stone-carvers turned from mytho-logical and historical themes to everyday occurrences. The combined impression from these bas-reliefs and Zhou Daguan's account is that many of the mundane aspects of Khmer life have remained similar almost to the present day, particularly in the countryside, where houses, markets, ox-carts and so on are almost identical to those carved in sandstone eight centuries ago. If there is any caution to be exercised here, it is in remembering that these few records afford just a glimpse of a society, not its totality. The images on these pages come from the Bayon, the quotes from Zhou Daguan.

INSCRIPTIONS

The inscriptions that the visitor can see in the temples are those carved on the door jambs of the entrances to the sanctuaries. Inscriptions were also carved on steles, but the majority of these are now housed in the Conservancy at Angkor to prevent them from being stolen. As documents they are of great historical importance, representing the sole archives on the ancient Khmer. While there were undoubtedly palm leaf manuscripts, all of them have disappeared.

More than 1,200 inscriptions have been discovered, but it is likely that many more have disappeared, or have not yet been found. The texts vary a great deal in length from as little as one line, to several hundreds. With some very rare exceptions, all related to the Hindu or Buddhist temples in which they were carved. Indeed, there are virtually no non-religious incriptions and it would seem that shrines to local divinities, which moreover were constructed in perishable materials, never had inscriptions.

Detail of the Preah Khan inscription

The script evolved over the centuries up to the Angkorian period. On the earliest inscriptions, dating to the 5th century, it is very close to that known as Pallava from Southern India, although an exact equivalent has not been found. However an individual style soon developed. By the beginning of the Angkorian period, the script had become typically Khmer and was often very meticulous in its execution. During the reign of King Rajendravarman a stencil was clearly used for royal inscriptions. After this time, the style changed very little, although, of course, not all carvers wrote in the same way. Then during the reign of King Jayavarman VII, the script took on its characteristic, rather squared up appearance. From then the script continued to evolve into that which is used today.

The texts were written in Sanskrit or Khmer, in more or less equal quantities, but their content was very different depending on the language used. The Sanskrit texts are poems addressed to the Hindu gods or the Buddha and had a more or less standard format: one or several verses of invocation to the deity of the temple would be followed by an eulogy on the founder of the temple, whether the king or an important dignatory. The eulogy was frequently formulaic, but nevertheless interesting details on the lives of the kings can be gleaned. The date of the installation of the principal divinity can usually be found, a date all too often confused with the actual building of the temple which would have begun before and frequently continued subsequently). Certain other dates may also be included such as when the king ascended the throne. The quality of the Sanscrit is extremely good, and sometimes of such finesse as to suspect an Indian author. Although the steles are frequently referred to as 'foundation steles', they seem to have been carved on the death of the person celebrated thereon and often many years after the foundation of the temple.

Khmer inscriptions were written in prose and are generally more like an inventory – listing the goods belonging to the gods, such as their land, animals or cult objects. Occasionally, we find long lists of the servants of the temple or the rice farmers working for the gods. These have often been referred to as slaves, but being listed in such a fashion, is more like appearing on a 'roll of honour'.

The difference in character between the two languages can be appreciated in the rare inscriptions incorrectly referred to as bi-lingual. Here the same facts are recounted in both languages but with a very different slant. While the sanscrit lists the gifts made to the gods by the founder, the Khmer emphasizes that the founder's family maintains the right to dispose of these gifts.

Some rare exceptions have been found among Khmer inscriptions such as that known as 'the oath of the servants of Suryavarman I' found on the door jambs of the *gopura* to the royal palace of Angkor Thom. After the oath formula, there follows a list of those who have pledged their allegiance to the king. There is evidence of some names being scratched out, suggesting that the loyalty of some oath-takers was short lived. One or perhaps two texts also contain short extracts of 'royal annals'. Such enticing glimpses as these afford, make even more regrettable the loss of palm-leaf manuscripts and other literary works.

The inscriptions allow us to some extent to trace the ancient history and civilisation of the Khmer. However, we must bear in mind the context in which they were carved and not expect information that is very comprehensive. Similarly, we should not draw conclusions from lack of evidence. A paucity of information does not necessarily imply that such and such and such an event or custom did not exist, nor that such and such a king was unimportant.

The stele of Preah Khan, until recently in its original location in the temple

Vandalised apsaras *with bullet holes, Angkor Wat*

Cleaning the S gallery, Angkor Wat

DISCOVERY & RESTORATION

It is frequently said that Angkor was 'discovered by the Europeans' but this is patently nonsense and simply reflects a Eurocentric view. The Khmers never forgot the existence of their monuments, and even if they neglected the majority of their temples, Angkor Wat always remained occupied and a place of worship.

It is nevertheless true that it was the posthumous notes made by the French naturalist Henri Mouhot, published simultaneously in Paris and London in 1863, that aroused Western interest in the wonders of Angkor. There had already been Western visitors such as Mouhot's immediate predecessor, Father Bouillevaux, or Portugese adventurers much earlier at the end of the 16th century. However, little attention was paid to their reports. After Mouhot, everyone wanted to see what he had described. John Thomson, working in Singapore, was the first to photograph the monuments. There was also the Mekong expedition, led by Doudart de Lagrée, with Francis Garnier, who made a detour to visit Angkor.

Pioneers were soon replaced by researchers. Several missions, largely French for historical reasons, took place before Siam ceded the northern provinces of Cambodia in the 1907 treaty, including that of Siem Reap where Angkor was located. The Ecole française d'Extreme-Orient, founded in 1899, assumed responsibility for the conservation of the monuments, initially under the direction of Jean Commaille. Thousands of cubic metres of soil were excavated, beginning with Angkor Wat and the Bayon, as well as the Elephant Terraces, etc. In 1916 Jean Commaille was assasinated by brigands, all for the miserable sum of a week's wages for a few coolies. His tomb is situated amongst trees in the SW corner of the Bayon.

Henri Marchal succeeded him as Head of the Conservation of Monuments at Angkor. For 20 years he toiled unceasingly, often

Planning the start of Preah Khan's restoration

Figure stolen from the Elephant Terrace

propping up monuments with cement beams, not the most aesthetic solution but frequently effective in preventing further collapses. At the same time, he wrote numerous articles. Although some of his hypotheses may have been superseded, they have proved invaluable for archaeologists. In 1930, he left for Java to study the method adopted by the Dutch known as anastylosis, applying it on his return to the temple of Bantaey Srei. Such was his love for Angkor that he moved there permanently at the end of 1947 when he was already 71, and died there in April 1970. Georges Trouvé took over from Marchal in 1931, but his tragic death in 1935 meant that his work there was all too short.

Maurice Glaize arrived in 1937. This meticulous architect was responsible for some remarkable restorations, in particular that of the central tower of Bakong, the tower of Neak Pean and Banteay Samré. It is even more remarkable when one considers the meagre funds available for such work during the Second World War.

The last two French conservators at Angkok, Jean Laur and, above all, Bernard-Philippe Groslier, transformed the Conservancy into a modern organisation and in addition carried out important works. It was they who began the immense task of restoring Bapuon, a work which the EFEO is about to complete, after a break of 20 years resulting from ensuing wars and the political situation.

Angkor became a World Heritage Site in December 1992.

As a result of an intergovernmental conference in Tokyo in 1993 an International Coordinating Committee was established to oversee restoration at Angkor, presided over by the Japanese and French

Even cement replicas have been vandalised as with this replica of the Leper King

The entire wall with this magnificent 32-armed Lokesvara was removed by thieves from the remote temple of Banteay Chhmar. While the local thieves are undoubtedly guilty they are acting on orders from antique dealers, who frequently show albums of choice Khmer pieces still in situ which they will steal to order

ambassadors with a secretariat provided by UNESCO. The committee functions successfully, meeting several times a year, whether in plenary session, or for technical meetings. Various teams from different countries work under the committee – a German team studying and restoring the *apsaras* of Angkor Wat; the World Monuments Fund of the USA working principally on Preah Khan; the Chinese working at Chao Say Tevoda, the French in coordination with EFEO researching and restoring the Terraces of the Leper King and of the Elephants and Bapuon; an Indonesian team on *gopuras* of the royal palace of Angkor Thom; the Italians at Pre Rup; the Japanese at the Bayon and Prasat Suor Prat and the University of Sophia working at Banteay Kdei.

The Khmers themselves have established APSARA (Authority for the Protection of the Sites and Administration of the Region of Angkor). After several problems in getting started, APSARA now seems ready to begin work.

Thefts

Damage caused to the sites during the period of civil war were comparatively few, as each Khmer faction respected the Angkor monuments. However, a major problem of theft arose at the beginning of the 1990s. Free-standing figures, lintels and pediments have been hacked away and removed, frequently via Thailand for sale to Western collectors. Until recently there was little concerted effort to crackdown on either the perpetrators or the middlemen, the latter operating quite openly at places such as River City in Bangkok. Stone guardian figures, large *nagas*, lintels and even inscriptions have all been for sale.

However some recent high profile scandals and seizures suggest that both the Cambodian and Thai governments are finally trying to prevent such outrages. Blocks from a 20m-section of the surrounding gallery at Banteay Chhmar which formed a magnificent Lokesvara were seized in lorries near the Thai-Cambodian border. Police raids have also taken place at River City and much Khmer material was seized. Those identifiable and attributable to specific sites will be returned or otherwise exhibited in a new museum, opening in Nakhon Ratchasima province in Thailand.

Convicts with stolen heads

Readers should on no account try to buy ancient Khmer artefacts whether in Cambodia or anywhere else. Such purchases simply encourage theft and wanton destruction.

A devata, whose face has been crudely hacked off

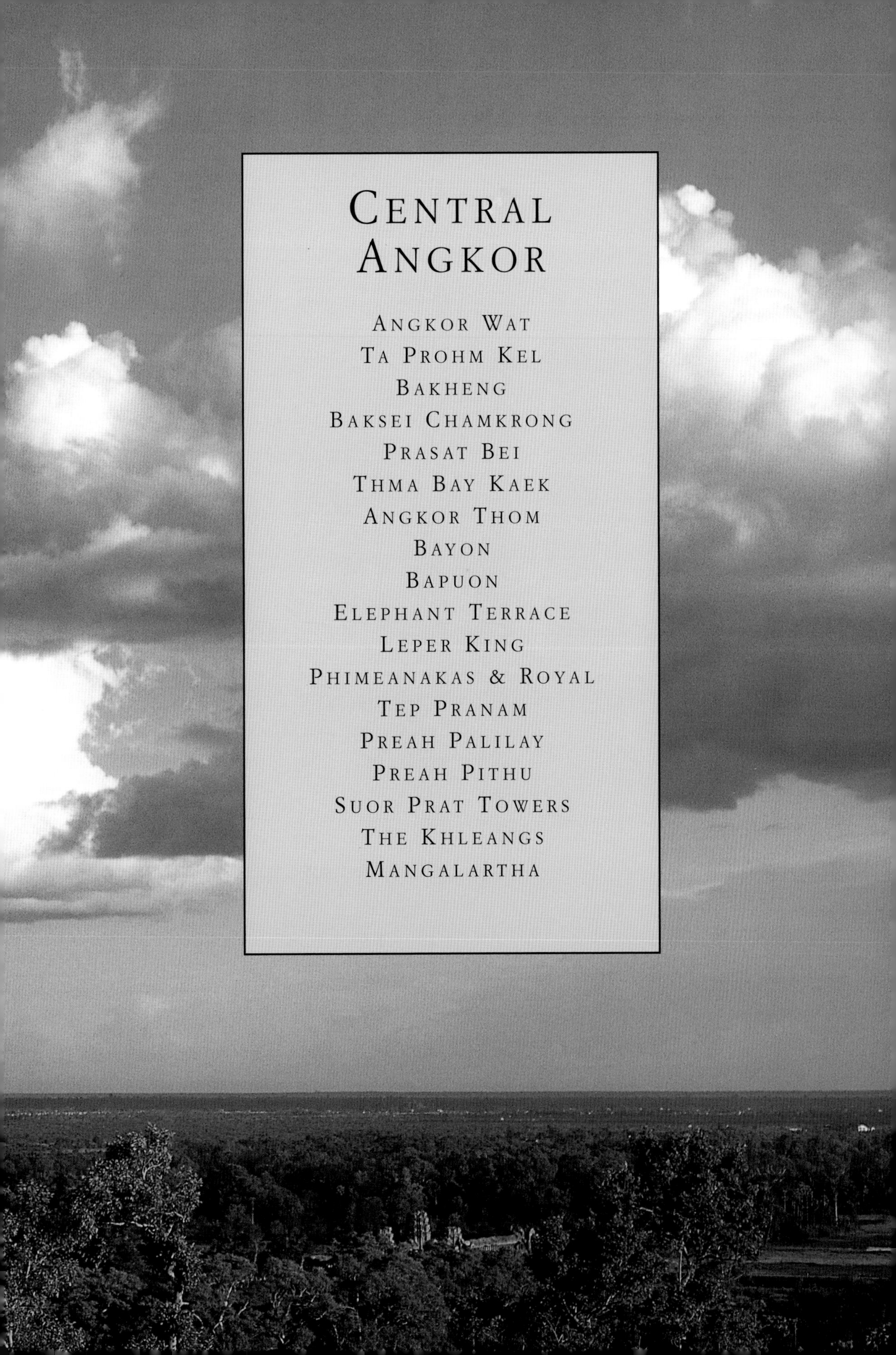

CENTRAL ANGKOR

ANGKOR WAT
TA PROHM KEL
BAKHENG
BAKSEI CHAMKRONG
PRASAT BEI
THMA BAY KAEK
ANGKOR THOM
BAYON
BAPUON
ELEPHANT TERRACE
LEPER KING
PHIMEANAKAS & ROYAL
TEP PRANAM
PREAH PALILAY
PREAH PITHU
SUOR PRAT TOWERS
THE KHLEANGS
MANGALARTHA

ANGKOR WAT ✤✤✤

Date: Early 12th century (between 1113 and 1150) with later additions
Style: Angkor Wat
Reign: Suryavarman II
Visit: Several hrs (more than one visit recommended)

Highlights
★ The world's largest religious monument
★ A completely realised microcosm of the Hindu universe, culminating in the five peaks of Mount Meru
★ Architectural masterpiece in fine proportions and rich in detail; the apogee of classical Khmer construction
★ Some 600 m of narrative bas-relief and nearly 2,000 *apsaras*

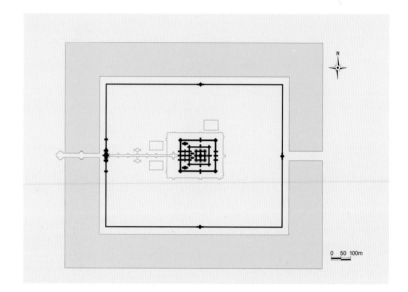

Right: Plan of the city
Below: Plan of the temple

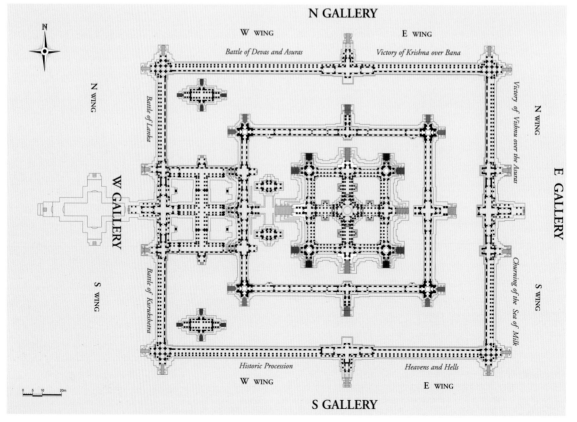

For once, the modern name of a temple is completely justified. Angkor Wat, the 'city [which became a] pagoda' , was not only the grandest and most sublime of all the Khmer temples, but also a city in its own right. It was built during the reign of Suryavarman II, in the first half of the 12th century, both as the capital and the State Temple dedicated to Vishnu.

Plan

The outer limits of Angkor Wat are set by its broad moat, faced in laterite and sandstone. Including this, the total area is almost 200 hectares – a rectangle of 1.5 km E-W by 1.3 km N-S, the largest temple at Angkor. Two causeways at W and E cross the 190m-wide moat to the outer enclosure, bounded by a laterite wall of 1025m by 802m. Because of Angkor Wat's unusual orientation, the W *gopura* of this outer enclosure is by far the largest of the four.

Within the 82 hectares of the outer enclosure, the temple itself stands in the middle on a terrace measuring 332 x 258m, nearly 9 hectares. The remaining 9/10ths of the area was taken up with the city, including the royal palace, although of course no trace remains of these buildings, presumably constructed in light materials. Following tradition, the palace would have been to the north of the actual temple.

The temple proper combines two major features of Khmer architecture: a pyramid and concentric galleries. Pyramids, which in most cases were created by means of stepped terraces, date back to the 8th century Ak Yum and the better known 9th century Bakong, and were the Khmer method of symbolising the centre of the Hindu universe, Mount Meru, in the form of a temple-mountain. Galleries, however, evolved later, around the beginning of the 11th century; they were the natural succession to a growing number of annex buildings surrounding the sanctuary. Angkor Wat is, to put it as simply as possible, a pyramid of three levels, each one enclosed by a well-developed gallery with four *gopuras* and corner towers. The summit is crowned with five towers in a quincunx.

The temple, whose moat, enclosures and towers represent the Universe

Right: The statue of Vishnu in the W entrance gopura *may originally have been in the central sanctuary. It has been restored several times*

Below: Half-pediment of the W entrance gopura *showing a battle scene from the* Ramayana

Bottom: Approach to the W entrance gopura

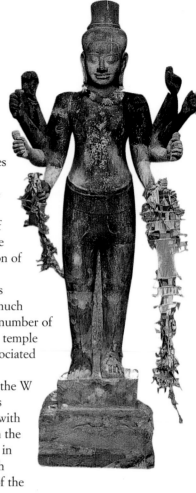

Symbolism

The scale of Angkor Wat enabled the Khmer to give full expression to religious symbolism. It is, above all else, a microcosm of the Hindu universe. The moat represents the mythical oceans surrounding the earth and the succession of concentric galleries represent the mountain ranges that surround Mount Meru, the home of the gods. The towers represent the mountain's peaks, and the experience of the ascent to the central shrine is, maybe intentionally, a fairly convincing imitation of climbing a real mountain.

Much has been made of Angkor Wat's orientation – facing W rather than the much more usual E – and this has attracted a number of explanations. The most likely is that the temple was dedicated to Vishnu, sometimes associated with the W.

The importance of this orientation to the W depends very much on how unusual it is considered to be – how abrupt a break with tradition. Other temples that break with the tradition of facing E are notably Phimai in NE Thailand, which faces SE, and Preah Vihear which faces N. At Angkor, two of the

Preah Pithu temples face W as does the Vishnu temple at Preah Khan.

Visit

Enter Angkor Wat city from the W by crossing the causeway over the moat. This causeway was, in fact, built more than a century later than the temple, as evidence the style of its round columns. Ahead is the W entrance *gopura* with the remains of three towers. At the left and right of this 230m-broad *gopura* are entrances large enough to have taken vehicles and elephants, and these may originally have been approached by wooden bridges across the moat. On entering the *gopura*, you can make a short detour to the right to the shrine under the southern tower, where an eight-armed statue of Vishnu (restored many times) fills the space. This image, which seems too big for this location, may originally have been worshipped in Angkor Wat's central sanctuary.

Return to the main entrance; the doorway leading to the enclosure frames a magnificent view – the towers of the temple at the end of a 350m causeway. At sunrise they are silhouetted against the morning sky, in the late afternoon they glow almost orange. As you step through onto the causeway, you can appreciate the scale of the city, which extended to the left and right. The balustrades of the causeway are in the form of *naga* serpents, their bodies raised on short square columns. At six points along its length, about 50m apart, steps lead to the ground level of the enclosure, and here the balustrades turn and end in rearing *naga*

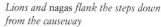

Lions and nagas *flank the steps down from the causeway*

Left: One of the original city streets

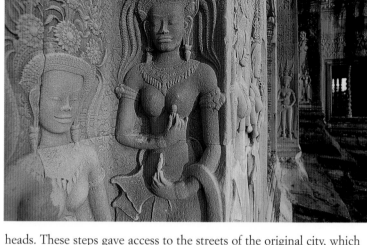

The single apsaras *at Angkor Wat showing her teeth*

Above right: Apsaras *on the inner wall of the W entrance* gopura

N 'library' of the outer enclosure

heads. These steps gave access to the streets of the original city, which was laid out in a grid, and, thanks to Groslier's restoration in the 1960s, the outline of some can be seen through the grass and trees.

Before walking down the causeway, however, turn round to examine the E-facing wall of the entrance *gopura* and its exquisite bas-relief carvings. The *apsaras* at the base of the wall are particularly fine, and look their best in early morning sunlight. Several metres S of the main entrance, the smile of one of these celestial maidens reveals a full set of teeth – uniquely among the almost 2,000 *apsaras* at Angkor Wat.

Continue along the causeway towards the temple proper. On either side are two large so-called 'libraries'. With four doorways at the cardinal points, these would have been shrines of some kind rather than repositories of manuscripts. Closer to the temple, also on either side, are two ponds (added later, perhaps in the 16th century); the views of the temple from their banks is one of the most popular. Just

before the temple, steps lead up from the causeway to a cruciform terrace. From its architectural elements, it was probably built after the original design.

You now face the entrance *gopura* of the temple itself, with galleries extending to the left and right. At this point, you have the choice of continuing up towards the towers of the central sanctuary, or of first walking around the Gallery of Bas-Reliefs. It is entirely a matter of personal preference, but for the first-time visitor we recommend leaving the bas-reliefs until later. We continue, for the sake of simplicity, with the architecture.

Enter and climb the steps which lead, in semi-darkness, to the temple's second level. These steps, together with four rectangular stone basins perhaps made water-tight with a layer of clay, are part of a structure known as the 'cruciform cloister'. This is an interesting architectural invention to connect the galleries of the first and second levels, and if you step to either side along the edges of the ponds, you can see how cleverly the three roofed stairways are stepped upwards to join the upper gallery. On the south side of the 'cruciform cloister' are the remains of a few Buddha statues, seated and standing. There were many more, placed in recent centuries by worshippers for whom Angkor Wat was a Theravada Buddhist pilgrimage site, giving this area the name 'Hall of the Thousand Buddhas'. Most were removed for safety in the early 1970s, others were destroyed by the Khmer Rouge during their reign of terror.

Lotus motif on column, gopura *III W*

Above left: The Gallery of Bas-Reliefs from gopura *III W*

One of the four basins in the 'cruciform cloister'

Below right: One of the remaining statues in the 'Hall of the Thousand Buddhas'

Footbridge and gallery wall, second level. The balusters are carved to imitate wood, while the small round columns supporting the terrace date to a later period

You can enter the enclosure of the second level through N and S doorways on the axis of the 'cruciform cloister', although only the two 'libraries' are of interest. Otherwise, continue climbing the steps up to the enclosure of the second level. You emerge from the darkness to another spectacular view – the massif of the central towers rising from the courtyard. A footbridge on stubby round columns, built in the second half of the 13th century, connects the entrance where you are standing with the central towers and with another two 'libraries' on either side. The clearest view of the towers is from either the NW or SW corner of this enclosure (at the extreme left or right), as the massif is set back slightly towards the E. *Apsaras* line the inner wall.

The uppermost level of the temple, which carries the five towers and surrounding galleries, really does look like the final ascent of a great mountain, and although the steps rise just 11m, their steep angle and the proportions of the massif make the climb memorable. The W stairways are less steep (50°) than those on the other three sides. However the S stairway does have a hand rail to assist the less able climbers. From the top of the steps, the view is commanding – the 'libraries' and galleries of the second enclosure below, and the half-kilometre approach from the W entrance beyond. Phnom Bakheng rises to the NW; from its summit there is a wonderful view back to Angkor Wat.

The summit is enclosed by a continuous gallery 60m square, four of the towers rising from the corners, and it is connected to the central shrine and tower (42m high) by axial galleries. All of this creates an effect similar to that of the 'cruciform cloister' below. The shrine itself has changed somewhat since its

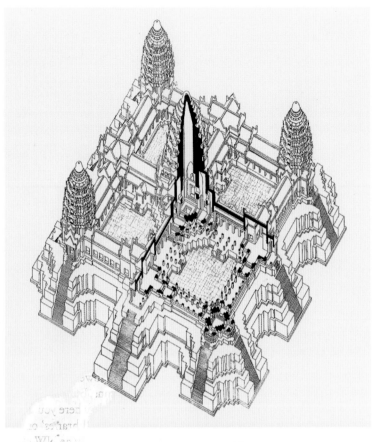

Apsaras, *gallery of the second level*

Upper level and towers from the courtyard of the second level

Krishna raising Mt. Govardhana, pediment of central tower

Above: Connecting gallery, upper level

foundation. Originally it was open on all four sides, and contained a statue of Vishnu (possibly that now found in the W entrance *gopura* by the moat). At some point in the 14th or 15th centuries, however, when the temple was converted to Theravada Buddhist worship, these doorways were blocked by walls carved with standing Buddhas, and the four vestibules turned into Buddhist shrines, as they are now. The doorway behind the standing Buddha on the south side was opened in 1908; inside, the space under the central tower is in pitch darkness, and dangerous, as the earth floor has been excavated into a 25m-deep pit. The sacred treasure buried here was pillaged long ago, and all that was found by the French in their 1934 excavation was a couple of gold leaves. Note the evidence of 16th restoration when columns from the cruciform terrace were reused here.

The bas-reliefs

These, arguably one of the most famous creations in Khmer art, cover the exterior walls of Angkor Wat's third enclosure, just above ground level. The carved area is immense: approaching 600m in length and 2m high with, in addition, the interior of two of the corner pavilions. Apart from two panels, the subject matter is from Hindu sources, mainly the *Ramayana* and *Mahabharata* epics. The exceptions are the Historic procession of Suryavarman II, and the Heavens and Hells carved on the W and E parts of the S Gallery respectively.

If you are pressed for time, you should at least take in the S half of the galleries, from the W *gopura* to that on the E. This includes the Battle of Kurukshetra along the S half of the W Gallery, the SW corner pavilion, the procession of Suryavarman II along the W half of the S Gallery, the Judgement of Yama and Heaven and Hell along the E half of the S Gallery, and the Churning of the Sea of Milk along the S half of the E Gallery. These are all of the highest order. If you have a little

Side elevation of Angkor Wat

more time, include the Battle of Lanka along the northern half of the
W Gallery and the interior of the NW corner pavilion.

Begin at the W *gopura* of the third enclosure, and turn right into the
Gallery of Bas-Reliefs. The viewing conditions are adequate, though
not perfect due to the method of construction of the galleries. In order
to keep the passage as broad as possible, yet structurally sound, the
builders used two rows of pillars. The inner row supports the outer
part of the corbelled vault, while an outer row of shorter pillars
supports a half-vault, similar in intention to the technique of
buttressing in European cathedrals. The disadvantage is that the 2m
high bas-reliefs are unevenly lit and darker towards the top. And, as

Plan of the SW quadrant

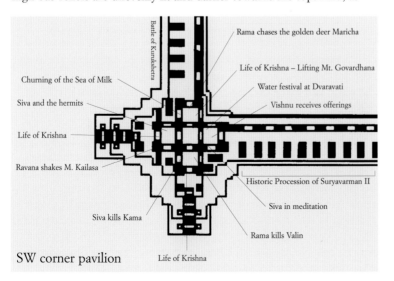

Battle of Kurukshetra

Rama chases the golden deer Maricha

Life of Krishna – Lifting Mt. Govardhana

Churning of the Sea of Milk

Water festival at Dvaravati

Siva and the hermits

Vishnu receives offerings

Life of Krishna

Ravana shakes M. Kailasa

Historic Procession of Suryavarman II

Siva in meditation

Siva kills Kama

Rama kills Valin

SW corner pavilion

Life of Krishna

The Kaurava army advances into the Battle of Kurukshetra

became apparent during recent structural restoration, the half-vaults did not do their job properly – the weight of the gallery roof has pushed the pillars out of alignment.

Battle of Kurukshetra (W Gallery, S section)

The Hindu epic, the *Mahabharata*, describes the struggle between the Pandavas and the Kauravas, two rival clans who, in the climax, fight the Battle of Kurukshetra in northern India. This 49m section of the W Gallery relates the battle, with the Kauravas advancing from the left and the Pandavas from the right. At the extreme N and S, the two armies march in an orderly fashion, with commanders riding horse-drawn chariots and elephants, and with musicians, but the action accelerates towards the centre. At the heart of the battle, the fighting is hand-to-hand and intense. As you walk along from the N, after 5m and near the top you can see Bhishma, the commander-in-chief of the Kauravas, laid dying on a bed of arrows at the end of the 10th day of fighting. 15m beyond this and also near the top, the brahmin Dronacharya, with his hair tied back in a topknot and wielding a bow, leads the Kauravas after Bhishma's death. 2m further on, near the bottom, Karna turns round in his chariot and tries to free the stuck wheel; as he does so he is killed by Arjuna, whom you can see 4m beyond and near the top, at the head of the Pandava army, firing an arrow from his chariot. His charioteer has four arms, identifying him as Krishna. You are now in the thick of the fighting, with hand-to-hand combat on all sides. Note the lunging horse between Karna and Arjuna. From here on are the Pandavas, and 8m further Bhima rides an elephant and carries a shield bearing the face of Rahu. The battle

Kauravas warriors

ended after 18 days, with all the combatants killed signifying the end
of that *yuga*, or world cycle.

SW Corner Pavilion

The interior spaces available for carving are the four bays that each
surround a doorway. The themes are principally mythological, with a
bias to the *Ramayana* and the Life of Krishna (both, therefore,
featuring *avatars* of Vishnu). For convenience, we describe the scenes
in anti-clockwise order, beginning with the W bay, on your right as you
enter the pavilion:

W bay, N side
A god-like figure stands in a doorway, surrounded by adoring women.
One interpretation of this scene is when Siva comes among the hermits
disguised as a beggar to test their pride in having overcome the world
of senses. The wives of the hermits, however, are all attracted to Siva,
causing the hermits to be jealous. Another possibility, suggested by the
reptile over the door, is the demon Ravana taking the form of a
chameleon in order to insinuate himself into the women's quarters of
Indra's palace. Against this, the reptile looks very much like a
crocodile, and compares with the equally enigmatic crocodile over the
image of Vishnu on the W wall of the central sanctuary of Prasat
Kravan (see p.152)

W bay, over door
From the Life of Krishna: The child Krishna crawls on the ground, his
foot tied to a stone by his foster mother Yashoda, who has had enough
of his mischief. He uproots two trees (in fact two gods transformed
into this state until they should see Krishna) by dragging the stone
between them, and they transform back into gods. The scene is framed
in a *naga* arch.

W bay, S side
A 20-armed, multi-headed Ravana shakes Mount Kailasa, enraged
when his path had been barred by Nadikeshvara on the instructions of
Siva who was spending time there with Uma.

S bay, W side
Kama, the God of Love, at the
request of Uma, fires an arrow at
Siva, in order to wake him from
meditation. Siva, who appears here as
a hermit with beard and rosary, is
understandably annoyed at being so
disturbed, and kills Kama. At the
bottom, next to the image of him
firing the arrow, you can see Kama
lying dead, mourned by his wife Rati.
According to the legend Kama was
reduced to ashes and would have had
no body. This representation shows
the Khmer sculptors adapting the
legend for their own purposes.

S bay, over door
From the Life of Krishna: two
consecutive scenes framed in a *naga*

The Battle of Kurukshetra

*Ravana shaking Mount Kailasa,
SW corner pavilion*

The death of Valin, SW corner pavilion

Cockfight at the Dvaravati water festival, SW corner pavilion

arch. At left, Krishna is seated with a hermit as a figure emerges from a wall of flames; at right, he fights with the same figure, who is unidentified. These scenes have not been linked to exact episdodes in Krishna's life and again may be a Khmer adaptation.

S bay, E side

From the *Ramayana*: The fight between the monkey brothers Valin and Sugriva. At the top Rama comes to the aid of his friend Sugriva by shooting Valin with an arrow. Below, Valin on his death-bed, mourned by his wife Tara (whom he had taken from Sugriva) and other monkeys. In four panels below, next to the window, are more monkey mourners with wonderfully expressive faces and gestures.

E bay, S side

Badly damaged bas-relief with Siva seated in meditation.

E bay, over door

Framed in a *naga* arch, a four-armed Vishnu receives offerings held on trays by different kneeling worhsippers, while *apsaras* fly overhead.

E bay, N side

The water festival at Dvaravati. On two registers, heavily decorated boats are rowed across water full of fish. In the upper boat a chess game is in progress (you can even make out differences between the pieces on the board; in the lower boat ladies play with their children).

N bay, E side

From the Life of Krishna: wearing a three-pronged headdress, and with his brother Balarama at his side, Krishna lifts Mount Govardhana to shelter herdsmen and their cattle from a torrential downpour sent by Indra (the cause of Indra's anger was that the people had mistakenly made a first offering to the Govardhana mountain rather than to him). Hermits pray in the forest of the mountain; cattle and villagers shelter below.

N bay, over door

From the *Ramayana*: At Sita's request, Rama fires an arrow at a golden deer – the demon Maricha in disguise so that Ravana can abduct Sita while she is alone in the forest. The scene is framed in a *naga* arch.

N bay, W side

The Churning of the Sea of Milk (partly damaged). At the bottom, over waves and fish, the *asuras* (left) and gods (right) pull alternately on the body of the serpent Vasuki, which is coiled around a pole which is Mount Mandara, to churn the ocean and eventually release *amrita*, the elixir of immortality. The mountain rests on the back of the turtle Kurma, an *avatar* of Vishnu, while Vishnu in human form controls the operation above with his leg around the pole. Indra sits on top of the pole to steady it, and the discs of the sun and moon appear on either side.

Monkeys mourn the death of Valin (shown opposite), SW corner pavilion

Procession of Suryavarman II (S Gallery, W section)

In contrast to Angkor Wat's other bas-reliefs, this 94m-long military procession has an historical basis, and shows King Suryavarman II, the temple's builder, and his army. It begins, at the W edge, with two registers: in the upper is a royal audience before the army sets off, in the lower a procession. 10m from the start, on the upper register, is the king, seated (in keeping with his rank, larger than any other figure). Below, princesses and ladies of the court are carried in palanquins. On the other side of the king are his ministers and army commanders, and after the audience they rise and leave, descending steps to rejoin the army. From here to the end, the army marches in a single register, its 20 commanders riding war elephants, their rank identified by the number of parasols and name identified in small inscriptions. The 12th elephant, exactly halfway along the bas-relief, carries the king, again the largest figure, with 15 parasols. The royal standard, a small statue

King Suryavarman II on his throne before the procession

Princess in a palanquin at the rear of the parade

of Vishnu on *Garuda*, precedes him. Military processions continued just like this throughout the different reigns; the Chinese diplomat Zhou Daguan's description from a century and a half later reads, *"The ministers and princes are all on elephant back; from afar their innumerable red parasols can be seen. ....Behind them at last comes the king, standing on the back of an elephant and holding in his hand the precious sword."*

18m in front of Suryavarman II, the royal sacrificer or *Rajahotar*, a brahmin, rides in a palanquin among priests, just behind the Sacred Fire on its ark (each end decorated with *naga* heads). A band precedes this: note the horns, conch shells, flute and a gong carried by two men. The small group of standard bearers just in front is excellent. The head of the procession is taken by more troops. 8m before the end Prince Jayasimhavarman on an elephant commands a provincial contingent from Louvo (now Lopburi in Central Thailand). Sloping out of step in front of these disciplined troops is a rag-tag body of Siamese mercenaries, wild-looking and armed with spears; their commander also rides an elephant.

Judgement of Yama, and Heavens and Hells (S Gallery, E section)

To the E of the S *gopura*, the theme is the judgement of souls and their consignment to heaven or hell. 66m long, this section is significantly shorter than the preceding Army of Suryavarman II because of the way in which the temple's enclosures are successively set back towards the E, away from the entrance. In order to keep a single N-S axis, all of the N and S *gopuras* are aligned with the central tower. Note the restored ceiling which shows how the space would have appeared originally. It was reconstructed based on a small piece of wood found there. The scene begins on two registers, with two processions, among them the great and good of Khmer society, carried on thrones and palanquins. They are confidently on their way to Heaven. Almost

Below right: Khmer foot soldiers

Siamese mercenaries at the head of the procession

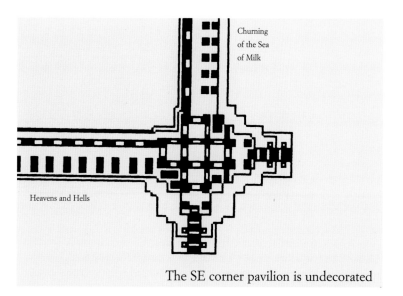

Churning
of the Sea
of Milk

Heavens and Hells

The SE corner pavilion is undecorated

The start of the judgement: the paths to heaven and to hell

immediately, both levels rise to make room for "the way down to the realms of hell" at the bottom, where demons waste no time in beating the damned and dragging them towards their just punishments. See how emaciated the sinners are; after 20m they are menaced by Yama's dogs – the hounds of hell – and beyond that they are savaged by wild animals, including a tiger and a beautifully observed Javan rhinoceros. Some of the damned are pulled along like cattle, with a cord through their nostrils.

The central register, after some 18m, shows the place where souls are judged by Yama, the God of Judgement and of the Underworld, 18-armed and riding his traditional mount, a buffalo. His two assessors Dharma and Chitragupta, 3m further on, listen without mercy to the pleas of sinners, who are thrown down into to Hell through a trapdoor. In fact, they are directed to sin-specific Hells – 32 of them, identified by short inscriptions. At this point, 22m into the bas-relief, the two upper registers end, and the 37 Heavens begin, considerably less interesting than the Hells, where the cruelty is extreme and the

Roasting sinners in the Hell of Avici

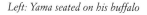

Left: Yama seated on his buffalo

Below: The trap-door to hell

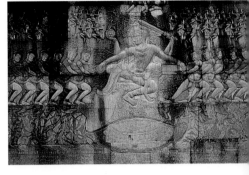

tortures imaginative. Supported by a frieze of *garudas*, the Heavens appear as a succession of palaces where not very much happens, and whatever delight the *apsaras* are supposed to give, they do it modestly. The inhabitants may, however, think it sufficient that they are spared the punishments below, some of which are spectacularly horrible.

Consider, for instance, the 3rd Hell, Vaitarani, the Hindu equivalent of the River Styx, where demons use long pincers to pull out the tongues of their victims (5m after the trapdoor); the 6th, Nirucchvasa, where the damned are slowly cooked; the burning lake of the 9th, Taptalaksamaya; bone-smashing in the 10th, Ashthibhanga. In the next, Krakaccheda, gluttons are sawn in two, which seems a little out of proportion, while in Puyapurnahrada immediately following, "those who steal strong liquor, seduce others' wives, go near the wives of scholars" (a strange combination) are torn to pieces by birds of prey and thrown into a lake of slimy pus. In the 23rd Hell, Kalasutra, demons roast a man on a spit. The 29th is Cita, the frozen Hell, where you can see thieves shivering. Between 3m and 2m from the end is a particularly unpleasant punishment in the Hell of Maharaurava: the victims are tied to frames, and nails hammered into their entire bodies.

Walk through the SE corner pavilion, which is undecorated, to the next section.

Churning of the Sea of Milk (E Gallery, S section)

Taken from the *Bhagavata-Purana*, this great Hindu creation myth is here spectacularly realised in one continuous 49m panel. By pulling alternately on the body of the giant *naga* Vasuki, which is coiled around Mount Mandara, the gods and *asuras* rotate the mountain for 1,000 years to churn the cosmic sea – the Sea of Milk – and so produce *amrita*, the elixir of immortality. In the event, this cooperation between gods and *asuras* is shattered as soon as the *amrita* begins to be produced. The gods go back on their promise to give half to the *asuras*, who then try to steal it. The scene shown here, however, is the actual churning.

For the first 5m, the army of *asuras* is lined up with horses and elephants; the churning begins directly after this, and the first you see is a giant multi-headed *asura* – Ravana – holding the five heads of the giant *naga* Vasuki. Beyond him stretches the team of 92 *asuras* pulling in unison on the serpent's body. The cosmic sea is represented by a swirling mass of marine life, caught up in the turbulence, all enclosed by a second representation of the *naga*, lying flat on the bottom of the ocean, its heads rearing up at the far left. In the sky above fly large numbers of *apsaras*, created as part of the process.

As you walk along, note the variety of marine life, most real, some mythical. It includes, among many kinds of fish, crocodiles, dragons, *nagas*, and turtles. Close to the centre of the panel the churning is so violent that many of them are sliced into pieces. In the middle, on the pillar-like Mount Mandara, four-armed Vishnu directs operations. He also appears below, as his turtle *avatar* Kurma, supporting the rotating mountain as it threatens to sink below the sea. The treatment here is full of incident and detail: above, a flying Indra helps to steady the top of the mountain, while close to Vishnu's discus are tiny images of the elephant Airavata and the horse Ucchaissravas, both created by the churning, like the *apsaras*. Notice that the area surrounding Vishnu is

Opposite
Top left: Ravana holds the head of the naga Vasuki
Middle: Asuras *pull on the serpent*
Below: Fish and a crocodile caught up in the churning
Top right: Vishnu supervises the churning

Below: One of the 88 gods pulling on the serpent's body

Hanuman, at the naga's *tail, encourages the gods to pull harder*

incompletley carved. The presence of Ravana and Hanuman on either side is quite unique and not part of the original legend. It represents the Khmer combining the ancient Vedic legend with characters from the *Ramayana*.

On the N side, as you continue, 88 gods pull the *naga*'s body in the opposite direction, commanded at the tail by a giant Hanuman. The last 5m of the bas-relief are taken up by the army of the gods.

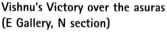

Vishnu's Victory over the asuras (E Gallery, N section)

N of the *gopura* (which has an inscription dated 23 February 1702, describing the building of the now-ruined 'chedi', or tomb, just outside the gallery), the next 52m of bas-relief show Vishnu fighting an army of *asuras*. Both the design and carving are markedly inferior to the preceding bas-reliefs, and it comes as a rather monotonous disappointment. It was carved much later, between 1546 and 1564. As in the Battle of Kurukshetra and the Churning of the Sea of Milk, the composition focuses on the centre, with the *asuras* converging from both sides on Vishnu, who stands four-armed on the shoulders of Garuda. One of the few points of interest is a group of *asuras* riding giant birds 3m beyond Vishnu, their legs wrappped around the birds' necks.

Krishna on garuda *during the battle with Bana. (Jaroslav Poncar)*

Plan of NE quadrant

Krishna's Victory over the asura Bana (N Gallery, E section)

Turn the corner through the (uncarved) pavilion. The next 66m section is also poorly executed, and shows Krishna defeating the *asura* Bana. 6m from the start, Krishna appears eight-armed and riding *Garuda*, with Pradyumna (left) and Balarama (right) carrying a plough. 3m beyond this, *Garuda* faces a wall of flames thrown up by Agni, the God of Fire, who rides a rhinoceros. Krishna appears riding *Garuda* again, on four different occasions in the battle, finally meeting the multi-armed Bana, who rides a chariot pulled by strange-looking lions, 10m before the end of the relief. Krishna, having cut off all but two of Bana's 1,000 hands with a single throw of his discus, emerges victorious, but finally, in the last 5m, kneels before Siva at Mount Kailasa and agrees to spare Bana's life. Siva's son Ganesha is seated at his feet. Below, *hermits* pray in grottoes in Mount Kailasa.

Battle between gods and asuras (N Gallery, W section)

This next bas-relief, well carved and running

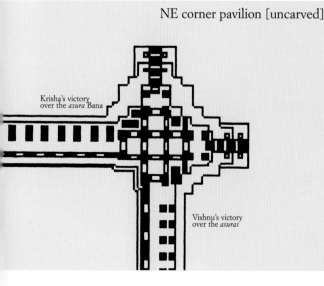

for 94m, shows an unspecified battle between gods and *asuras*. The battle is engaged immediately, with the gods facing W, the direction in which you are walking, and is interesting chiefly because it details the 21 important gods in the Hindu pantheon, with their *varanas*, or mounts. They include:

Kubera, God of Wealth, on a *Yaksha* (27m from the start)
Agni, God of Fire, in a chariot pulled by a rhinoceros (33m)
Skanda, God of War, on a peacock (37m)
Indra, King of the Gods, on the elephant Airavata (44m)
Vishnu on *Garuda* (54m)
Yama, Judge and King of the Dead, on a chariot pulled by buffalos (63m)
Siva in a chariot pulled by the bull Nandi (67m)
Brahma on a *hamsa* (71m)
Surya, the Sun God, in a chariot pulled by horses (76m)
Varuna, God of the Ocean, on a 5-headed *naga* (86m)
The multi-headed *asura* Kalanemi appears 60m from the start, in a horse-drawn chariot.

Krishna pays respects to Siva at the end of the battle with Bana. (Vittorio Roveda)

NW Corner Pavilion

Identical in construction to the SW Corner Pavilion, its four bays are all carved. nine of the 12 scenes have been identified as being from *Ramayana* and it is likely that the remaining three are also. They are, in anti-clockwise order, beginning with the N bay, on your right as you enter the pavilion:

N bay, E side
Unidentified scene with two noble figures, one of them wearing a three-pronged headdress, seated in a palace, surrounded by courtiers. There are two prone figures, with hair flowing outwards, below the palace.

N bay, over door
From the *Ramayana*: Within a *naga* arch, Rama and Lakshmana, grimacing fiercely, use bow and arrow to slay the demon Viradha, who has captured Sita in the forest. The demon holds Sita in his left arm, and attacks the brothers with a spear.

The god Kalanemi in the scene showing the Invitation to the Descent of Vishnu

Plan of NW quadrant

N bay, W side
From the *Ramayana*: (badly damaged) the scene in which Sita submits to trial by fire to prove her faithfulness to Rama during her period of captivity. No trace of Sita remains in the relief, but you can see the flames clearly above and to the right of where her figure was.

W bay, N side
From the *Ramayana*: the return in triumph of Rama to Ayodhya, following victory in the Battle of Lanka. He rides the chariot Pushpaka, belonging to Kubera, drawn by *hamsas* which appear as a

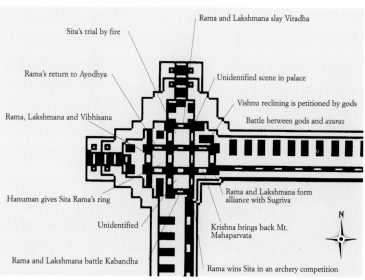

Rama and Lakshmana slay Viradha
Sita's trial by fire
Rama's return to Ayodhya
Unidentified scene in palace
Vishnu reclining is petitioned by gods
Battle between gods and *asuras*
Rama, Lakshmana and Vibhisana
Rama and Lakshmana form alliance with Sugriva
Hanuman gives Sita Rama's ring
Krishna brings back Mt. Mahaparvata
Unidentified
Rama and Lakshmana battle Kabandha
Rama wins Sita in an archery competition
N

frieze over the window. To the right of the window, monkeys dance and play musical instruments in celebration.

W bay, over door

From the *Ramayana*: Rama (centre) and Lakshmana, with a monkey troop behind them at right, forge an alliance with the demon Ravana's brother Vibhisana (with a typical demon headdress, on the left of Rama). The scene is framed in a *naga* arch.

W bay, S side

From the *Ramayana*: (partly damaged) Hanuman, having found Sita held captive by Ravana on the island of Lanka, introduces himself by offering Rama's ring. The *rakshasi* Trijata sits on the other side of Sita.

S bay, W side

Unidentified scene in which a four-armed Vishnu, or Krishna, is seated in meditation, with a smaller figure seated on the right, surrounded by *apsaras* dancing on either side and below, and flying above.

S bay, over door

From the *Ramayana*: Framed in a *naga* arch, Rama and his brother Lakshmana battle the demon Kabandha, who appears as a giant disembodied head (similar to Rahu).

S bay, E side

From the *Ramayana*: at the royal court of King Janaka, Rama wins the hand of the King's daughter Sita in an archery competition, aiming up at a bird perched on a wheel. None of the other competitors were strong enough to draw the bow, which formerly belonged to Siva.

E bay, S side

From the Life of Krishna: Krishna, riding *garuda* and with his wife Satyabhama on his right side (standing on *garuda*'s hand) returns victorious from having wrested Mount Maniparvata from the *asura* Naraka. The mountain, a broad triangle with trees, is behind Krishna, while the ranks of his army around and below him carry the spoils of war.

E bay, over door

From the *Ramayana*: Framed in a *naga* arch, Rama and Lakshmana make an alliance with the monkey king Sugriva. Rama is holding a bow in the centre; Sugriva faces him.

E bay, N side

Vishnu Reclining. Near the top, with *apsaras* flying overhead, the god rests on the serpent Ananta, his feet supported by his wife Lakshmi. The serpent floats on the cosmic ocean, represented by shoals of fish. Below, a procession of gods, riding their mounts to ask Vishnu to appear on earth. They are probably acting as guardians of the eight directions (*dikpalas*). They are, left to right:–
Kubera on the shoulders of a *yaksha* (N)
Varuna on a *hamsa* (W)
Skanda on a peacock

Krishna bringing back Mt. Mahaparvata (Photo: EFEO)

Above right: Rama with bow and arrows, standing on the shoulders of Hanuman during the Battle of Lanka

Monkey warriors defeating asuras *in the Battle of Lanka*

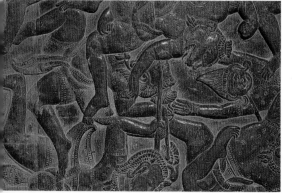

Vayu on a horse
Indra on his elephant Airavata (E)
Yama on a buffalo (S)
Agni on a rhinoceros
Ketu on a lion
On two panels below, next to the window, a frontal view of Surya (the Sun) and Candra (the Moon) on their horse-drawn chariots.

Battle of Lanka (W Gallery, N section)

The final bas-relief (if you have made the complete circuit from *Gopura III W*) is a marvellously vital depiction of the climax of the *Ramayana* – the Battle of Lanka, in which Rama and his allies, including the monkey troops, defeat Ravana and rescue Sita. The standard of carving is excellent, and the details of the hand-to-hand fighting closely observed. The main characters are near the centre of the 51m panel. 21m from the start, Rama wields his bow while standing on the shoulders of Hanuman. Next to Hanuman stand the demon Vibhisana (Ravana's brother, with whom Rama has forged an alliance) and Rama's brother Lakshmana. 5m further on is the first of a series of duels spaced 2-3m apart: the monkey Nila vs. the *rakshasa* Prahasta; Valin's son Angada vs. Mahodara (Angada wrenches out the tusk of Mahodara's elephant); 20-armed Ravana on a chariot drawn by lions; Angada vs. Vajra-damstra; Angada vs. Narantaka; another monkey vs. two dragons, which he holds up by their hind legs; Hanuman vs. Nikumba; and Sugriva vs. Kumba.

The galleries and towers from the west

Other monuments of the period
At Angkor: Banteay Samré, Thommanon, Chao Say Tevoda. Elsewhere: Beng Mealea (40km E); Phimai, Phnom Rung, Sikhoraphum, Ku Suan Taeng, Yai Ngao (all Thailand); much of Wat Phu (Laos).
Best times to visit
Angkor Wat is of sufficient complexity that at any time of day there are features to be seen at their best. Equally, it is too large to take in at one specific time.
Sunrise: silhouette of the central sanctuary from the W entrance *gopura* and, with reflections, from either of the water-filled basins on either side of the causeway; the towers from the E side of the second level; the panorama from the W entrance of the 3rd terrace. *Morning*: the E-facing *apsaras* on the walls of the W entrance *gopura* and the S-facing *apsaras* on the N side of the gallery of the 2nd terrace. *Late afternoon*: the W-facing bas-reliefs of the *Ramayana* and *Mahabharata* on the Gallery of Bas-Reliefs; the W entrance *gopura* and moat from the road. *Sunset*: The towers and W galleries from the causeway; the towers from the NW corner of the 2nd terrace. *Full-moon*: the central sanctuary from the W entrance *gopura*; the towers from the 2nd terrace. *Any time*: the Gallery of Bas-Reliefs; the cross-shaped galleries connecting the lower and 2nd terraces; all interiors. There are also fine views from the summit of Phnom Bakheng, particularly early in the morning and late in the afternoon.
Location and access
5.5 km north of Siem Reap on the main road to the monuments — the first temple reached. There is a T-junction at the end of this road, opposite the S outer *gopura* and moat. Turn left, following the moat, and at the SW corner turn right; the entrance to the causeway across the moat is 650 m ahead.

TA PROHM KEL

Date: 1186
Style: Bayon
Reign: Jayavarman VII
Visit: 10 mins

Ta Prohm Kel looking west

This small ruined sandstone monument was one of the 102 chapels added to hospitals, some of which were already in existence, by Jayavarman VII all over the empire. The sanctuary, with its now-collapsed tower, opened to the E and had false doors on the other three sides. It was preceded by a small sandstone *gopura* a little to the E, of which traces remain. The decoration is in the style of the Bayon, with *devatas* and small roundels enclosing figures. A *somasutra*, or channel for draining lustral water out of the shrine, exited through the N wall of the sanctuary.

Similar monuments of the period
At Angkor: Hospital chapel near Ta Keo and also chapels to the N and W. In Thailand: Prang Ku, the Kuti Reussis, Ta Muen Toch, Phimai.
Best times to visit
Any time.
Location and access
450m N of the entrance to Angkor Wat, to the left of the road.

Bakheng plan

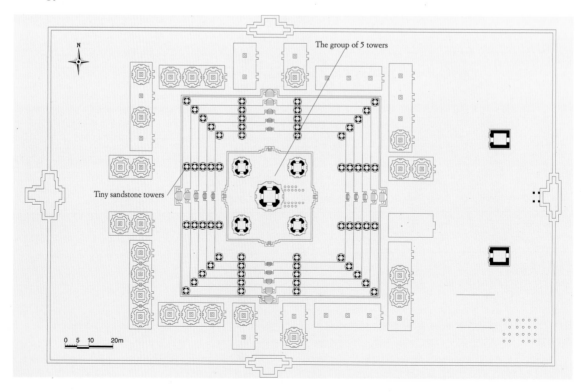

The group of 5 towers

Tiny sandstone towers

PHNOM BAKHENG ✥

Date: Late 9th to early 10th century (dedicated about 907)
Style: Bakheng
Reign: Yasovarman I
Visit: 1 hr, including climb

Highlights
★ State temple of the first
  capital at Angkor
★ Spectacular views, particularly
  of Angkor Wat

As the State temple of the first city at Angkor, Phnom Bakheng has a special importance, even though many of its buildings are in poor condition. It was to here that Yasovarman I moved his capital from Roluos, 13 km southeast of Siem Reap. The city, called Yasodharapura, was 4 km square (larger than the later Angkor Thom) and enclosed by an earth bank. It was centred on the isolated hill of Phnom Bakheng.

With some important differences, Bakheng imitates the temple of Bakong at Roluos, built some two decades earlier – a pyramid of ascending square terraces surrounded by subsidiary sanctuary towers. Work began at the end of the 9th century, the *linga* of the central shrine was dedicated in about 907, but building continued after that. The name of the divinity and of the temple was Yasodharesvara –'the Lord of (the one) Who Bears Glory'. It was abandoned after 928, but briefly rehabilitated in about 968 by Jayavarman V.

The small towers and lions flanking the eastern staircase, from the base of the pyramid

Small divinity at the base of a pilaster on the central sanctuary

Devata *on the W side of the central sanctuary*

Plan

There was an outer enclosure surrounding the hill, in the form of a rectangular moat 650m x 436m; parts of its earth bank survive. At the foot of the hill were four *gopuras* in brick and laterite at the cardinal points; some of their foundations can still be traced. Stairways lead up from the E, N and W *gopuras*, though oddly not from the S (there may not have been enough time to complete all four). The E entrance was the principal one, and at the foot of the staircase are the remains of two large guardian lions.

The temple itself occupies the summit, which was first substantially levelled, leaving a pyramid of rock in the centre from which the terraces were cut. In addition, the core of the temple has been carved as a stepped pyramid from the hill itself, as can be seen from the SW side. The 13m-high pyramid, set back slightly to the W in the enclosure, is made of five terraces, the lowest of which is 76m square, the topmost 47m square. Around the base of the pyramid are 44 brick towers in groups of 2, 3 and 4. On the terraces of the pyramid above are another 60 tiny towers in sandstone, arranged symmetrically (pairs flanking each stairway, and one on each corner of each terrace). On the summit itself was a quincunx of towers built on a low platform, 1.60m high, 31 m square, and set back slightly to the W. Thus in total there are 108 towers plus one, the principal tower, which subsumes the rest. The number 108 is considered sacred according to Hindu and, indeed, Buddhist cosmogony.

Visit

Begin the ascent from the east side, at the foot of the hill, close to the road. As you reach the top of the staircase, you can appreciate the extent of the levelling that the builders undertook: in front of you is a wide open space crossed by a broad pathway, some 100m long. This space was perhaps occupied by priests' dwellings; there would have been a substantial number because of the Bakheng's many shrines to be tended. In the middle of this path is a later Buddha footprint. Beyond this are the remains of the E *gopura* of the inner enclosure, 190m x 120m, originally walled in laterite. For those wishing to make a more leisurely ascent rather than straight up the steep steps, there is on the S side slightly left of the steps a winding path, referred to by the Khmer as 'the elephant path'.

The elongated proportions of this enclosure were dictated by the oval plan of the hill, and the N and S *gopuras* are noticeably squeezed up to the base of the pyramid. To your left and right are two 'libraries', which as usual open to the W but also have secondary E entrances; their side walls are pierced with small diamond-shaped holes. The pyramid, with its 60 small shrines arranged symmetrically around all of the five levels, rises in front of you. The builders enhanced the impression of its height by manipulating perspective – the elevation of each terrace is less than that of the one below, and the size of the lions which flank the four staircases also decreases.

At the summit, all that remains of the towers is the shell of the central one, and some ruins. The central tower of this group of five was the largest, but little now remains. Note, however, its fine carvings of full-bodied *devatas*. An attempt in the 16th century to build a large seated Buddha used most of the sandstone blocks from these central five towers, and this largely accounts for their present condition: the NE and SE towers are in ruins, and the NW and SW towers are completely gone.

The view from the summit is magnificent, particularly of Angkor Wat to the SE, and is popular at sunset. Further to your right, S, is the hill of Phnom Krom, 16 km distant on the shores of the Tonlé Sap. The three prominent hills of the area – Phnom Bakheng, Phnom Krom and Phnom Bok (14 km WNW) – were all crowned with temples at around the same time. Over to the W are the waters of the West Baray; the islet in the middle (depending on the level of the water) is West Mebon. The E edge of the *baray*, closest to where you are standing, was made from part of the W earth wall of the city of Yasodharapura – the work was done in the 11th century.

Linga of the NE sanctuary on the summit

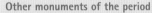

Other monuments of the period
At Angkor: Phnom Krom, Phnom Bok. In Thailand: parts of Phnom Wan. In Laos: Huei Thamo.
Best times to visit
Sunrise and early morning for the temple itself and stairway. Sunrise, early morning, late afternoon and sunset for the views from the summit (but take care if descending the steep stairway after dark)
Location and access
On the summit of Phnom Bakheng (67m), 1.7 km NW of Angkor Wat. Use the E staircase, which is 1.2 km N of the W entrance to Angkor Wat, on the left of the road. If approaching from the Bayon and the N, stop on the road 400 m S of Angkor Thom's S Gate. The climb is quite steep: allow 15-20 min. By the 'elephant path' the time is about the same.

View east to the Buddha's footprint from the pyramid's E staircase

BAKSEI CHAMKRONG

Date:	Early and middle 10th century (re-dedicated 948)
Style:	Bakheng to Koh Ker
Reigns:	Harshavarman, restored by Rajendravarman
Visit:	15 mins

Highlights
★ The only pyramid temple at Angkor that was not a state temple

The brick pyramid and tower, facing E

The name Baksei Chamkrong, meaning 'the bird with sheltering wings' is modern and irrelevant. This small, elegant pyramid temple stands at the foot of Phnom Bakheng, not far from the (later) S Gate of Angkor Thom. A single brick tower on a stepped pyramid of laterite, it was built to house statues of Siva and his spouse Devi and dedicated to the memory of his parents by King Harsharvam I.

After the interlude in which the capital moved from Angkor to Koh Ker, Baksei Chamkrong was restored by the new king, Rajendravarman, and the shrine's god dedicated at 9.40 in the morning on Wednesday 23 February 948. However, the elements described in the inscription have long vanished: 'a splendid stucco decoration' to the tower, and the 'gold' statue of Paramesvara (referring to Siva, represented as a statue rather than a *linga* as in Preah Ko).

Plan

Although now almost completely disappeared, a brick enclosure originally surrounded the pyramid, with a stone *gopura* on the E side. The pyramid, which measures 27m square at the base, rises in four laterite stages to a summit measuring 15m square and 13m high. Four stairways reach the summit at the cardinal points, but their condition at the time of writing is not good, and one should be careful in making the climb.

The brick sanctuary tower, 8m square on a sandstone base, opens to the E, with the usual blind doors on the other sides. The E door frame is carved with an important inscription, which details the dedication mentioned above, and praises the early Khmer kings from Jayavarman II onwards, as well as earlier legendary kings, including the ancestor of the nation, the hermit Kambu. The lintel above shows Indra on a three-headed Airavata. *Devatas* in niches are lightly incised in the brickwork at the corners of the tower; these would have been a guide for the stucco decoration that covered them but which has disappeared.

Other monuments of the period
At Angkor: Prasat Kravan.
Best times to visit
Morning, for the light filtering through the trees on this E-facing temple.
Location and access
Between Phnom Bakheng and the S Gate of Angkor Thom (150 m N of the E entrance to the former, 300m SW of the causeway of the latter). The temple is set back from the road on the W side and easily visible. The 4 steep stairways are an awkward climb – that on the N side is the least difficult.

PRASAT BEI

Date: 10th century
Style: Bakheng
Reign: Yasovarman I
Visit: 5 mins

The three brick towers of Prasat Bei

Prasat Bei means 'three towers' and here the brick towers stand in a N-S row, facing east and on a 24m x 10m laterite platform. This probably unfinished temple was partly restored by Groslier at the end of the 1960s. The central tower contained a *linga*; the flanking towers reach no higher than the doorways. Only the lintels of the central and S towers were carved, both showing Indra on the elephant Airavata (three-headed on the central, one-headed on the S).

Other monuments of the period
Bakheng, Phnom Krom, Phnom Bok
Best times to visit
Any time. Combine with Thma Bay Kaek.
Location and access
Between Baksei Chamkrong and the moat of Angkor Thom, 300m W of the road and 175m W of Thma Bay Kaek. Follow the path just before the row of gods at the approach to the S Gate of Angkor Thom, and continue past Thma Bay Kaek.

THMA BAY KAEK

Date: 10th century
Style: Bakheng
Reign: Yasovarman I
Visit: 5 mins

All that remains of this temple which must be one of many that originally surrounded the Bakheng are the ruins of a square brick tower, E-facing and preceded by a laterite terrace. A sacred treasure consisting of five gold leaves arranged in a quincunx, the central leaf carrying the image of Nandi (Siva's bull) was found here.

Best times to visit
Any time.
Location and access
Between Baksei Chamkrong and the moat of Angkor Thom, 125m W of the road. Follow the path just before the row of gods at the approach to the S Gate of Angkor Thom.

ANGKOR THOM ✤✤✤

Highlights
★ One of the largest Khmer cities ever built, 9 sq km in area
★ Face-towers and causeways of the city gates
★ With the Bayon at its centre, a microcosm of the universe

Date: Late 12th century and later (excluding some earlier monuments inside, such as the Bapuon and Phimeanakas)
Style: Bayon (excluding some earlier monuments inside)
Reign: Jayavarman VII and successors
Visit: Several hours (see entries for individual monuments)

This, one of the largest of all Khmer cities, was founded by Jayavarman VII and probably remained the capital until the 17th century. For most visitors, the first sight of this monumental construction is the magnificent S Gate, with its towers with four faces pointing in each of the cardinal directions and elephants, preceded by the no less impressive avenue of gods and *asuras* lining the bridge across the moat.

Angkor Thom overlaps the SE corner of the first capital of Yasodharapura (end of 9th century), and incorporates temples of previous centuries, notably Bapuon and Phimeanakas. And, as it remained the capital of Jayavarman's successors, there are many later additions and some re-modelling. Its name which dates at least from the 16th century, appropriately enough, means 'Great City'.

The S gate of Angkor Thom, from inside the city

Plan

The city walls, surrounded by a moat, enclose a square, approximately 3km on each side. The total area, therefore, is 900 hectares, most of it now forest but originally a considerable city. These walls are pierced by four gates at the cardinal points, and the roads that pass through them converge on the central State Temple of Jayavarman VII, the Bayon. A 5th gate, known as the Victory Gate, pierces the E wall of the city 500m N of the E Gate, and its road leads directly to the Royal Palace (by tradition, the palace was always sited N of the State Temple).

Visit

The usual approach is from the S, passing through the S Gate and on to the Bayon in the exact centre of the city. There are, however, so many other monuments, most of them in the area N of the Bayon, that a single visit is rarely sufficient. Moreover, temples in

the N, NE and E of the Angkor region are usually reached by driving through Angkor Thom, so that many people stop off at monuments inside the city while passing through. Because of this, individual monuments are dealt with separately in this guide in the following pages.

The S Gate

On the road from Angkor Wat and Siem Reap, this is the first point of entry to the city for most visitors. All five gates are similar, but the S Gate has been the most extensively restored and is the most complete. Constant use has helped to save the statues of gods and *asuras* that line its approach; most of the heads at the other gates have been stolen, and only the N Gate retains a number of complete figures.

The approach to the gate, crossing the moat, is lined by an avenue of statues. On the left and on the right, two rows of figures each carry the body of a giant serpent – a seven-headed *naga* – almost in the attitude of a tug-of-war. The figures on the left are gods, while those on the right, with fierce grimaces, are *asuras* (demons). The parallels with the Churning of the Sea of Milk, particularly as sculpted on the gallery of Angkor Wat, are obvious; even the headdresses are the same. The

Head of asura *from the entrance to the S gate*

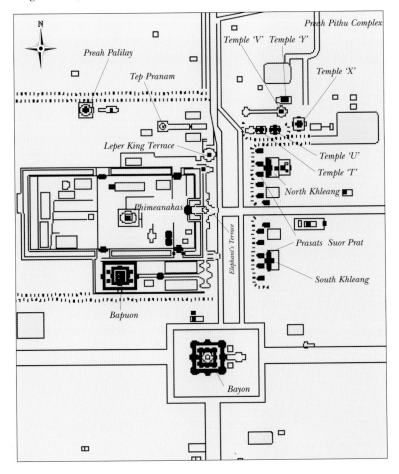

Map of Angkor Thom, showing the NW and NE areas close to the Bayon.

Head of god from the entrance to the N gate

question then remains, where is the actual churning taking place, with Mount Mandara as the pivot? The most likely focus is the State Temple of the city itself – the Bayon. Support for this theory is the absence of enclosing wall and moat around the Bayon, suggesting that the walls of the city and its moat take their place. If so, this is a grand conception of religious symbolism, covering an entire city.

The symbolism does not stop there, however. The use of *naga* balustrades lining the approach to a temple and usually across a moat was common, and it is believed that the purpose was to link the world of men (outside the temple) to the world of the gods (inside). According to George Coedès and Paul Mus, such '*naga* bridges' correspond to a rainbow, which provides the same function in Hindu tradition. So, even with the addition of gods and *asuras*, the approaches to the gates of Angkor Thom are '*naga* bridges'. Another suggestion is that the *nagas* are the guardians of the city's royal wealth.

The gates themselves, 23m high, have a triple tower carved with four faces – a foretaste of the Bayon. The faces, like all of those on the towers of this period, closely resemble the known statues of Jayavarman VII. These could be representations of Lokesvara, and their position at the cardinal points of the city may also signal his control over the far reaches of the empire. The faces were added late than the main construction.

At the base of the gate-tower, on either side, is another wonderful invention: a three-headed elephant plucking lotus flowers with its trunks, which form pillars. The elephant is none other than Airavata, the mount of the god Indra. As Indra is the god of the sky, as well as king of the gods, this may re-inforce the idea of the '*naga* bridge' representing a rainbow.

Other gates
These were identical in construction to the S Gate, the difference nowadays being in the condition – most of the heads of the statues of gods and *asuras* are missing. Note that the original paving stones remain under the W Gate.

Asura holding the naga's *body, entrance to the N gate*

The walls

Built of laterite with an earth embankment on the inside, the city walls are 8m high and 3km long on each side; an inscription confirms that they were built for defence. It is possible to follow the parapet on foot, and the view over the moat is at the same time peaceful and impressive. The natural drainage of the region is towards the SW. Thus drainage tunnels were constructed at the NE corner to bring water in and in the SW corner to take the water out. The latter, very well done, is worth a visit.

The Prasats Chrung

At each corner of the city, on the earthern embankment that reaches almost to the top of the walls, is a small temple known as Prasat Chrung –'Shrine of the Angle' in modern Khmer. These four sandstone temples, in the style of the Bayon, were Buddhist and dedicated to the Bodhisattva Lokesvara, as was the Bayon and the city. Cross-shaped in plan and facing E, each was surrounded by a wall with a single opening on the E side. The sanctuary is surmounted by a tower and originally steles with a poem praising the king were housed in small adjacent structures. Each stele has four different authors. Today these are housed in the Conservation office.

The best-preserved is that in the SE corner: once inside the South Gate, turn right and climb the earthen bank up to the parapet, then follow this for 1.5km. Some of the originally Buddhist pediments were defaced in the late 13th century during the reign of Jayavarman VIII and the figure of the Buddha was transformed into a *linga*.

Other monuments of the period
At Angkor: Bayon, Ta Prohm, Banteay Kdei, Preah Khan, Neak Pean, Ta Som, Srah Srang, Ta Nei, Ta Prohm Kel. Elsewhere in Cambodia: Banteay Chhmar.
Best times to visit
There is much to see at any time of the day – see entries for individual monuments.
Location and access
The S Gate is 1.7 km north of the W entrance to Angkor Wat; the N Gate is 1.6 km SW of Preah Khan; the Victory Gate is 1km W of Ta Keo. These are the three driveable entrances.

The E entrance of the SE Prasat Chrung

THE BAYON ✦✦✦

Date: Late 12th to late 13th centuries, construction probably starting about 1200
Style: Bayon
Reign: Jayavarman VII to Jayavarman VIII
Visit: 2 hrs

This, the State Temple of Jayavarman VII and his immediate successors, is one of the most enigmatic and powerful religious constructions in the world. The temple is extremely complex both in terms of its structure and meaning, having passed through different religious phases from Pantheon of the Gods, Hindu worship and Buddhism. It uses, uniquely, a mass of face-towers to create a stone mountain of ascending peaks. There is some dispute about the number of towers. There were originally 49 towers even though Paul Mus thought there should be 54. Today only 37 are standing. Most are carved with four faces on each cardinal point but sometimes there are only three or even just two. The central tower has many more. Readers are invited to write in when they have counted them all. Whatever the final number the overall effect is quite overwhelming.

Plan

The Bayon has gone through several architectural changes, with additions that are responsible for the complexity and crowding at its centre. This is because the city of Angkor Thom was so well fortified

Aerial view from the NE

Face towers in the SE part of the upper terrace

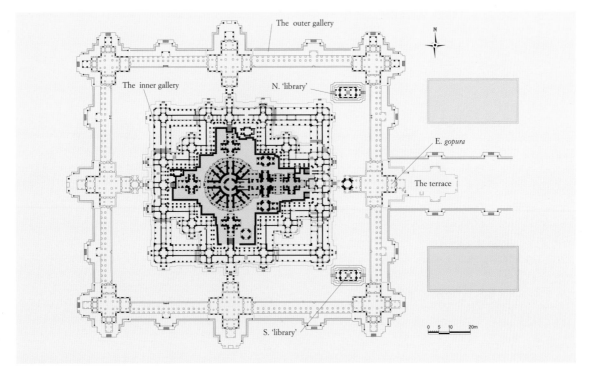

The outer gallery

The inner gallery

N. 'library'

E. gopura

The terrace

S. 'library'

0 5 10 20m

that later kings found it simpler to re-model the Bayon rather than
remove it and build their own new State Temple which would have
had to have been in the same place at the centre of the city. Its plan is
distinctive and has many peculiarities.

The temple itself is composed of two galleried enclosures, which are
almost square, but also on three levels, because of the rebuilding
described below. The approach, which is probably later, is a broad,
two-tiered terrace, 72m long and guarded by lions, leading to the
eastern *gopura* of the outer enclosure, which measures 156m x 141m.
This is the first, at ground level and is surrounded by a gallery with
corner pavilions and *gopura*s. Within this, the inner enclosure is 80m x
70m, and is slightly offset, in common with most Khmer temples, away
from the entrance. Between the 3rd and 2nd enclosure, can be clearly
seen traces of 16 large chapels where Buddhist and local divinities
were housed. They were demolished by Jayavarman VIII.

The confusion of the Bayon begins inside the inner enclosure, where
additional construction has made a complex arrangement of galleries
and towers on the second level. Within the almost-square surround of
galleries, another set of redented galleries in each corner enclose a
cross shape. It is generally agreed that the original gallery was cross-
shaped, and that the corners that make it now rectangular were added
later.

Almost filling the cross-shaped gallery walls is the 3rd level – the
upper terrace, also later – and in the centre of this rises the central
massif, which is, very unusually, round. 25m in diameter, it reaches a
height of 43m above ground-level, and is connected to a series of small
chambers to the east. In fact, it was originally cruciform in plan, but
later radiating chapels filled in the 'circle'.

Dominating the whole arrangement of galleries and terraces are the
face-towers, some over the *gopura*s, others over the corner angles, yet
others free-standing on the upper terrace. As mentioned above the

Guardian lion at the E approach

number of faces are in dispute. Equally, the actual numbers of towers
do not have any symbolic significance as many were added later. Their
different individual heights combined with the different levels of the
temple create the impression of a forest of towers rising towards the
centre.

The temple from the E

Visit

The Bayon is sufficiently compact to
encourage any order of visit, particularly
as the absence of a surrounding wall
makes it easy to enter at any point. Not
only this, but one of the special pleasures
of this unique temple is to immerse
yourself in its maze-like qualities. The
confusion of the inner enclosure, with its
narrow chambers, corridors and
stairways, giving occasional surprise
glimpses of the enigmatic faces, is itself a
fascinating experience. The itinerary that
we propose here is just a suggestion; as
with Angkor Wat, a tour of the extensive
bas-reliefs competes with an exploration
of the temple's architecture.

We begin at the E, climbing the steps
up to the long terrace that approaches the
temple, with guardian lions and *naga*
balustrades on either side. From here, the
face-towers appear as a confused jumble
of stone, and only begin to resolve
themselves as you get closer. The terrace
ends at the eastern *gopura*, which is partly
collapsed. Note the lightly incised
carvings of dancing *apsaras* on the pillars.
You now face the outer bas-relief gallery,
4.5m high.

How much time you spend with the
bas-reliefs will depend on your level of
interest. The S section of the E Gallery
and the E section of the S Gallery are
generally considered the most interesting,
and this fits in conveniently with a short

Dancing apsaras *on a column of the
outer gallery*

tour of the temple. For this, turn left at the main east entrance to the
SE corner, then turn right and continue as far as the *gopura* in the
middle of the S Gallery. This will give you the best introduction to the
bas-reliefs (for a description, see the separate section on the bas-reliefs
below), and you can then enter the temple from the S. As you start,
note that the gallery wall is pierced at intervals with small doorways. In
fact, there are 16 of these, and they originally gave access to chapels on
the inside, which housed Buddhist guardian divinities. These, however,
have all disappeared; they were part of the temple's original plan, and
pulled down in middle of the 13th century.

After you have followed the bas-reliefs on the S Gallery to its
middle, enter the outer enclosure, where you can see to your right the
S elevated 'library' in the corner. This 'library' and the N one are from
the last phase of the Bayon's construction in the second half of the
13th century. The complete restoration of the N 'library' by the
Japanese government team will be finished shortly. Ahead is the gallery
of the inner enclosure, with its religious and mythological bas-reliefs.

The S inner gallery, with the central massif beyond

You can see from here that the level of the galleries at the far left and right is lower than in the middle. This is due to rebuilding, when the corner galleries were added to the original cross-shape.

Turn to the right and follow these from the outside, round the south-east corner to the middle of the E side, or enter and follow the redented galleries inside the SE angle to reach the same spot (see the plan on p. 79). From here you have a choice of two stairways leading to the upper terrace; this pair replaced the original central steps (the S stairway, on the left as you face the temple, has an additional set of concrete steps that are easier to climb). The famous scene supposedly relating the Legend of the Leper King, described in detail at the end of the section on the bas-reliefs (p.101), is in the small chamber to the right (N) of the central doorway.

On the upper terrace, you are in a different world. After the claustrophobia of the lower levels, this terrace has an atmosphere of peace and calm, with wonderful views of the face-towers set against a background of trees. The free-standing face-towers, which are shrines, allow a close inspection of the faces as you walk around. There are countless views of these faces – some in profile, others framed by

Inside the northern section of the E inner gallery, with a linga *whose date of installation is not known*

Devatas *on the wall of the S 'library'*

*The SW part of the upper terrace,
central sanctuary at right*

*Evidence of rebuilding: a partly hidden
Buddhist pediment of the inner gallery*

doorways, yet others juxtaposed in series – and the aspect changes
throughout the day as the sunlight falls on and off different parts of
the temple.

Fine *devatas* adorn the walls of the central massif which, strikingly,
appears round in plan. In fact, originally there were just four
projecting porches at the cardinal points, but at a later stage the angles
were filled in with four more radiating chapels. Walls connect all eight
and complete the circumference. Small inscriptions detail which
divinity inhabited that particular shrine. Former kings were venerated
in the shrines on the S of the massif, Vishnu on the W, and Siva on the
N, as at Preah Khan. The 5m-diameter sanctuary at its heart can be
entered from the E, through a series of connecting
chambers. Here was housed the Bayon's principal
image, a 3.6m Buddha. It was discovered in 1933 at
the bottom of the central well, where it had been
thrown, broken into pieces, during Jayavarman
VIII's destruction of Buddhist images in the
middle of the 13th century. Remarkably, every
piece of this beautiful image was recovered
enabling its restoration. In 1935 it was relocated
to a small pavilion just south of the Victory Way,
immediately to the E of the S Khleang, where
it remains today.

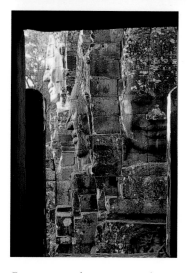

The bas-reliefs
Uniquely, the Bayon has two sets of bas-reliefs,
carved at different times. Those on the walls of
the outer enclosure were carved earlier,
perhaps at the beginning of the 13th century,
and deal with historical subjects, from
battles with the Chams to scenes of daily
life. The inner bas-reliefs cover the
interrupted walls of the inner enclosure,

*Face-towers on the upper terrace from
one of the small chapels*

*The reconstructed 3.6 m high Buddha
now stands in a small pavilion which
stands on one of the 60 'Buddhist
terraces' dotted around the area of
Angkor Thom. They were the bases of
Theravada temples and are proof of an
active spiritual presence in Angkor after
the 13th century*

84

Plan of outer gallery
SE quadrant

1 *Khmer army on the march*
2 *Khmer army; interior scenes*
3 *Unfinished carvings*
4 *Naval battle between Khmer and Chams*
5 *Nautical and genre scenes; palace scenes; further battles*

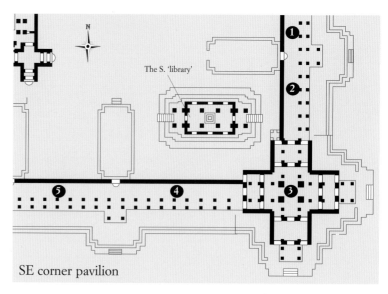

The S. 'library'

SE corner pavilion

and were carved in the second half of the 13th century when, under Jayavarman VIII, the Bayon was converted to Hindu worship. Their subjects are from Hindu mythology, and the complications of rebuilding meant that the carvers had to work on small, irregular surfaces – short sections of gallery, the angles and corners of the *gopuras* and corner pavilions, and some interiors.

THE OUTER BAS–RELIEFS

There are eight sections of bas-relief along the gallery of the third enclosure, each of them 35m long and 3m high, between a corner pavilion and a *gopura*. Each section is, in turn, interrupted by doors that give access to the courtyard inside. Begin at *Gopura III E* and turn left. Various suggestions have been made as to the correct way to view the reliefs but the structure of the temple precludes a logical clockwise or counter-clockwise procession. No-one disagrees that the Outer Galleries illustrate mainly historical events, but which ones exactly remains an open question.

The problem is that, whatever historical continuity there might be, it does not necessarily follow a Western linear progression around the

The lower two registers of the army on the march, S section E outer gallery, N of the doorway (1)

temple. Traditionally the battle scenes are described as opposing
Khmer against Cham. In fact, as with much else at the Bayon, the
reality is more complex, with the battles showing Khmer and Cham
against different groups of Khmer and Cham. There were several
kingdoms in the area of Champa and different alliances were forged
with diverse Khmer factions. Various battle scenes are shown on the E
of the N Gallery and on the N side of the E Gallery, but quite distant
from the naval battle on the S Gallery. This argues against the latter
being that of 1177, when the Chams took Angkor (and on the W of
the scene, the Khmers are shown having the upper hand after the
Chams disembark); it is more likely to be the later battle, sometime
before 1181, when King Jayavarman VII was victorious. But if so, what
is the land battle on the E Gallery? There seem to have been a
succession of battles, and from the inscription at Preah Khan, the final
one took place at that site.

   Whichever direction you take, there are discontinuities. Scenes of
war alternate with daily life at court and in the city. On the S side of
the E Gallery the Khmer army marches in opposite directions on either
side of the small door. There remains much that is not completely
understood among the bas-reliefs, and this undoubtedly adds to their
interest. Remember that there are some special conventions used by
Khmer artists. One is that on most of the walls, the scenes appear in
two, three or four registers; they are often related. Another is that the
carvers usually dealt with perspective by placing the foreground
underneath the background; this is easy to confuse with the normal
superimposition of registers. A third convention is that important
figures, such as a king or an army commander, are simply shown larger
than others.

*Khmer soldier with shield and spear,
S section E outer gallery*

*A woman passes a turtle to a man in
the train of the army, S section E outer
gallery*

E Gallery, S Section
The reliefs begin with the Khmer army on the march, on 3
registers (1). From where you are at *Gopura* III E to the
door in the middle of the section, the army is moving from
left to right. Most of the soldiers, armed with spears, have
short hair and wear a loincloth and a distinctive
arrangement of rope or thick cord looped across the chest.
Note, however, a group of soldiers on the lower register
with beards, topknots, and patterned tunics, giving them a
distinctly Chinese appearance. The commanders ride
elephants, with the number of parasols signifying rank. In
addition there are cavalry, riding bareback, and musicians,
including a small figure beating a gong. On the upper
register are details reminiscent of the Procession of
Suryavaman II on the S Gallery of Angkor Wat: three
princesses born on palanquins, and the Sacred Fire. In the
train of the army, next to the door in the middle of the
gallery, are women, children and provisions, with ox-carts
exactly the same as used today. There are several well-
observed scenes: a crouching figure blows on a cooking
fire, a woman hands a tortoise or turtle to the man in front,
two men cut up a small deer for food.

   Beyond the door is a similar treatment of the army, but
this time moving from right to left (2). Some of the soldiers

'Chinese' soldiers, S section of the E outer gallery, (2)

wear short tunics, there are musicians and provisions carried in ox-carts. At the far end, on the second register, a buffalo has been tied to a post, probably for a sacrifice. The span and shape of its horns, with recurved tips, suggest that it is a buffalo, rather than an ox as suggested by Glaize.

There then follow interior scenes on four registers. Birds perch on roofs of the buildings, which have decorative gables and finials on the ridges. Parasols and other objects are stored by being tied to the rafters. Some of the inhabitants, by their appearance and behaviour, may be tradespeople. Most are Khmer, but some are clearly Chinese, including a group of men inside one building where food is being cooked in a pot; the carcass of a small deer hangs from the top of a post.

A buffalo tethered for sacrifice, S section E outer gallery, (2)

SE Corner Pavilion

Here the bas-reliefs are incomplete (3). The principal scene surrounds a temple with three sanctuary towers, the central one taller than the others, each one topped with a trident finial. The structure of these towers, ogival in shape and with antefixes in receding layers, is remarkably similar to those of Angkor Wat. In the central sanctuary is a *linga*, suggesting it was carved in the second half of the 13th century. Immediately to the right of the towers are three uncarved blocks that were clearly intended to carry the figure of an important person (the parasols and banners signs of rank). Climbing steps to approach this unknown figure are ladies in waiting, carrying large fans and a betel-nut container; note the *naga* balustrade on short columns, again exactly like those at Angkor Wat. Under the stairs is a finely carved *kendi*, or spouted drinking vessel, on a stand.

Around the corner towards the S Gallery is the unfinished carving of a large boat with oarsmen.

S Gallery, E section

Probably the best-known of the Bayon's bas-reliefs, this section features a battle between the Khmers and the Chams, perhaps following the capture of Angkor by the latter in 1177 (4). It could have occurred in 1181, the year that Jayavarman VII took the throne. Immediately after the SE Corner Pavilion, the upper half of the wall is taken up with a palace scene; surrounding the ruler are attendants, musicians, a dancer and two gladiators fighting. Below, Khmer boats row into battle.

There now begins the naval battle in the Great Lake: warships of both sides, manned by oarsmen, ram each other, while the marines, armed with spears, attempt to board the enemy boats; only two of the boats are Cham. The Khmer warriors have close-cropped hair and wear the usual loin-cloth and arrangement of ropes around their chests and necks; the Chams have short-sleeved tunics and curious helmets in

Chinese cooking, with a deer carcass, S section of the E outer gallery, (2)

the shape of an inverted flower, and carry pronged shields. As part of the boarding technique, the boats are secured with ropes thrown around the prows. The slain fall into the water, providing a free meal for the lake's crocodiles. The scale of the naval battle is conveyed in the usual Khmer way for treating perspective – by showing boats arranged one above the other rather than overlapping. At the bottom, and so nearest the viewer, is the shore, with vegetation. Along this, and oblivious of the battle raging above, are scenes from daily life.

These little vignettes are some of the most interesting of all Khmer bas-reliefs, and most are readily identifiable. Two figures grill skewered meat over an open fire, while others eat with their hands inside wooden buildings. There follows a forest scene, with a hunter about to fire a crossbow at a deer. Then, another barbecue and men carrying rice panniers. Next, in another forest, not always a safe place in ancient Cambodia, a tiger has leapt onto a man and is biting his head while gouging his abdomen with the hind claws. Cranes perform a courtship display. More simple habitations follow: a woman scratches a kneeling man's head; a mother plays with her children; female servants attend a lady with an elaborate coiffure; a woman is shown giving birth and writhing in pain, held by another; a hunter aims a crossbow at a buffalo.

Beyond the door, there is a similar arrangement of subjects: nautical above, genre scenes along the bottom (5). However, the boating incidents are, for the time being, peaceful. They begin with a naval parade, with five large boats arranged vertically: the bottom two carry soldiers, the third musicians and a dancer, the fourth more soldiers, the fifth a ruler seated in an elaborate cabin. Next, a large junk carries a Chinese crew, the captain seated and giving orders. At the stern a sailor operates a long rudder, while at the prow, another raises (or lowers) an anchor in the form of a large stone tied with rope. Above, fishermen cast nets; a crocodile takes advantage of this and seizes one of the fish.

On the bottom row, daily life in town and village continues. Women sell fruit; further on is a beautifully observed cockfight, at the start

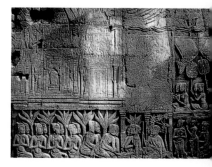

Temple with linga*, and palace attendants, SE corner pavilion (3). The principal character remains uncarved*

Left: Woman playing with children, E section S outer gallery, (4)

A crocodile seizes a man who has fallen overboard during a naval battle with the Chams, E section S outer gallery, (4)

Market women weighing goods, while two Chinese men pass comments, E section S outer gallery, (5)

when the two owners present the fighting cocks to each other and bets are made. Next, a market, where one woman is selling a hen, and two others weigh their goods, causing comment from two Chinese men.

There then follow palace scenes on four upper registers. A ruler, in an unfinished carving, reclines on the topmost register in his palace, surrounded by women and attendants. Below are other scenes, with princesses, musicians and dancers. The bottom of the wall is again taken up with vignettes from daily life, including a chess game, wrestlers, gladiators and a boar fight for sport.

Further on, the battle between the Khmers and Chams continues, on the lake and on land. On the lower register, the Cham boats, in full battle order and with flags flying, row apparently unopposed; the

Two monkeys in a tree, E section S outer gallery, (4)

bodies of some dead Khmers float in the water. In the register above – later in time sequence – the Chams have landed and the battle is engaged, but now the Khmers have the upper hand. Beyond this, the Khmer king, victorious, presides in his palace over the preparations for celebration. Cooks prepare a banquet: one lowers an animal into a cauldron while another tends its fire, and two men barbecue skewers of meat on an open fire. Potters make large numbers of ceramic ridge finials used on temple and palace roofs.

South Gallery, west section
Only the lower two registers are complete, carved with a military procession and lacking the small, beautifully observed details of the preceding section. Note, however, the large-scale military weapons: a giant, elephant-

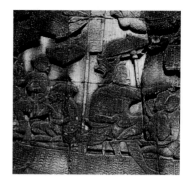

Left: Cham warships row into battle, E section S outer gallery, (4)

Bottom: The Khmers defeat the Chams in a land battle at Angkor, E section S outer gallery, (5)

A cockfight is about to begin, watched by Chinese who place bets, E section S outer gallery, (5)

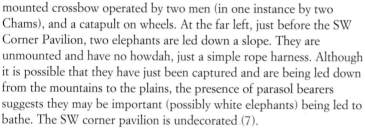

mounted crossbow operated by two men (in one instance by two Chams), and a catapult on wheels. At the far left, just before the SW Corner Pavilion, two elephants are led down a slope. They are unmounted and have no howdah, just a simple rope harness. Although it is possible that they have just been captured and are being led down from the mountains to the plains, the presence of parasol bearers suggests they may be important (possibly white elephants) being led to bathe. The SW corner pavilion is undecorated (7).

W Gallery, S section
From here until you reach the E Gallery, much of the carving is unfinished. At various points you can see the different stages of

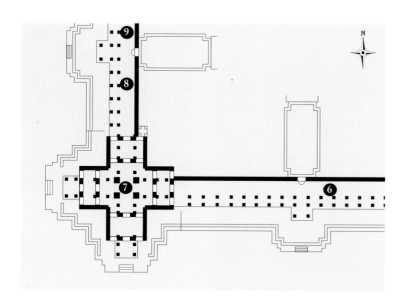

SW quadrant

6 *Military procession; upper registers incomplete*
7 *The SW corner pavilion is undecorated*
8 *Army in the forest; temple construction*
9 *Civil war*

Two Khmer warriors

producing the bas-reliefs: first the outline is lightly incised, then the background is cut back to give the basic shape, and finally the details are added. All stages are present in what looks like a haphazard fashion: at any one time, different scenes around the temple were being started and finished. It is for this reason that some of the work looks crude.

A scene from the civil war, S section W outer gallery, (9)

At the start of this section, on the lower register an army passes through a forest with mountains behind, its commanders riding elephants (8). In an inconsequential aside, two hermits climb a tree to escape attack by a tiger. On the register above are scenes of temple construction: workers (perhaps slaves) drag a block of sandstone, urged on by a foreman with a cane standing on the block. Others carry materials; yet others grind blocks of stone suspended from a kind of frame. Further on are scenes with hermits.

Beyond the door are scenes which could be related. Of great historical interest, they are enigmatic (9). They show, first in a panel of three registers, then of four, what George Coedès believed to be a civil war, with crowds of people gesticulating, others armed and about to

Cham soldiers in the Khmer army operate a kind of crossbow on the back of an elephant, W section S outer gallery

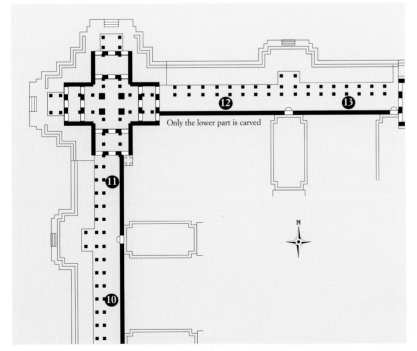

Only the lower part is carved

NW quadrant
10 *The battle continues*
11 *Procession on two registers*
12 *Entertainments; palace scene*
13 *Fighting between Khmer and Chams*

*Civil war battle by a lake,
N section W outer gallery, (9)*

fight. In the third register, two decapitated heads are held aloft – this exact scene also occurs at Banteay Chhmar. Further on there is fighting between Khmer combatants indistinguishable in appearance one from another. This may be the documented 1182 revolt in Malyang, south of present-day Battambang.

W Gallery, N section

The battle continues, on two registers, with one Khmer army pursuing another north – in the direction in which you are walking (10). The losing army is clearly in flight, the men looking over their shoulders; they carry distinctive small round shields. At the beginning they pass a lake where there is a curious incident: a large fish is about to swallow a small deer. The brief inscription in rough script states "the deer is its food" indicating that this was an instruction to the carver which should have been removed at the end. A similar explanation would apply to the inscription saying "the King pursues and fights the defeated", where the principal figure can be seen riding an elephant.

   Beyond the door is a procession on two registers, the ark of the Sacred Fire at the head, and women and children at the rear (11). Among soldiers, a ruler rides on an elephant, surrounded by many parasols. An inscription says, "the king then withdraws to the forest to celebrate Indrabhiseka (the coronation", which may refer to the actual coronation or an annual commemoration of the event).

N Gallery, W section

Only the lower part of the wall has been carved, and many of the figures are unfinished. It begins with entertainments in two registers (12): on the upper level there are fencers, a tight-rope walker,

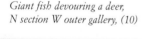

*Giant fish devouring a deer,
N section W outer gallery, (10)*

wrestlers; on the lower level musicians, an acrobat supporting three children, a juggler spinning a wheel with his feet. This is presided over by the king, seated in a palace, and his court. Under the palace (meaning in front, according to the Khmer use of registers to deal with perspective) passes a line of animals, including a rhinoceros, flightless bird, buffalo, deer and so on.

Further on, in the shade of some trees, hermits, identifiable by their chignons and pointed beards, are meditating. One sits in front of a low table with a round object on it. A group of men, accompanied by women, are nearby.

Between here and the door are two rivers, with fish, separated by a mountain; on its slopes are two palaces, each close to one of the rivers. In the centre of this scene, at the foot of the mountain, stands a large male figure, accompanied by two women, possibly his wives. On either side, by the river banks, a group of women carry objects which may be gifts.

Beyond the door, more fighting between Chams and Khmers (13).

N Gallery, E section

At the time of writing, all but the western and eastern ends of the wall had collapsed. On these remains are more scenes of conflict with the Chams (14). These, however, show the Khmers in defeat: the Cham troops attack in ranks from the west, and the Khmers flee to the mountains. This could be the occasion in 1177 when the Chams took Angkor, before Jayavarman's successes of 1177. It is tempting to see the entire outer bas-reliefs of the Bayon as an historical sequence; at least the events relating to the Chams appear to begin here and to end round the corner, at the N end of the E Gallery.

NE Corner Pavilion

Khmer soldiers and elephants on the march, possibly related to the battle scenes that follow on the East Gallery.

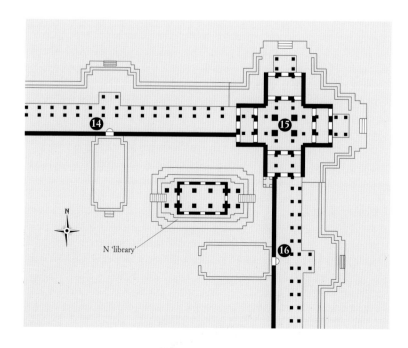

Wrestlers, W section N outer gallery, (12)

A court scene, W section N outer gallery, (12)

A circus scene with jugglers, W section N outer gallery, (12)

NE quadrant

14 *Khmers battle with Chams*
15 *Khmer soldiers and elephants on the march*
16 *Battle between Khmers and Chams*

E Gallery, N section

Another great battle between the Chams and the Khmers, both armies converging on the centre, where the fighting is at its most intense. The Khmer army, advancing from the south, is a direct continuation of the army shown in the S section of this gallery. Even the elephants fight: one uses its trunk in an attempt to tear out the tusk of an opposing elephant. The Khmers are shown to be winning. Note the large grilled panels held upright, whose use is so far unexplained. Although these scenes may be historic they date from the reign of Jayavarman VIII and their precise meaning remains unclear.

Khmer soldiers attacking Chams, N section E outer gallery

Above: Battle, N section E outer gallery

Siva and hermits, E inner gallery

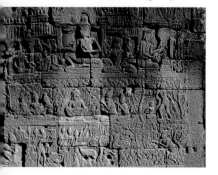

THE INNER BAS-RELIEFS

We follow the same procedure for visiting the inner bas-reliefs (plan on p. 99) – of the second enclosure – by walking clockwise from the E entrance. Here, however, the construction of the gallery, with its wide three-doored *gopuras*, leaves no long panels. Instead, the bas-reliefs are broken up into small sections, covering angles and corners as well as the walls, and even inside some of the small vestibules. The subjects are for the most part from Hindu mythology, and many are obscure, though they include events from the Indian epics that had long been popular among the Khmer. Clearly scenes grouped together are linked in some way but their exact relationship is often unclear.

E Gallery, S section

1 *Between the central and S towers* facing S : a number of small scenes showing the life of hermits, including some collecting water, others reading holy texts. Forest animals surround them. Siva also appears in a door. Facing E, on three registers: a palace scene with a ruler, wives and members of the court being entertained by dancers, musicians and singers. On the left, also on three registers: another palace scene on the upper register, with ruler in the middle; below, men talk or argue.

2 *Small gallery next to the S tower* On the right facing S, on three registers: above, Siva as an ascetic, seated in a palace with hermits, one of whom cuts into a fruit; in the middle, hermits pray before a figure seated in a cave; below, a hermit collects lotus flowers in a lake, while a hunter, camouflaged by wearing a deer's head, fires an arrow at a fleeing deer. Adjacent facing E, on two registers: above, two priests in a temple empty the contents of bowls onto a fire; below, figures (in poor condition).

3 *Gallery wall* On the right of the door: princesses and their servants in a palace. To the left, on two registers: an army on the march, but while the leaders are Khmers, the majority of the soldiers are Chams (distinguishable by their headdresses), together with a royal figure riding an elephant, and the Ark of the Sacred Fire in front.

SE corner
4 Soldiers marching, their commander on an elephant.

S Gallery, E section
5 *Gallery wall* (in poor condition) Begins with an army on the march; on the right, a commander rides an elephant. Then, combat between two princes, followed by a palace scene, and more soldiers marching. Next, a mountain, on its summit a ruler or god seated; below a *garuda* between the head and tail of a giant fish; all around are hermits and animals. This is followed by more soldiers, and finally two palaces, empty except for the rulers' wives. One princess is looking in a mirror, another combs her hair.

6 *Small gallery next to the E tower* Adjacent, on two registers: above, a

Below: Siva, seated with attendants, S inner gallery

Hermits kneeling in prayer, S inner gallery

Court attendant holding casket, S inner gallery

Ladies of the court relaxing around a lake, S inner gallery

king or prince fights a lion with his bare hands; below, spectators. On the left, also on two registers: above, a similar scene, with another figure fighting an elephant which he has seized by the legs; below, soldiers and musicians.

7 *Between the E and central towers* On two registers, a group of related scenes, telling a story that George Coedès believed to be that of Pradyumna, the child of Krishna and Rukmini, who is thrown into the sea by a demon, eaten by a fish and saved by fishermen when they open up the fish. The story starts in the middle of the wall and reads (with difficulty) from left to right On the upper register, three princesses kneel before a (damaged) figure seated on a throne, which is surrounded by fans, parasols and fly-whisks; *apsaras* fly overhead. In the lower register, a princess places a child in a chest. Next, a fisherman casts a net, with a richly clothed princess watching from a boat. On the right, men carry a giant fish and raise it towards a king seated in his palace above – the figure of a child is lightly incised on the fish, perhaps to show that it is inside. Finally, a man holds the child in his hands.

Beyond these scenes, two registers: above, servants carry a throne towards a palace with an empty central chamber; below soldiers and musicians. Beyond the small door, facing: a figure seated in his palace, accompanied by women; below him water and a building in which a fire burns. Beyond this, a battle scene with two leaders. Finally, a figure (probably one of these combatants) leaving his palace, in which his wives remain.

S Gallery, W section

8 *Between the central and W towers* On the right facing W, two registers in poor condition: below, a ruler with his wives in a building; above, in another building, a man lying on a bed, with a woman seated by him. Facing S: Siva represented twice, on a throne and also seated on a lotus. Worshippers surround the god, one of them prostrated. Facing E: another poorly carved Siva carrying a trident, attended by *apsaras* and musicians.

9 *Small gallery next to the W tower* On the right, in poor condition: the interior of a building with birds on the roof and people seated; in the register above, a three-towered temple with Vishnu inside and Siva outside. Adjacent facing S, also in poor condition: a temple with seated figures and a figure walking down steps.

10 *Gallery wall* First, a worn tableau of a bearded Siva standing with attendant priests and flying *apsaras*. Next, a forested mountain with a temple, surrounded by wild animals; a tiger attacks a man. Then, Siva again, holding court, with women and priests. Below, boats carry ladies of the court across a lake, where a group of three *apsaras* dance on lotus plants. This is followed by yet another representation of Siva, this time standing in a temple set in a lake, surrounded by animals and hermits, one of whom is being chased by a tiger; others talk in small palaces, yet others bow to the god. In the centre of the wall, a statue of a four-armed Vishnu is surrounded by flying *apsaras*, while a figure, possibly a king by his dress, prostrates himself. Beyond, a procession approaches from a palace at the far end of the wall, with horses and a ceremonial container on wheels. In the palace, with steps guarded by

statues of lions, the ruler gives orders to servants, while others
go about their duties below: one opens a chest, others carry
objects, while one man is ill and is tended by two others, one
of who holds his head. At the far left, a lady is rowed in a
small boat by a servant, gathering lotus flowers; other women
walk in the garden above.

W Gallery, S section

11 *SW corner* Two registers: on the lower, soldiers with spears
and shields; on the upper, women in a palace from which the
ruler is leaving. A cushion and fan are on a bed in the palace.

12 *Between SW corner and S tower* Up to the small door: a battle scene
with a four-armed Vishnu on *Garuda* at its centre. He faces the army
marching towards him from the SW corner, but at its head, some of
the soldiers are in positions of prayer, apparently submitting. On the
other side of Vishnu is his army. Beyond the small door, two registers:
on the lower, men carry fly-whisks; on the upper, a palace with men
and women.

Vishnu on Garuda *at the head of an army, W inner gallery*

13 *Small gallery next to the S tower* Facing W, three badly worn
registers: on the lower, two *apsaras* and their musicians; on the second,
a ruler in a palace with his court; on the upper, figures of rank (with
parasols) on either side of a temple with blind windows. On the left
facing S, two registers: below, women bathing and picking lotuses, with
a hermit by the water's edge. Above: dancers, a fight between two men
in which one grasps the ankle of the other, and a man firmly holding
the arms of a woman.

14 *Between the S and central towers* On the right facing N, three
registers all show the building of a temple: on the lower, men carry
stones on their shoulders, with guards carrying sticks; on the second,
slaves drag a block on which stands a foreman with a cane (compare
with the similar scene on the West Outer Gallery), while others grind
blocks, assisted by a system of levers and ropes; on the upper level, the
four-armed figure must be the statue of Vishnu which would have been
installed and dedicated at the very beginning of the temple building
process.

A man grasps a woman by her wrist and arm, W inner gallery

Statue of Vishnu in a temple, W inner gallery

Adjacent facing W, up to the small door: a damaged scene in which
Vishnu stands four-armed in a temple or palace, surrounded
by figures with *apsaras* flying overhead. Beyond the small door,
a boating scene, damaged but apparently similar to the water
festival at Dvaravati featured in the SW Corner Pavilion of
Angkor Wat. A decorated boat, with a *makara* prow and a
curtained cabin, carries two figures and is accompanied by
smaller boats. On the left facing S, three registers: on the lower
(damaged) hermits meditate in caves; on the second a hermit
swims among lotus leaves, while others carry lotuses, a
cormorant flies off with a fish, and a deer comes to drink; on
the upper, Siva, with Vishnu dancing on one side and their
consorts Uma and Lakshmi.

W Gallery, N section

15 *Between the central and N towers* On the right, three badly
worn registers: on the lower, a figure seated in a building; on

Detail from Churning of the Sea of Milk, showing the jar of amrita *and Vishnu as a turtle at the bottom, N section W gallery*

the second, men seated; on the third, a god (indicated by the *apsaras* above) seated in a palace. Facing W and continuing to the left: three registers of a military procession, mainly cavalry, with two main figures in horse-drawn chariots. The scene continues on the short wall facing S.

16 *Small raised gallery N of the N tower* On the right: a badly worn scene of two figures, one with a three-pointed headdress, in a palace set among trees and coconut palms; princesses being dressed; a temple containing a kind of tabernacle. Adjacent facing W, three registers: on the lower, priests carrying various objects converge on a central area (where the carving has disappeared); on the second, more priests, two of whom hold a tray with round objects; on the third, a temple, with a priest and two bearded figures seated in front, an archer of rank (indicated by parasols and banners) with two priests kneeling before him, another archer flexes his bow.

17 *Remainder of gallery up to the NW corner* Up to the small door: a ruler in a palace, attended by others. Behind him an archer stands ready to fire an arrow, accompanied by two other archers. Beyond the small door: The Churning of the Sea of Milk. The *naga* Vasuki is pulled on the right by *asuras* and on the left by gods, the latter exhorted by Hanuman at the tail. Vishnu, 4-armed, oversees the churning in the centre, where Mount Mandara is shown as a column, resting on the back of the turtle *avatar* of Vishnu. Below, a row of fish indicates the ocean, with another representation of the *naga*. Indra can be seen in the sky above, with flying *apsaras* and birds. The sun and moon are seen as discs, and a flask for the *amrita*. Further left is an army of *asuras*, their leader in a chariot drawn by lions; above them a god rides a bird. If it is Skanda the bird is a peacock.

NW corner
18 Soldiers marching

Hanuman urges on the gods during the Churning of the Sea of Milk, N section W gallery

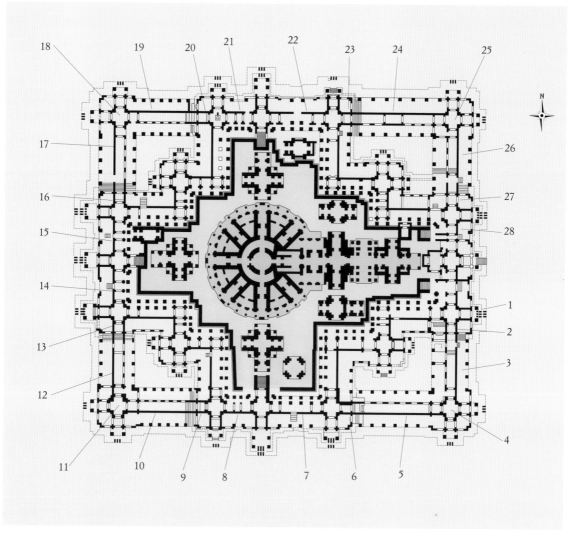

Plan of inner gallery

N Gallery, W section

19 *Gallery wall* Three registers of palace scenes, followed by two registers of a procession carrying offerings towards a mountain, whose wildlife includes an elephant, rhinoceros, *nagas*, deer, birds and wild boar. A temple is on its summit. Next, a larger temple with guardian *dvarapalas*. Another procession, with two leaders carrying tridents, is received by priests. Then three large sailing boats, each carrying an important figure, attendants and crew. Finally, several figures in a palace on the slopes of a hill, one of them carrying a trident.

20 *Small gallery* Two versions of the Hindu Trinity. In one facing N, a 10-armed Siva dances (Siva *Nataraj*) between Vishnu and Brahma (with four heads); Siva's son Ganesha, and Rahu below. In the other facing W, Siva is between Vishnu and Brahma; a giant boar below.

21 *Between the W and central towers* On the right facing E: Siva seated with his wife Uma, among hermits and women, with the bull Nandi just discernible on the left. Facing N: a woman arranging her hair in a doorway, between two men, one bearded; hermits are in prayer. In the middle of the wall, Kama fires an arrow at Siva, in meditation with

A dignatory seated in a dragon-headed boat, W section N Gallery

Siva on Nandi, W section
N inner gallery

Uma at his side; Siva kills Kama, who lies mourned by his wife Rati (also see pages 57 Angkor Wat and 212 Banteay Srei). In the third scene, a figure with a three-pointed headdress sits in a palace, carrying a stave in his right hand and gesticulating with his left to the seated figures at his side. On the short wall facing W: Siva on Nandi.

N Gallery, E section
(This section was closed for restoration at the time of writing).
22 *Between the central and E towers* On the right, two registers: above, Siva on Nandi again, with Uma, in front of a palace, with a *naga* king; below, musicians, singers and *apsaras*. Facing N, on two registers: above, a temple with a tabernacle, in front of which seated figures perform rite; below, servants carry objects on their heads. Next, the scene from the *Mahabharata* in which Krishna's ally Arjuna and Siva (disguised as a hunter) both fire arrows at a charging boar and then dispute. Siva, though victorious, pardons Arjuna his temerity and gives him the magical weapon Pasuputa. On the left: A ruler in his palace, with women and a servant carrying an object of some sort. Then, the well-known scene in which the demon Ravana, with 10 heads, 20 arms and four legs, shakes Mount Kailasa, on the summit of which sits Siva and two other figures (see p. 57 at Angkor Wat). Finally, on the left panel, in two registers: a ruler in a palace, being fanned, with women and attendants; below, a long building with figures.
23 *Small gallery next to the E tower* On three registers, a procession of people carrying objects, possibly offerings to the temple in the next gallery. Most are on foot, some in ox-chariots, others in palanquins.
24 *Gallery wall* All on two registers: above, a three-towered temple whose central sanctuary is empty and the other two contain statues of Vishnu and Lakshmi; below, priests and soldiers. Next, Siva amidst worshippers and flying *apsaras*. Beyond this, an army marching, with a chief and elephants. Then, on the upper register, a palace with an empty central chamber and a ruler about to leave on a six-wheeled chariot; below, ladies of the court on palanquins, an ox-drawn chariot, a small building and a closed temple. The last scene on the facing wall is a ruler seated in his place on the upper register, a sword in his right hand, his left raised towards kneeling figures; on the lower register, a long building with figures. Finally, on the left panel, a hunter aims at a deer, another watches a tiger, and two porters carry goods.

The Ark of the Sacred Flame, N section
E inner gallery

NE corner
25 Soldiers marching

E Gallery, N section
26 *Gallery wall* The army on the march, on two registers: below are soldiers, cavalry, musicians and chariots drawn by horses and oxen. Above, a ruler and two wives ride in a large six-wheeled chariot mounted on *hamsas*, other ladies ride in

palanquins; the Ark of the Sacred Fire; an empty throne; a ruler with a bow on an elephant followed by two other commanders. Beyond the door: a ruler by his throne, prostrating himself at the feet of Siva, while below, *nagas* appear to be coming out of the water.

27 *Small gallery next to the N tower* Two scenes that appear related, and for which the most plausible explanation is of an important statue vandalised by the Chams and thrown into the moat, then later recovered by the Khmers. If so, it reads left to right, as follows. On the left: the statue of a female divinity is in the middle, with three registers on either side. On the

A king fights with a giant serpent, N section E inner gallery

upper register, men strike the head with axes. On the middle, elephants pull on ropes tied to the statue's arms. On the lower, men fan the flames of a fire with bellows, while others attack the statue with spears. Facing: two large boats in a basin bordered with stepped embankments. On board, men carry a throne for an object that has disappeared, while in the water two figures raise their hands towards it. Below, a diver has something (indistinguishable) in his hand. *Apsaras* fly above the entire scene, indicating that the subject is sacred. The missing object may be the statue or a broken part of it.

Between the N and central towers These scenes also seem intended to be read from left to right, and are usually referred to as the 'Legend of the Leper King': a ruler fights a giant serpent with his bare hands, with onlookers below. Next, seated, he orders his servants off and they descend a staircase. He is then seen with his hands being examined by women. Finally he lies ill. The assumption, according to legend, is that he contracted leprosy from the serpent's venom, and the last scenes show the progression of the illness.

Other monuments of the period
At Angkor: Angkor Thom, Ta Prohm, Banteay Kdei, Preah Khan, Neak Pean, Ta Som, Srah Srang, Ta Nei, Ta Prohm Kel. Elsewhere in Cambodia: Banteay Chhmar.
Best times to visit
The complexity of the monument, ensures that the play of light changes throughout the day. Early morning and late afternoon can give marvellous and unexpected views of the faces. Because of the trees, almost no direct sunlight strikes the Bayon during approximately the first hour after sunrise and the last hour before sunset. Shortly before midday, the bas-reliefs of the E Gallery are strongly and precisely lit. The bas-reliefs of the S Gallery receive sunlight for most of the day, those on the W Gallery are sunlit in the afternoon, while those on the N Gallery receive some sunlight around midday only in mid-summer.
Location and access
In the centre of Angkor Thom, 1.5km from both the S and N Gates of the city. In the absence of an enclosing wall, the monument can be entered at will from any direction – the road makes a complete circuit around it.

Part of the procession, E section N inner gallery

BAPUON ✥

Highlights
★ State temple of Yasodharapura in the 11th century
★ Bas-reliefs in small individual panels
★ View from the summit

Date: Middle of the 11th century (1060)
Style: Bayon
Reign: Udayadityavarman II
Visit: 1 hr

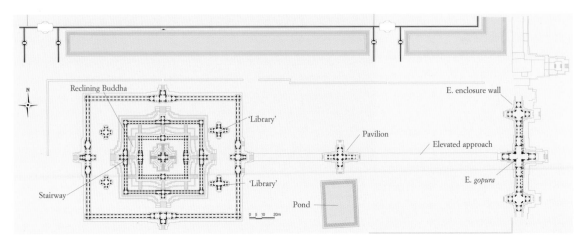

*Below: The collapsed pyramid behind
the restored* Gopura III E

A hunter looses an arrow at a wild boar, from the pavilion on the causeway

Left: Short round pillars support the causeway from the E entrance

Below: Scenes decorating the walls of the pavilion on the causeway

This enormous temple-mountain (to the NW of the Bayon) was the state temple of the Yasodharapura of King Udayadityavarman II, and still sufficiently impressive (or recently restored) at the end of the 13th century to merit this description by the Chinese diplomat Zhou Daguan: *"North of the Golden Tower [Bayon] at a distance of about two hundred yards, rises the Tower of Bronze, higher even than the Golden Tower: a truly astonishing spectacle, with more than ten chambers at its base."* Its present ruined condition obscures its former importance: it is now in the process of being restored, but the problems are severe. The restoration is meant to be finished by 2002 but it may well take longer. During this time parts of the temple may be closed for work. For now, its chief interest is in its bas-relief panels.

Plan

Bapuon is essentially a massive five-tiered pyramid set within a long enclosure, but its ruined state makes it difficult to appreciate. The outermost (4th) enclosure, 425m x 125m, borders the Royal Palace to the N, while its main E entrance *gopura* and the E wall are in a direct line with the Elephant Terraces to the N (although these last were built two centuries later).

A raised causeway 172m long leads from the E entrance *gopura* to the temple-mountain itself, but this causeway is a later addition. In fact, the cross-shaped pavilion that interrupts it was probably the outer *gopura* originally, which would have made the overall proportions less elongated at 238m x 125m. This rectangular pyramid rises in five levels to a summit 24m above ground-level. Three concentric galleries, on the 1st, 3rd and 5th levels, demarcate the three inner enclosures. The base of the pyramid, which coincides with the gallery of the 3rd enclosure measures 120m x 100m. Each of the three successive galleries had *gopuras* at the cardinal points and corner towers. Part of them collapsed and the stone was used for other buildings, but currently they have been dismantled for restoration.

Visit

Approach from the E, through the E entrance *gopura* and along the causeway raised on round pillars, passing the ruined pavilion in the middle. Pause to examine the tiny scenes carved in small panels on its walls: animals, duels between warriors and men fighting animals. These

Dvarapala, Gopura III S

bas-reliefs, each containing one scene, are highly characteristic of the Bapuon style, a little naïve and carved with great charm. At the end of the causeway, climb to the *gopura* of the 3rd enclosure, the most elaborate of all, with three widely spaced entrances. There are more carvings here: note in particular the motif of open lotus flowers.

Pass through this *gopura* into the third enclosure, which surrounds the actual pyramid. As elsewhere the two 'libraries' which stood on the left and right are being restored and will be reinstalled. They were connected to each other and to the *gopura* by a causeway raised on short columns dating to the 13th century. Turn left and make your way to the south side. The S *gopura* of this enclosure is in fairly good condition, having been restored, and its walls are decorated with more small carved panels, many showing animals, some of these fighting, and the open lotus flowers.

Continue round to the W of the pyramid, where we can see the outline of an unfinished giant reclining Buddha begun in the sixteenth century. This construction accounts for the missing gallery and other parts. Access to the pyramid is possible from the middle of the figure. The famous narrative bas-reliefs of Bapuon (as distinct from the many vignettes you have already seen) are on the *gopuras* of the second enclosure. Those on the W *gopura* have scenes from the *Ramayana* and the *Mahabharata*, including one from the latter in which Siva gives Arjuna magic weapons. At the time of writing only the restoration of the E *gopura* is complete and the other three are not visitable.

In contrast to the bas-reliefs at Angkor Wat, which cover the same subjects, episodes are divided into panels, rather as in a comic book and they read from bottom to top. The N *gopura* also has scenes from the *Ramayana*, including a number of episodes from the Battle of Lanka. On the E *gopura* there is Rama's triumphal return to Ayodhya and the trial of Sita, and from the *Mahabharata* details from the Battle of Kurukshetra (including the death of Bhishma) and the dispute between Arjuna and Siva. The S *gopura* has scenes from the Life of Krishna, including the god battling with the *naga* Kaliya and other monsters sent by his evil uncle King Kamsa, and the death of Kamsa himself. All of these known narratives are interspersed with various scenes of daily life, such as hunting, a tiger chasing a hermit, or a woman playing with her child.

Rama and Lakshmana, Gopura II W

Collapse makes climbing the pyramid difficult and maybe forbidden, but you can continue up to the first enclosure on the top level. Little remains on this upper platform, 42m x 36m, of the galleries, *gopuras* and central tower. In the 13th century it seems that attempts were made to change the cruciform base of the central sanctuary to a square, but this work was uncompleted.

The view, however, is very good, with the long causeway to
the E, the Bayon to the SE, Phnom Bakheng to the S and
Phimeanakas. One strange feature is that the surrounding
gallery had a wall running down its middle on the inside,
which supported the roof but must have made the gallery
impractical to use and suggests that it may have been
purely for visual effect. It seems that stones from the
central tower were used for the reclining Buddha.

Other monuments of the period
In Thailand: Muang Tam (part), Ta Muen Thom, Phnom Wan (part),
Preah Vihear (part), Kamphaeng Yai, Narai Jaeng Waeng.
Best times to visit
Early morning for the view from the E entrance; late afternoon for
views from the summit; any time for the bas-reliefs.
Location and access
400m NW of the Bayon, inside Angkor Thom. The E entrance
gopura is on the left of the road 300m N of the Bayon. For access
to the summit for its views S, E and N, use (with caution) the W
staircase leading from the middle of the reclining Buddha.

Above: Reclining Buddha on the W side of the pyramid

*Arjuna receives Siva's magic weapons,
and Rama and Lakshmana, Gopura II W*

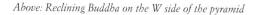

ELEPHANT TERRACE ✤

Date: Late 12th century, with late 13th century additions
Style: Bayon
Reign: Jayavarman VII, added to by Jayavarman VIII
Visit: 20-30 mins

This long terrace at the heart of Angkor Thom, looking out over the Royal Square, was the foundation for royal reception pavilions; the carvings of elephants along its walls give it its modern name.

Plan

300m long, the terrace runs north from the entrance of the Bayon as far as the Terrace of the Leper King, and forms the W edge of the Royal Square. There are five projecting stairways symmetrically placed: three in the centre, and the other two at either end. The central stairway is the largest. The ones on either extremity are later in date and the one on the S extremity projects 10m more than that on the N. Recently discovered lead tiles behind the terrace confirm the report of the late-13th century Chinese diplomat Zhou Daguan that "the tiles of the king's main apartments are of lead".

Visit

Immediately after the E entrance to the Bapuon, you see first the southernmost stairway, which projects into the Royal Square, as do the

Elephant with mahouts on the main wall

other four. Like the S Gate of the city, the staircase is flanked by three-headed elephants with their three trunks pulling lotuses from the ground. Beyond this, the 3m-high wall is carved with one long, continuous scene of elephants with their mahouts, in hunting scenes.

The next projecting stairway is similar to the southern one, with flanking three-headed elephants. Beyond this, the shorter section of wall leading to the main central stairway is sculpted with lion-headed figures and *garudas*, all with raised arms. Climb the main staircase, the upper part of which has *naga* balustrades and guardian lions. To the E, the Victory Way leads east through the Victory Gate of the city. To the W, the raised platform, set back 4m, has a frieze of *hamsas* (the sacred geese) along its edges, a sure sign that it was designed to support the Palace. Beyond the platform, to the west, is the entrance *gopura* leading to Phimeanakas and the Royal Palace. At this point, if you choose to enter, see the entry for Phimeanakas on p. 111. One option is to make a clockwise circuit of Phimeanakas, the pond to its N, then Preah Palilay, Tep Pranam and the Terrace of the Leper King, ending with the concealed reliefs of the northern stairway of the Elephant Terrace (see below).

To the north of the central stairway, the same elements are repeated: lions and *garudas* on the wall as far as the next stairway, then elephants as far as the northernmost stairway. This stairway, most extensively modified over the centuries, is worthy of particular study. The architect Christophe Pottier has summarised the changes as follows and as shown on the small diagram. 1) a simple 3m high base dates to the 11th century. 2) during the reign of Jayavarman VII this was encased in

Alternating garudas *and lion-headed figures*

Plan showing the succesive enlargement of the N stairway. (Courtesy Christophe Pottier)

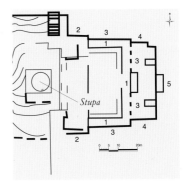

A game of polo on the wall of the N staircase

Five-headed horse on the hidden wall at the N end

sandstone carved with a three-headed Airavata on the E framed by seven-headed horses, whose mythological origin is unknown. The lateral walls show hunting on elephants as before. 3) Perhaps in the first half of the 13th century the second stage was enlarged and the sculptural elements were re-used with the addition of a three-headed elephant on the E panel and a five-headed horse; side panels with various sporting scenes. 4) After the mid-13th century, the final extension eastwards of the stairway; two stairways frame a three-headed elephant while the side panels are decorated with *garudas* and lions. 5) Then perhaps in the 16th century or later, a panel of bas-reliefs was added at the back of the stairway platform by re-using the three-headed elephants from phases 2 and 3. 6) After the 16th century, a badly-built *stupa* was added behind the 16th century panel.

Other monuments of the period
At Angkor: Angkor Thom, Bayon, Ta Prohm, Banteay Kdei, Preah Khan, Neak Pean, Ta Som, Srah Srang, Ta Nei, Ta Prohm Kel. Elsewhere in Cambodia: Banteay Chhmar.
Best times to visit
Early morning, for the light. A little before midday, the hidden relief of the five-headed horse is sunlit.
Location and access
N of the Bayon, inside Angkor Thom and facing the Royal Square. The Terrace runs for a little over 300m, from just N of Bapuon's E entrance as far as the Terrace of the Leper King.

LEPER KING TERRACE ✦✦

Date: 13th century
Style: Bayon
Reign: Jayavarman VII, added to by Jayavarman VIII
Visit: 20 mins

This massive terrace, named after the 15th century sculpture that was discovered on top, stands more or less independent of the other buildings that surround the Royal Square of Angkor Thom. Like the Elephant Terrace it has certain dating problems. It probably dates to the reign of Jayavarman VIII and was part of significant alterations made to the royal palace during his reign, including the extension of the Elephant Terrace with the Bapuon entrance *gopura*. After a partial collapse, its surface area was extended and the wall entirely rebuilt, although the former sculptures were left intact within the new embankment. Recent excavation and restoration now allow both sets of reliefs to be appreciated.

Plan

The sides of this terrace, which projects into the Royal Square, measure 25m, but the corners are strongly redented, making it more octagonal than square in plan. A trench-like path follows the outline of the 6m walls from the SW corner to the NW corner, 2m behind the outer walls, and its inner surface is carved with the scenes described below.

King, consorts and sword-swallower, N wing

Visit

The three outer faces of the terrace – S, E and N – together with a short E-facing section to the N, are all carved in deep relief with mythological scenes. These are in six and seven registers, and feature deities carrying swords, *devatas* and other figures; the lowest tier has *nagas* and marine creatures. The best of the reliefs is on the E-facing extension wall immediately to the N of the terrace, and we recommend that you begin there. The style of the carving has similarities with those on the S wall of the large pond of the Royal Palace, confirming a date in the second half of the 13th century.

To see the hidden reliefs, enter the trench by the narrow entrance in the SW corner and follow its zig-zag course around the terrace. The carvings are similar to those

Nagas and deities of the underworld, the hidden wall

Other monuments of the period
At Angkor: Angkor Thom, Ta Prohm, Banteay Kdei, Preah Khan, Neak Pean, Ta Som, Srah Srang, Ta Nei, Ta Prohm Kel. Elsewhere in Cambodia: Banteay Chhmar.
Best times to visit
Any time for the hidden reliefs, which are in a deep, narrow trench. Morning for the east-facing bas-relief with four registers on the N side of the Terrace.
Location and access
The north continuation of the Elephant Terrace, inside Angkor Thom and facing the Royal Square. There are 2 entrances to the hidden reliefs – in the SW corner and in the NW corner.

on the outside: seated male figures with drawn swords are flanked by attendant *devatas*. Below are powerfully executed five-, seven- and nine-headed *nagas*, on the lower registers of the walls and the corner angles.

The reasons for making a second set of reliefs (the trench was filled with laterite rocks and rubble when it was discovered) are probably that the first walls started to collapse and it was decided to enlarge the terrace. Gaps in the exterior wall, show that numerous blocks of stone were reused.

You leave the hidden reliefs by climbing the steps at the NW corner. On top of the terrace, a statue of Dharma or Yama, the god of the Underworld was found in the centre: a naked male figure (but with no sexual organs), he is portrayed in a seated position, with the right knee raised, carrying a mace on his right shoulder. Possibly because of the strangeness of the figure and the corrosion of its surface by patches of lichen, it later became known as the 'Leper King', following an old folk-legend that one of Angkor's kings was a leper. The original is in the National Museum in Phnom Penh, for safety – with good reason, as even the cement copy which replaced it has been decapitated. The inscription on its base is 14th century, or later, and this is probably the date of the statue.

PHIMEANAKAS & THE ROYAL PALACE ✤

Date: Late 10th to early 11th centuries (Phimeanakas); 12th to 13th centuries (other parts)

Style: Khleang (Phimeanakas); Bakheng to Bayon (other parts)

Reign: Jayavarman V and Udayadityavarman I (Phimeanakas); Suryavarman I onwards (other parts)

Visit: 30 mins–1 hr

The site where Suryavarman I built his royal palace continued in use, almost uninterruptedly, from the 11th to the end of the 16th century. During that time, the area underwent many transformations and restorations. Recent excavations have revealed many remains, some of which are even earlier, such as a temple from the beginning of the 10th century built by a minister to Yasovarman I and sturdy posts which may have been the residence for this minister.

The majority of the buildings here would have been non-religious in nature, and as such were constructed in perishable materials. The disappearance of these structures means that what remains today gives an impression of great disorder.

Plan of Phimeanakas

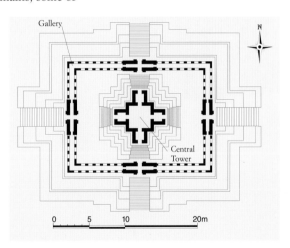

Plan

The rectangular site of the royal palace was surrounded by a very well-built 5m high laterite wall, 246m along the N-S axis and 585m along the E-W, enclosing an area of more than 14 hectares. Five large sandstone *gopuras* with steps gave access, two on the N, two on the S and one on the E, larger than the others and aligned with the Elephant Terrace and Victory Gate. The compound was only

Phimeanakas from the E

Guardian lion on the east staircase of Phimeanakas

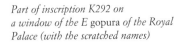

Part of inscription K292 on a window of the E gopura of the Royal Palace (with the scratched names)

accessible on foot. The first group of buildings, built by Suryavarman I, was surrounded by a moat of which some traces remain, in particular on the E. The ground inside the palace compound is 1.2m higher than outside, necessitating a double course of stone on the exterior of the entrances. In places, the ground has been raised even higher. Although evidence of many buildings remain, only a few are of interest to the tourist – the temple of Phimeanakas, the Large Pond whose S wall is carved with bas-reliefs; a smaller pond and various terraces, ponds and small sanctuaries

Visit
Phimeanakas
The laterite pyramid is relatively modest, measuring only 35m E to W and 28m N to S. Rising in three levels of 12m each, it is not aligned with the E axis of the palace entrance *gopura* and therefore was not planned as the central feature. Stairs lead up on all four sides, although much has crumbled and we recommend those on the W. They are flanked with guardian lions, while there are elephants on the corners. At the top, inside a small continuous sandstone gallery, is the remains of a base some 2.5m high which was probably a sanctuary whose date is more recent than the pyramid.

One of the door jambs has been re-used from another temple and bears an earlier inscription, possibly relating to a temple built by a minister to Yasovarman I. The stele relating to the actual temple was found smashed beneath an embankment, indicating that its burial was the work of Jayavarman VIII, who also built the embankment 2.6m high over the first two courses of the base which extends to the Large Pond.

It was inside the sanctuary of Phimeanakas, that according to Zhou Daguan, the Khmer king lay every night with a woman who, as the incarnation of a nine-headed *naga*, had power over the lands of the kingdom. It is reasonable to assume, however, that this legend held sway mainly among the Chinese population of Angkor.

The Large Pond
The 125m x 45m pond, probably built by Jayavarman VIII, is faced with sandstone around its circumference. 13 tiers of steps descend 5.32m to the laterite paving. On the S and to a lesser extent on the W, a wall was constructed, presumably to retain the embankment which extends to the pond from Phimeanakas. Dominating the pond on top of the wall is a paved terrace where one can imagine the king installing himself to watch aquatic sports.

The walls are completely carved with bas-reliefs: the lower regions show crocodiles and fish, some with horse's or cow's heads; in the middle, two rows of princes and *naga* princesses, similar to those on the Leper King Terrace; and above winged figures and male and female guardians.

The East Pond
Near the E northern entrance *gopura* is a 40 x 20m sandstone pond, 4.5m deep. It was probably part of the first palace to be built here.

The Large Pond of the palace

Terrace and Pond W of the Large Pond

To the W of the Large Pond, one passes firstly the W northern *gopura* and then a laterite wall in poor condition to reach a small pond and low terrace, whose walls are carved with attractive bas-reliefs of a procession of people, elephants and horses above a frieze of *hamsas*, probably dating to the 16th century.

Terrace to the E

This cruciform terrace with round columns and overhanging top, typical of the 16th century, is often hard to reach as it is engulfed in vegetation.

Four small sanctuaries to the E

These four small sanctuaries, opening to the W and parallel to the SE of the second part of the royal palace, date to the early phase, evidenced by their lower floor level. Their purpose is unclear.

Other monuments of the period
At Angkor: North and South Khleangs, Ta Keo. Elsewhere in Cambodia: Preah Vihear (part). In Thailand: Muang Tam (part).
Best times to visit
Any time; the surrounding trees cut off much of the light.
Location and access
200m directly N of Bapuon, inside Angkor Thom and near the centre of the grounds of the Royal Palace. It is set back 300m W of the Elephant Terrace, and is most easily reached either from here or from Preah Palilay.

Marine creatures on the frieze surrounding the Large Pond

TEP PRANAM ✣

Date: Circa16th century
Style: post-Bayon
Reign: Unknown
Visit: 10 mins

A giant seated Buddha, built from sandstone blocks is still worshipped here. The interior of the figure re-uses many stone blocks, while the head appears somewhat later.

Plan
To the N of the Terrace of the Leper King and the Royal Enclosure, the image is approached from the E along a 75m laterite causeway, 8m wide. This causeway ends on the west in a 50m x 14m terrace, with double *sema* (Buddhist boundary markers) at the corners and on the axes. The building housing the image would have been in wood, long since disappeared, and was constructed on a 30m x 30m cruciform foundation.

The seated Buddha

Visit
Walk 100m N from the Terrace of the Leper King, and then W along the laterite causeway. At the terrace, note the *naga* balustrades and lions that flank the E approach. The lions are in the style of the Bayon, and so considerably later. A modern structure takes the place of the orignal building, as Tep Pranam is now a site of Theravada Buddhist worship, as indeed it probably was until the 18th century. Inside is the Buddha, seated on a lotus and in the *bhumisparsa-mudra*, calling the Earth to witness. Behind the building is another stone Buddha, standing but headless, 4m tall.

Guardian lion on the E approach

Other similar statues
The large reclining Buddha of Baphuon
Best times to visit
Any time — the monument is surrounded by trees.
Location and access
Inside Angkor Thom, 100m N and 120m W of the Terrace of the Leper King. Combine with a visit to Preah Palilay, 280m to the west and slightly north.

PREAH PALILAY ✤

Date: 13th or 14th century
Style: Bayon
Reign: Perhaps Jayavarman VIII or
           later
Visit: 15 mins

This small Buddhist sanctuary in the
wooded area north of the Royal
Enclosure in Angkor Thom has a
number of attractive features, and is
well worth the short detour when you
visit the other monuments on the W
side of the Royal Square.

Plan

Enclosed by a 50m-square laterite
wall with a single sandstone *gopura*
on the east side, the sanctuary, also
sandstone, is 5m square with 4
entrance porches. Its tapering,
partially collapsed tower is
characteristic of its later date.

A 33m-long causeway (maybe a
later addition) connects the *gopura* to
a cross-shaped terrace to the east.
This terrace, 8.5m x 6m, is in
particularly good condition.

Visit

If approaching from Tep Pranam,
walk 200m W and about 50m N
through the forest until you reach the
terrace, easily recognisable by its
excellent *naga* balustrades. If you are
coming from Phimeanakas, leave the
Royal Enclosure through its N *gopura*
and walk N for 200m to the laterite-
walled enclosure of the sanctuary
(visit the terrace later).

The *nagas* are particularly fine,
seven-headed and crowned. There were originally also two statues of
guardian *dvarapalas* here, since vandalised. The large seated Buddha is
modern. From the terrace, take the causeway west to the *gopura*.
Cross-shaped and with three entrances, this has excellent pediments
with scenes from the Buddha's life. As you approach, see the E-facing
pediment over the N entrance (to your right), which shows the
'offering of forest animals' including monkeys and elephants. The
forest in question was called Parilyyaka, and this name was corrupted
to become 'Palilay'. The N-facing pediment shows the Buddha

The sanctuary and tower

Highlights
★ Buddhist pediments on the
   gopura
★ *Naga* balustrades of the terrace
★ Attractive forest setting
★ Chimney-like tower

Head of a naga *from the terrace balustrade*

subduing the enraged elephant Nalagiri. The other pediments carry further representations of the Buddha.

Inside the laterite walls of the enclosure, the unadorned tower rises from the ruins of the sanctuary. Unlike any other tower at Angkor, it may have been faced with other materials. Glaize was of the opinion that the base may have been earlier with the tower a later addition. Pediments from the sanctuary lie on the ground and include 'the assault of the army of Mara' and Indra on Airavata. This co-existence of Buddhist and Hindu imagery is only part of the problem of dating this temple. If it was built in the reign of Jayavarman VII, it is difficult to explain how its Buddhist images could have escaped destruction under the Hinduist king Jayavarman VIII in the late 13th century, bearing in mind how many other Buddha images were destroyed. One possibility is that it might have been built at the end of the latter's reign, when he may have begun to accept Buddhism.

The Buddha subduing Nalagiri, on the N pediment of the gopura

Other monuments of the period
At Angkor:
Angkor Thom, Bayon, Ta Prohm, Banteay Kdei, Preah Khan, Neak Pean, Ta Som, Srah Srang, Ta Nei, Ta Prohm Kel. Elsewhere in Cambodia: Banteay Chhmar.
Best times to visit
Any time — the monument is surrounded by trees.
Location and access
Inside Angkor Thom, 280m west and slightly north of Tep Pranam; 400m north and slightly west of Phimeanakas.

PREAH PITHU ✣

Date: 13th century
Style: Bayon
Reign: Suryavarman II, Jayavarman VIII
Visit: 30 mins

Although traditionally regarded as a group of five temples, in fact they were in all probability not designed as a group. Despite their ruined state, the remains have good decorative carving, and although they are among the most ignored monuments at Angkor, their semi-wooded setting is attractive and peaceful. They are worth strolling around if time permits.

Plan

Two of the five were probably built together and interestingly face W rather than the usual E. They are referred to either numerically or by letter. The first (Temple T) and second (Temple U), with enclosures of 45m x 40m and 35m x 28m respectively, are surrounded by the same moat and are on the same W-E axis. To the W of Temple T, the moat has been replaced by a cruciform terrace. E of Temples T and U, and slightly to the N, Temple X, probably the latest and dating from the 14th century, is surrounded by an even larger moat as far as is physically possible; it connects at its SW corner with the previous moat; it has no enclosure, but rises in two tiers from a 40m-square terrace 4m high.

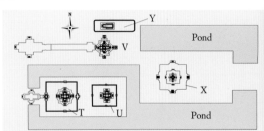

Temple V, without an enclosure, lies to the N of Temple U and is preceded on the W by a large terrace and a causeway some 70m long. 30m N of this temple lies Temple Y, perhaps of a later date than T, U and V; it consists of a sanctuary, *antarala* and *mandapa*, all connected and facing E.

Temple V, across the moat surrounding Temples T and U

Naga *balustrades on the terrace leading up to Temple T*

Temple X from the west

Visit

Approach Temple T by climbing the cruciform terrace that is almost directly opposite Tep Pranam on the other side of the Royal Square. Note the round decorated columns that support it, and the elegant *naga* balustrades similar to those of Preah Palilay and Angkor Wat. On either side are two arms of the moat. Enter the enclosure through its W *gopura*. The sanctuary rises above a 6m three-tier foundation and is set back to the E of the enclosure. Four stairways give access to the 3m-square shrine, in which was found a *linga* on its pedestal. It has four porches with windows, the walls decorated with *devatas* and floral motifs, and on the ground fragments of a lintel showing the Churning of the Sea of Milk. The tower has collapsed.

Leave the enclosure by the eastern *gopura* and cross over to the enclosure of Temple U. This is like a smaller version of the first. *Dvarapalas* guard the doors. The W-facing lintel has Siva, Vishnu and Brahma over a *kala* head; the N lintel shows the Churning of the Sea of Milk.

If the moat is dry, which depends on the season, cross it and walk over to Temple X, some 100m to the east and 30m to the north. Otherwise, retrace your steps, turn left (S) at the entrance terrace to Temple T and follow the banks of the moat around to the E. Temple X, rising above a broad terrace, is similar in design to the first two, although much larger and the decoration is incomplete. It is distinct from the other temples, all of which were Hindu, in being Buddhist, with a frieze of Buddhas inside the shrine and a Buddhist lintel. This change of religious use suggest a 14th century date for this temple. A laterite terrace E of the temple has Buddhist *sema* stones.

From Temple X, walk back to the W and N to reach Temple V, which is more or less due N of Temple U. This has the largest shrine of all, almost 4m square, entered from the east through a small hallway. It contains a large *linga*. The decoration is incomplete.

Finally, Temple Y sits some 30m to the N on an earthen platform. Much simpler than the others, it lacks tiers, stairways and porches, but has the same arrangement as Temple V, but with a larger *mandapa*, facing E. It, too, contained a *linga*. Pediments and half-pediments include Krishna's defeat of the *asura* Bana, Vishnu Crossing the Ocean and the fight between Sugriva and Valin.

Leave the Preah Pithu complex by taking the causeway W from Temple V, descending the steps of the cruciform terrace at its end to the NE corner of the Royal Square.

Best times to visit
Afternoon
Location and access
Inside Angkor Thom, E of the NE corner of the Royal Square. Enter either from here, or by taking the path N of the Victory Way opposite the Buddha of the Bayon (300m E of the central staircase of the Elephant Terrace) – this path reaches the Preah Pithu group after 250m.

SUOR PRAT TOWERS

Date: Early 13th century
Style: post-Bayon
Reign: Indravarman II
Visit: 10 mins

A row of 12 small identical towers lining the E side of the Royal Square, of unknown function. The modern name means 'towers of the rope dancers' (that is, tightrope walkers) and is clearly nonsense. Although they are shrines of some sort, they do not correspond to the normal styles of Khmer shrines. There is a direct reference to these towers by the 13th-century Chinese diplomat Zhou Daguan, but this also has a suspicious ring to it. He wrote: "*Take the case where two men are in dispute, without its being known who is in the right or in the wrong. Opposite the royal palace there are 12 small stone towers. Each of the two men is made to sit in a tower, and each is watched over by members of his family. They remain there for one or two, or even three or four days. When they emerge, the man in the wrong has inevitably caught some disease, either afflicted by ulcers, or by catarrh or noxious fever. The man in the right has not the slightest illness. In this way they decide who is innocent and who is guilty, and they call this 'celestial judgement'* ".

The northernmost towers, with the N Khleang behind

The S side of one of the southern towers

One of the pediments on the ground at Mangalartha shows the Three Steps of Vishnu

Plan

The 12 towers are arranged symmetrically on either side of the Victory Way. Two rows of five are in on the same N-S line; the remaining two are set back slightly at the centre. Each is square in plan, built of laterite with stone lintels and pediments. Apart from some pediments carved with *naga* arches, the stonework is undecorated. The two upper levels are in diminishing proportions and were decorated with antefixes in the form of *nagas* and hermits, a few of which remain. The door in each tower opens via a porch to the W – that is, onto the Royal Square – but unusually for a shrine, each cell has large open windows on the other three sides.

Visit

Unless you have an exceptional interest in the towers, there is little reason for a close inspection. The best views of the towers are as a row from an angle near the N or S end.

MANGALARTHA

Date: Late 13th century (1295)?
Style: Bayon
Reign: Jayavarman VIII
Visit: 20 mins

The last known monument of the Angkor period, consists of a small shrine on a high foundation mass. It was built in honour of a Brahmin scholar called Jayamangalartha, the son of one of the *guru*s of Jayavarman VII, born towards the end of the twelfth century, and who attained the remarkable age of 104. The images of its gods were 'brought to life' on Thursday 28 April 1295, at about 8.45 a.m.

Visit

Mangalartha is in Angkor Thom, almost hidden between the two eastern causeways. It is difficult to find, lying at the end of a footpath some 200m before the Victory Gate and only worth visiting if you very keen. The shrine is overgrown with vegetation.

Pediments lying on the ground show carvings of Reclining Vishnu and the Three Steps of Vishnu, in which he steps over the Ocean.

THE KHLEANGS

Date: Late 10th to early 11th centuries
Style: Khleang
Reign: Jayavirvarman (North), Suryavarman I (South)
Visit: 20 mins

Highlights
★ Stylistically important lintels

The name of these two similar large buildings on the east side of
Angkor Thom's Royal Square, standing symmetrically with the
triumphal way leading to the Palace, is modern. It means either 'the
warehouse temples' or the 'temples of the royal treasure'. Their siting
and purpose are unclear.

The N Khleang, 40m x 4.7m and with 1.5m thick walls, is earlier
than its companion and thus their symmetry was not part of the orginal
plan. It houses several inscriptions mentioning Jayaviravarman. Later
the large hall was split into two by the addition of a central tower
shaped edifice. On the E an arrangment of galleries enclosed a
courtyard.

The unfinsihed S Khleang dates to the reign of Suryavarman I,
whose architect doubtless wished to improve the symmetry of the royal
square. It is less slightly narrower than the N Khleang, being only 4.2m
wide, less carefully built and unfinished.

The style of these buildings has been considered sufficiently
distinctive to give rise to a specific style – the Khleang style, which is
also applied to Ta Keo and Phimeanakas.

Other monuments of the period
At Angkor: Phimeanakas, Ta Keo.
Elsewhere in Cambodia: Preah
Vihear (part). In Thailand: Muang
Tam (part).
Location and access
On the E side of the Royal Square
inside Angkor Thom, behind the
Suor Prat towers. Both the N and S
Khleang are set back some 150m
from the road running W-E from
the Royal Square to the Victory
Gate. The easiest access is from the
Royal Square.

The W wall of the N Khleang

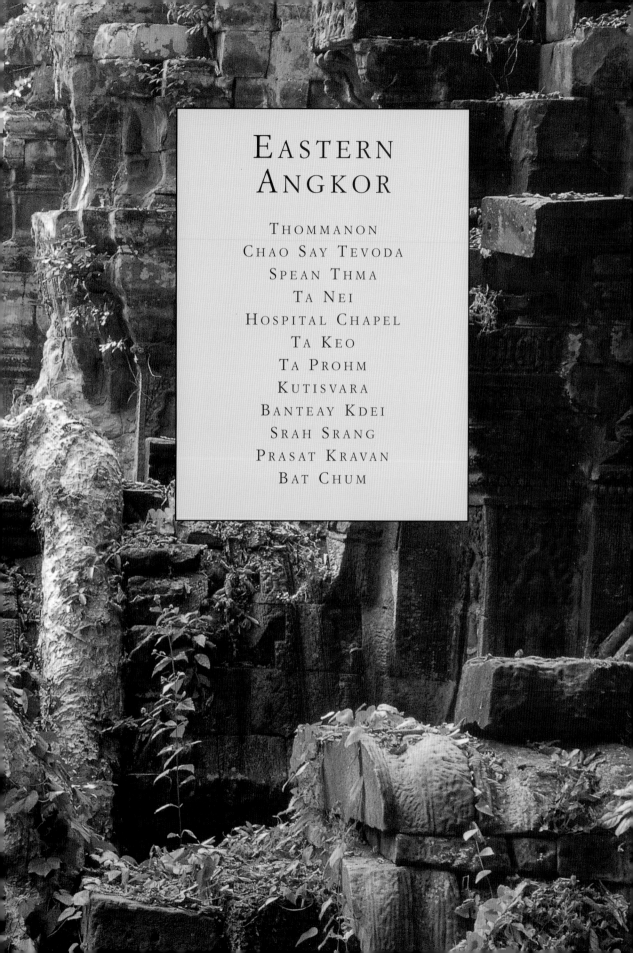

EASTERN ANGKOR

THOMMANON ✧✧

Highlights
★ Compact temple in the style of Angkor Wat, well-preserved and in an attractive setting
★ Fine relief carvings, particularly the *devatas*

Date: Early 12th century
Style: Angkor Wat
Reign: Suryavarman II
Visit: 30 mins

This minor but elegant temple, situated just off the Victory Way a short distance E of Angkor Thom, is immediately recognisable as being of the period of Angkor Wat. It was completely restored in the 1960s when Groslier added concrete ceilings to the buildings in order to create the correct interior space. Its ogival tower and the elaborately costumed carved *devatas* are the most obvious dating signs. In fact, stylistically, Thommanon appears to have been built at the beginning of the reign of Suryavarman II, when work on Angkor Wat was begun.

Directly opposite Thommanon, on the other side of the road, is Chao Say Tevoda, a temple of more-or-less similar proportions, layout and style, although in a semi-ruined condition. They are often referred to as a pair, but this cannot be so as Chao Say was built at the end of Suryavarman's reign. Furthermore, they pre-date both the Victory Gate and the Royal Palace at Angkor Thom, and so cannot have been sited to flank the Victory Way.

Pages 121-23: A silk-cotton tree amidst Ta Prohm

The mandapa *with the sanctuary behind from the* E *gopura*

Plan

Although incomplete, Thommanon has the typical layout of a single-towered temple of the period. The E-facing sanctuary is topped with a tower, and connected by a short corridor, or *antarala*, to a substantial antechamber, or *mandapa*. The three make a central unit, set in an

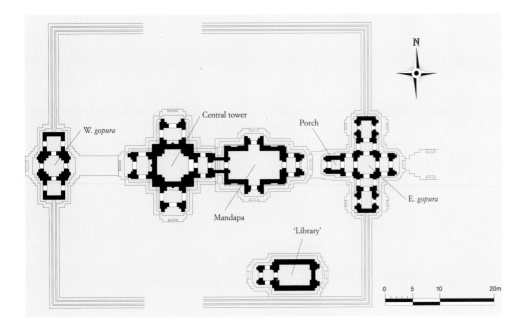

60m x 45m enclosure. *Gopuras* on the E and W give access to the enclosure (there is no trace of N and S *gopuras*, but gaps in the wall show that they were intended), which was surrounded by a moat, now dry. There is a single 'library' in the SE corner.

Visit

Only traces of the enclosure wall's laterite base remain, so that the sanctuary, *gopuras* and 'library' appear as isolated buildings. The sanctuary tower, in the shape of those at Angkor Wat, surmounts the shrine, which has three false entrance porches on the S, W and N. The base of the building is high, at 2.5m, and the carving on the walls and porches of the sanctuary is extremely fine. In particular, note the *devatas* with their elegant costumes and headdresses in the Angkor Wat style. The shrine opens east into a short corridor and antechamber. This last, the *mandapa*, has a stone roof imitating tiles, and is at a lower level than the sanctuary (1.8m). Many of the lintels and pediments are worn and damaged, but those worthy of attention include: the E interior lintel of the sanctuary showing Vishnu on *Garuda*; the interior pediment of the *mandapa* showing the death of Valin from the *Ramayana*; the S-facing pediment of the *mandapa* with Ravana shaking Mount Kailasa (both these latter scenes are also close at Angkor Wat, in the SW corner tower).

The E *gopura* is larger than the W, in keeping with the temple's orientation, and has

Dvarapala and devatas, *south side of the sanctuary*

three doors. An interesting vaulted roof surmounts the centre. Vishnu appears on the N and S pediments, while the E pediment is uncarved.

Just to the south of these buildings is a fine 'library' in the style of the *mandapa*, complete with false aisles and false windows (the cramped interior comes as a surprise). It opens to the W.

The W *gopura* stands well apart fom the other buildings and is less elaborate than its counterpart on the other side, but has reasonably well preserved, deeply carved pediments. Vishnu appears in battle riding *garuda* on the W pediment; Siva as an ascetic on the S upper pediment. A well carved Churning of the Sea of Milk is on the N upper pediment.

Opposite: Head of a devata *with elaborate headdress*

The main sanctuary

Below: Frieze of praying hermits, W *gopura*

Other monuments of the period
At Angkor: Angkor Wat, Banteay Samré, Chao Say Tevoda, some of Preah Pithu. Elsewhere: Beng Mealea (40km E); Phimai and Phnom Rung (Thailand); most of Wat Phu (Laos).
Best times to visit
Early-to-mid-morning for the light; easily combined with a visit to Chao Say Tevoda opposite.
Location and access
500m E of Angkor Thom's Victory Gate. Follow the road E from the Victory Gate (towards Ta Keo); Thommanon is situated 100m N of the road.

128

CHAO SAY TEVODA ✤

Highlights
★ Compact temple in the style of Angkor Wat

Date: Middle 12th century
Style: Angkor Wat
Reign: Suryavarman II, continued by Yasovarman II, additions by Jayavarman VIII
Visit: 15 mins

Just across the road from Thommanon, Chao Say Tevoda is another minor temple of the Angkor Wat period, though in a more ruined state. Recently its restoration has been begun by the Chinese. As mentioned under the entry for Thommanon, the two temples are often wrongly thought to be a pair. Stylistically, Chao Say Tevoda appears to have been built towards the end of Suryavarman II's reign, and so is later than Thommanon. Nor were they planned to line the Victory Way leading from the Royal Palace of Angkor Thom, which was built much later.

The S side of the sanctuary (right) and mandapa (left). The strangler fig is no longer in situ

Plan

The layout is essentially that of Thommanon, except that Chao Say has four *gopuras* and two 'libraries'. The central buildings follow the same pattern: sanctuary tower connected by an *antarala* to a *mandapa*. The scale of everything is a little smaller than Thommanon: the enclosure measures 50m x 40m and the ground plan of the sanctuary is reduced.

The E *gopura* is, as usual, larger and more elaborate than the others, with three entrances, and the 'libraries' (in very poor condition) are in their normal positions: the NE and SE corners of the enclosure.

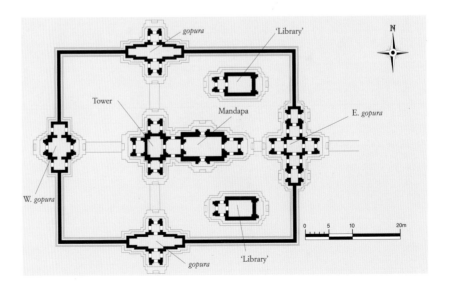

Visit

The ruined state of the temple gives it a different atmosphere to that of Thommanon, and it is interesting to compare the two in this light. There is more of the feeling of exploring an abandoned site. The path leads to the N side of the monument; make your way to the left towards the E *gopura*. The S pediment shows the Death of Valin in good condition. Note the slightly raised causeway on pillars connecting this *gopura* with the sanctuary. This causeway, together with others connecting the sanctuary with the other three *gopuras*, was added at a later date. The W *gopura* is in the best condition, having been restored in the 1960s, although the N pediment is badly damaged and the Churning of the Sea of Milk is only just discernible.

A strangler fig which had taken root in the S porch of the central sanctuary, contributed to the collapse, and has now been removed. Only the lower part of the tower remains standing. The standard of carving is of the same high order as at Thommanon, although the vandalised condition of the *devatas* is regrettable. Note also the floral motifs in square panels around the walls of the *antarala*, *mandapa* and E *gopura*. An interesting pediment on the ground to the S seems to show a maternity hospital.

To the E of the temple is a large cruciform terrace and causeway leading to the Siem Reap river which was probably added by Jayavarman VIII.

Damaged devata *on the south porch of the sanctuary*

Other monuments of the period
At Angkor: Angkor Wat, Banteay Samré, Thommanon, some of Preah Pithu. Elsewhere: Beng Mealea (40km E); Phimai, Phnom Rung, Sikhoraphum, Ku Suan Taeng, Yai Ngao (all Thailand); most of Wat Phu (Laos).
Best times to visit
Early-to-mid-morning for the light; easily combined with a visit to Thommanon opposite.
Location and access
500m E of Angkor Thom's Victory Gate. Follow the road E from the Victory Gate (towards Ta Keo); Chao Say Tevoda is situated 100m S of the road.

The E gopura of Chao Say Tevoda

SPEAN THMA

Date: 16th century
Style: post-Bayon
Reign: Unknown
Visit: 5 mins

The N side of Spean Thma

To the left of the road leading from the Victory Gate towards Ta Keo, where it crosses the Siem Reap River, are the remains of the original Khmer stone bridge (Spean Thma means 'stone bridge' in modern Khmer). The builders here used exactly the same method for spanning space as in the temples, that is, narrow corbelled arches. This necessitated a bridge that was twice as wide as the river in order to achieve sufficient passage for the water to flow through. Even so this later proved insufficient and, since it was built, the canalised river has changed course to go around the bridge. Another problem exacerbating the water flow problems is the sand on which the bridge was built, making the river bank unstable. If you take the trouble to inspect the supports, of which there were originally 14, you will see that the stones are carved, indicating that they have been reused from temples of several epochs, in particular those of the post-Bayon period.

Best times to visit
Any time
Location and access
700m east of Angkor Thom's Victory Gate, and 200m E of the point on the road opposite Thommanon and Chao Say Tevoda; 350m NW of Ta Keo.

25

TA NEI ✦✦

Date: Late 12th century
Style: Bayon
Reign: Jayavarman VII, enlarged by Indravarman II
Visit: 30 mins

This Bayon-style temple lies deep in the forest N of Ta Keo and 200m west of the East Baray. A restoration project is about to start under the auspices of the Conservation department.

A lichen-covered devata

Highlights
★ A little visited temple in an overgrown setting
★ Interesting pediments

Plan

The temple was originally designed to be 35m x 26m. It was then extended initially towards the E to measure 46m x 26m and then later enlarged to 55m x 47m, with three small *gopuras* on the N, W and S and a large E *gopura* that is essentially a part of the inner, galleried enclosure. As at Ta Prohm, city walls were begun but were probably never finished. Today only two outer *gopuras* exist to the W and E. The length of the urban enclosure was 190m. Inside are two long, narrow 'tank moats' on the N and S. The original E *gopura* now stands isolated, and the original NE and SE corner towers are now part of the gallery. The plan explains this best. There is a single collapsed 'library' near the S side, and a chamber connects the sanctuary to the N *gopura*.

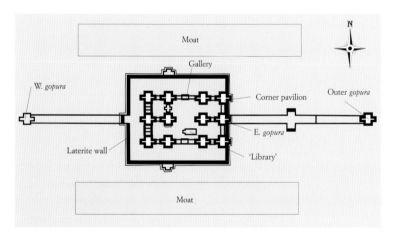

The central sanctuary surrounded by fallen blocks

The W gopura

Visit

The forest path from Ta Keo leads to the W *gopura* of the outer enclosure. From here, follow the remains of a causeway 45m E to the laterite wall of the second enclosure, and enter through the small *gopura*. Immediately in front of you are the galleries that make up the inner enclosure. The sanctuary (cross-shaped with four porches), *gopuras* and corner towers are in sandstone, but the connecting walls of the gallery are in laterite. The collapsed library uses both materials.

Note the Buddhist pediments and lintels, some of which are in place. They include a standing figure in a boat with flying figures carrying parasols (N pediment of the sanctuary); a kneeling figure blessing two children (N pediment of the the south *gopura*); an armed figure on horseback (S pediment of the N *gopura*).

The central Buddha from this pediment at Ta Nei was probably defaced in the mid 13th century

Armed figure on horseback, S pediment N gopura, Ta Nei

Hospital Chapel

> **Other monuments of the period**
> At Angkor: Bayon, Angkor Thom, Ta Prohm, Preah Khan, Banteay Kdei, Neak Pean, Ta Som, Srah Srang. Elsewhere in Cambodia: Banteay Chhmar
> **Best times to visit**
> Morning
> **Location and access**
> Where the road that passes Ta Keo turns S towards Ta Prohm, take the forest path directly N for 900m. By car, it may be possible to turn left onto a small track running N just after Ta Keo. This leads to the main enclosure rather than the W *gopura*.

HOSPITAL CHAPEL

Date: Late 12th century
Style: Bayon
Reign: Jayavarman VII
Visit: 10 mins

Like Ta Prohm Kel, almost opposite Angkor Wat, this small ruined sandstone monument was one of the four *arogayasalas*, or chapels of hospitals, built by Jayavarman VII around Angkor Thom. In all 102 were constructed throughout the empire. The sanctuary, with its now-collapsed tower, opened to the E, and had false doors on the other three sides. It was preceded by a small sandstone *gopura* a little to the E, of which the N and S door frames remain. The decoration is in the style of the Bayon, with *devatas* and small circular medallions enclosing figures. A *somasutra*, or channel for draining lustral water out of the shrine, exited through the N wall of the sanctuary.

Fragments of various pediments and lintels with Buddhist elements stand on the ground.

> **Other hospital chapels**
> At Angkor: Angkor Thom, Bayon, Ta Prohm, Preah Khan, Ta Prohm Kel.
> **Best times to visit**
> Any time.
> **Location and access**
> 150m directly W of Ta Keo.

TA KEO ✛✛

Date: Late 10th to early 11th century
Style: Khleang
Reign: Jayavarman V and Jayaviravarman
Visit: 45 mins - 1 hr

Highlights
★ State temple of Jayavarman V
★ The five massive towers on top of the imposing temple mountain construction

A giant 'temple-mountain' in the tradition of the Bakheng and Pre Rup, Ta Keo stands out for being the first of these great undertakings to be built entirely of sandstone. Its appearance is all the more massive for being incomplete. Indeed, the temple carving had only just begun when worked stopped.

The location chosen for the state temple of Jayavarman V, who succeeded his father Rajendravarman II, builder of Pre Rup and East Mebon, was the W edge of the great East Baray. Jayavarman here broke with tradition by not placing it in the centre of his new capital, Jayendranagari, but in other respects followed his predecessors – the royal palace was sited due N, at the centre of the W bank of the *baray*, and Ta Keo was designed as a representation on earth of five-peaked Mount Meru. Indeed, its name from the inscriptions was Hema-sringagiri, 'the Mountain with Golden Peaks'. Work began in 975 and it was dedicated some time around 1000. When Suryavarman I came to the throne in c.1010 he gave the temple to Yogisvara Pandita, who used only the lower parts, considering himself unworthy of occupying the upper terrace.

The temple from the W

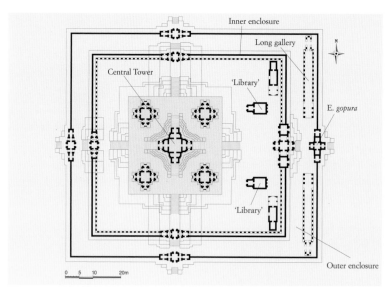

Inner enclosure

Long gallery

Central Tower

'Library'

E. gopura

'Library'

Outer enclosure

0 5 10   20m

Plan

A causeway lined with boundary stones connects the E entrance of the temple with the East Baray 500m away, where there is a small terraced landing stage. The temple is surrounded by moats, the outer banks of which measure 255m E-W by 195m N-S, faced with steps of laterite and sandstone. Within these sit the temple and two ponds to its E. The outer enclosure is a raised platform, 122m x 106m, surrounded by a stone-on-laterite wall and *gopuras* at the cardinal points. The inner enclosure is another platform, 5.5m higher, measuring 80m by 75m, with a continuous gallery instead of a wall.

The pyramid proper rises 14m from this second terrace in three tiers; its total height above the ground is 21.35m. The base is 60m square, the summit 47m square, and the pyramid is crowned by five towers in a quincunx, the central tower being larger and on a higher platform than the others, according to tradition.

Visit

Because the road runs around the W and S sides of Ta Keo, these are the most easily accessible entrances. The S stairway is considered easier to climb, but all the ascents are steep compared with other temples. If you enter from the S, turn right after you pass through the *gopura* of the outer enclosure and walk to its E side. On either side of the E *gopura* with its three doorways are two raised long galleries. These each have an entrance porch facing inwards towards the *gopura*, a small chamber at the back, and balustered windows along each wall.

Climb the steps up to the E *gopura* of the inner enclosure. In the courtyard you face the pyramid; the general absence of decoration makes its lines seem clean and simple, and so particularly massive. If you approach the E face you can see where some decorative carving was started – floral patterns, some in repeating diamond shapes. At the foot of the staircase is a statue of a kneeling Nandi. On either side are substantially built sandstone 'libraries', facing W and with false windows on the recessed upper storey. In the corners on your far left and far right are shorter

Kneeling Nandi

Detail of diamond pattern decoration on the mouldings at the base of the pyramid

Left: The S 'library' in the inner enclosure

versions of the long galleries on the lower terrace. Architecturally, however, the most interesting feature of this enclosure is the gallery, with windows facing inwards. Walk around and you will see that what makes this gallery peculiar is the absence of doors making it seem entirely decorative. There is no trace of stone vaulting over the gallery, and it is likely that the roof would have been of brick or tiles. In fact, this is the point in the evolution of Khmer temple design at which true galleries first appear. Before Ta Keo there were long buildings lining the enclosure, the so-called 'long galleries', as at Pre Rup. Henceforth, the galleries are continuous.

On the summit, the NW (left) and central tower

Climb the steep staircase, which covers the three tiers in a single flight. At the top, the five towers crowd the summit. The massive stones are plainly dressed, with no trace of decoration, and this undoubtedly gives a monumental feeling to the towers. It is important to remember nevertheless that this was not intentional, simply incomplete. It is not a new aesthetic, as has sometimes been suggested. Climb any of the 4m-high staircases of the central tower for a rewarding view over the forest particularly peaceful towards sunset.

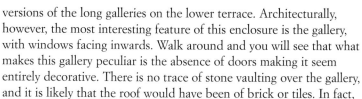

Other monuments of the period
At Angkor: Phimeanakas, the Khleangs. Elsewhere in Cambodia: Preah Vihear (part).
Best times to visit
Early morning, late afternoon, particularly for overall views and for the summit towers.
Location and access
1 km E of Angkor Thom's Victory Gate and 500m W of the W edge of the East Baray, on the road between Angkor Thom and Ta Prohm. The road turns S after crossing the Siem Reap River and runs along the W and S sides of Ta Keo. Overall views of the monument are from either of these sections of the road.
The E and S staircases offer the easiest approach to the summit, but the climb is steep.

TA PROHM ✤ ✤ ✤

Date: Late 12th to 13th centuries
Style: Bayon
Reign: Jayavarman VII, enlarged by Indravarman II
Visit: At least 1 hr

One of the major temples of Jayavarman VII – in fact, a temple-monastery – Ta Prohm features a set of concentric galleries with corner towers and *gopuras*, but with many other additional buildings and enclosures. The complexity of its layout is increased by its partly collapsed state, with trees interlaced among the ruins. According to its stele, which until recently was *in situ*, the principal divinities of Ta Prohm were installed in 1186 to transfer merit to the king's mother. The principal deity, Prajñaparamita, the 'Perfection of Wisdom', was carved in her likeness. (Similarly, the principal deity of Preah Khan, Lokesvara, was carved in the likeness of the king's father). This was only five years after Jayavarman's accession, making it clear that much of the building work took place throughout and after his reign. Ta Prohm's original name was Rajavihara, 'the royal monastery'. In the initial plan for Ta Prohm, 260 divinities were called for; many more were added later.

This was the temple chosen by the École Française d'Extrême-Orient to be left in its 'natural state', as an example of how most of Angkor looked on its discovery in the 19th century. This was an inspired decision, and involved a significant amount of work to prevent further collapse and enough clearing of vegetation to allow entry. It has been maintained in this condition of apparent neglect. All in all, Ta Prohm has the romantic appeal of, say, a Piranesi ruin: partly overgrown and gently declining.

The trees that have grown intertwined among the ruins are especially responsible for Ta Prohm's atmosphere, and have prompted more writers to descriptive excess than any other feature of Angkor. There

The NW corner of Gopura *IV E*

Courtyard of the 'cruciform cloister', in its 'natural state'

are two species: the larger is the silk-cotton tree (*Ceiba pentandra*) distinguished by its thick, pale brown roots with a knobbly texture, the smaller is the strangler fig (*Ficus religiosa*), with a greater mass of thinner, smoother grey roots. In both cases, the plant takes hold in a crevice somewhere in the superstructure of a building, usually where a bird had deposited the seed, and extends roots downwards to the soil. In doing this, the roots work their way between the masonry, so that as they grow thicker, they gradually wedge open the blocks. Eventually, the tree becomes a support for the building, but when it dies, or is felled by a storm, the loosened blocks collapse. In this way, the trees are agents of destruction. In the itineraries below, we point out some of the prominent trees, but remember that they are temporary features.

Overall plan of the city of Ta Prohm

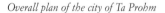

Plan

Because of the jumble of closely-spaced buildings and galleries at the heart of Ta Prohm, most published plans omit to show the outer enclosures. This helps to give a false sense of the scale, in particular of the great size of the urban area beyond the temple

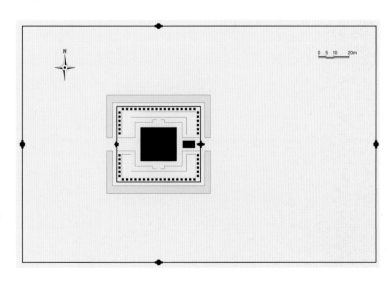

138

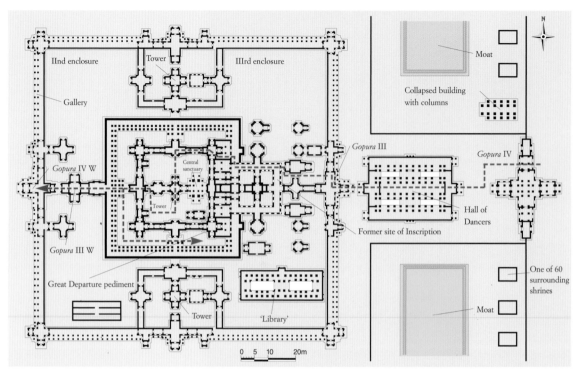

Detailed plan of Ta Prohm showing many later additional shrines

Fallen masonry and silk-cotton tree in the third enclosure, next to the E Gopura

proper. Now forested, apart from some occasionally farmed areas in the east, this outer area was, in its day, a fully inhabited city. Beyond it, 3,140 villages and 79,365 lay people helped to maintain the whole enterprise. The outer wall measures 1 km E-W and 650m N-S, certainly big enough to accommodate the 12,640 people mentioned in the temple's inscription. Within, another wall 250m x 220m marks the fourth enclosure (numbered, as usual with Khmer temples, from the centre outwards). Similar proportions are repeated at Preah Khan and Banteay Kdei, which were built at about the same time.

The temple proper occupies only 1 hectare out of the total 60, in a series of three concentric galleried enclosures inside a moat. Each of these is, as usual, offset slightly towards the west – away from the main entrance – and each has four entrance *gopuras*, at the cardinal points. The outermost – the third – measures 112m x 108m, and is preceded on the E by a large rectangular building in the form of four courtyards, known as the Hall of Dancers.

In the space between the wall of the third enclosure and the second enclosure, which is 50m square, are a number of other structures. In the E part, a cross-shaped gallery and an extension of its axial gallery to the E connects the two enclosures; on either side are several small sanctuary towers, some of them free-standing. In the N and S parts, are two satellite temples. The S temple housed the image of Jayamangalartha-deva, the guru of Jayavarman VII and perhaps the grandfather of the builder of the Mangalartha Temple. The N temple housed an image of Jayakirtideva, Jayavarman VII's elder brother. On the W an axial gallery connects the main enclosures, with two free-standing towers, one on either side.

The 30m-square inner enclosure is bounded by a gallery with corner towers and *gopuras*, and is joined to the second gallery on its eastern side by some later additions which appear now as a confusing jumble. The central sanctuary, no larger than most of Ta Prohm's other shrines and corner towers, is connected to the enclosure gallery on the E and W. In the southeast corner is a 'library'.

Visit

The intentionally unrestored state of Ta Prohm, coupled with the size and complexity of its layout, makes orientation a

The 'house of fire' on the E approach to the temple

Detail of bas-relief, NE wall of Gopura IV E, *showing an episode from the life of the Buddha. This detail shows the earth goddess, Bhumidevi, wringing her hair.*

little difficult. Traditionally, visits began on the W side, but now that the E of the temple has been cleared, and the road approach to it is easy, there are good arguments for entering from this direction. Not the least is that Ta Prohm, like almost all Khmer temples, is oriented to the E. If you have a driver, the best is probably to ask to be dropped at the E *gopura* and then picked up at the W *gopura*. We recommend the route marked on the plan on p. 138.

Ruins of the Hall of Dancers

Itinerary from the E

Enter through the outer eastern *gopura*, next to the road. This is one of four *gopuras* that break the outer laterite wall at the cardinal points, and originally had a tower carrying the four faces of Lokesvara, like those at the Bayon – here it has collapsed completely. As in Banteay Kdei, the face towers were added later, probably during the first half of the 13th century. The path ahead, with trees on either side, leads for 500m to a large, raised cross-shaped terrace in sandstone that leads across the moat. Just before you reach the terrace, you can see on your right a fine stone 'house of fire', similar to that in the same position at

Dvarapala at the entrance to Gopura III E

Preah Khan. Its south pediment shows the *bodhisattva* Lokesvara. See the entry for Preah Khan for a description of these buildings.

Ahead, beyond the terrace, is *Gopura* IV E – the most important of Ta Prohm's entrances. More substantial than any of the others, it is cross-shaped with double rows of pillars inside, and its most interesting features are the tall bas-reliefs with scenes from the life of Buddha on the outer and inner walls. Enter through the right-hand of its three doorways. On the other side, which also has reliefs carved on either side, in the NW angle of the *gopura*, the roots of an enormous silk-cotton tree envelope part of the wall; one of them runs vertically right next to a *devata*.

To the N may be seen a collapsed building with columns, similar in form and in the same location to that which has been restored at Preah Khan. Note the remains of small shrines (of which there are 60 in all) placed at regular intervals around the walls.

Immediately ahead of you is a large unroofed building measuring 20m x 30m, containing four small courtyards, each surrounded by 24 pillars that would have formed a small gallery. This is the Hall of Dancers, equivalent to that at Preah Khan and at Banteay Chhmar (in NW

Cambodia – see *A guide to Khmer Temples in Thailand and Laos*). The interior lintels each carved with a row of dancing *apsaras* suggest that at least part of its function was for ritual dances. Walk around it to the right: the large wall on this northern side (and also on the south) has an impressive blind door. Over the low walls on either side you can see the beginning of the inner moat.

Walk through the central doorway of *Gopura III* into the third enclosure. Looking up, you can see one of the classic views of Ta Prohm, of silk-cotton trees rising over the central towers. Climbing up the pile of blocks just in front of you to the gallery roof is not safe – masonry in this condition can and does fall. Do not do it even if your guide encourages you. Firstly, you may well break your leg, or worse. Secondly, it will damage the temple. Turn to the right and then almost immediately left, where there is a space between the gallery wall on your left and a tower on your right. Here, another silk-cotton tree has worked its way around the tower, the adjacent roof and some blocks on the ground.

As you pass the tower, you find yourself in the relatively open NE corner of the third enclosure. Immediately in front of you are two free-

The roof of the 'cruciform cloister' with a small sanctuary tower beyond

The S gallery of the 'cruciform cloister', looking W to the inner enclosure

The central sanctuary from the SW corner of the inner enclosure

Devatas in the SW corner of the inner enclosure

standing sanctuary towers, similar to the one behind, perhaps a later addition. Beyond the right-hand sanctuary, around the corner of the second enclosure, is a satellite temple with galleries and towers (see page 138). If you wish to see where the stele once stood, squeeze through a narrow gap under a silk cotton tree on the left-hand wall.

Retrace your steps and exit the northeast courtyard into the second enclosure by a small east-facing door close to the corner. Go straight on into the gallery, with its double pillars, and after 20 m turn left into the first enclosure. The central sanctuary is in the middle. Enter its projecting porch and cross through to the other side. Note the modest size of the central sanctuary, even smaller than that of the two satellite temples. This S half of the inner enclosure is distinguished mainly by a 'library' tucked right into its SE corner. On the W side of the sanctuary, stands two isolated square columns, which probably carried wooden altars for offerings. The walls of the gallery ahead are carved with *devatas* in niches – notably attractive ones are on the corner of *Gopura* II S ahead near the middle of the wall, and to your right on the wall facing E. The *devatas* continue even behind the 'library', where they are almost impossible to view.

Leave the courtyard through the small doorway in the W gallery wall, close to the SW corner. Inside, turn right and make your way carefully to the main axis. Here, at *Gopura* I West, turn left and after a few paces turn left again into the small open space between the second and first enclosures. To your right is a magnificent example of a silk-cotton tree with a cascade of roots falling over the roof of the double-pillared gallery. Cross through this gallery into the third enclosure just after the roots of the tree and just before the corner.

Detour to see The Great Departure Pediment
The way out is diagonally to your right, but first turn left, past the corner of the gallery you just left, and walk back E to the group of galleries and towers ahead. This S satellite temple, partly ruined and with trees growing up from it, mirrors the one on the N. The entrance is on the W side, to where the path leads. Cross through, and work your way to the right around the central sanctuary (the left is blocked by fallen masonry). Ahead, in the middle of the E wall, above a tumbled blocks and facing west, is a fine pediment of the 'Great Departure' – the moment in the life of the Buddha when Siddhartha leaves the city to begin his quest; divinities hold the feet of his horse to muffle the sound.

Retrace your steps back to the SW part of the third enclosure, and cross over to its *gopura* on the main axis. This – *Gopura* III – carries detailed decorative carving which repays

The 'Great Departure' pediment

Above: Silk-cotton tree roots over the double-pillared W gallery of the second enclosure

Left: Stegosaur-like animal on the wall of Gopura III W

Face-tower over Gopura *V W, from the W*

Above right: Divinity riding a mythical bird, on the wall of Gopura *III W*

The central section of Ta Prohm showing the fallen masonry and a large strangler fig

Opposite: Strangler figs and silk-cotton trees on the N side of the third enclosure

close examination. On the angles and corners of the porch are numerous small scenes and representations of animals, both real and mythical. Among the vertical strip of roundels in the angle between the south wall of the porch and the east wall of the main body of the *gopura* there is even a very convincing representation of a stegosaur.

Leave the temple proper through this *gopura*, over a cross-shaped stone terrace, to *Gopura* IV West. Continue through this, passing the moat on either side, and walk another 300m along the forest path to exit through the outer western *gopura* (*Gopura* V West) with its face-tower. Your taxi should wait for you here. The road here goes left towards Banteay Kdei, Srah Srang and beyond, or right towards Ta Keo.

Other monuments of the period
At Angkor: Angkor Thom, Bayon, Banteay Kdei, Preah Khan, Neak Pean, Ta Som, Srah Srang, Ta Nei, Ta Prohm Kel. Elsewhere in Cambodia: Banteay Chhmar
Best times to visit
At any time because of the temple's ruined state and complex layout of buildings and passageways, although early morning is probably the most peaceful time.
Location and access
Just S of the SW corner of the East Baray; 1.7 km east of the eastern city wall of Angkor Thom. The usual entry is from the W — the W outer *gopura* with its face-tower is on the road exactly 1 km S of Ta Keo. Alternatively, the temple can be entered through the larger E outer *gopura* — stop on the road 850m W of the NW corner of Srah Srang, at the point where the SE corner of Ta Prohm's wall meets the NW corner of Banteay Kdei's wall, and walk north for 300m.

KUTISVARA

Date: Early 9th century to mid 10th century
Style: Preah Kô (central tower), Pre Rup (others)
Reign: Jayavarman II, Rajendravarman
Visit: 20 mins (including walking from the road)

Now in ruins, this small brick temple of three towers is of more historical interest than architectural. It is only worth a visit if you are keen to see as many monuments as possible. It is buried in vegetation and difficult to find. It is the site of Kuti, mentioned in the stele of Sdok Kok Thom in connection with the 9th century of Jayavarman II. Besides, an inscription found on a stone re-used for the building of Banteay Kdei next door mentions a dedication to Siva and the erection of two statues, of Vishnu and Brahma, by Sivacarya, one of Rajendravarman's priests in the 10th century.

Plan

There are three collapsed brick towers, arranged in a north-south row on a raised earth bank, all facing east. The platform of the central tower is brick, those of the other two laterite.

Visit

Walk 200m from the road passing the north outer wall of Banteay Kdei, as described in the directions below. The shrine of the central tower is almost 3m square, and contained a *linga* on its pedestal. The door-frame and lintel are stone, with octagonal colonettes. The other two towers are a little later in style; the lintel of the northern one featured the Churning of the Sea of Milk, while that of the southern one had a seated Brahma. A statue of Brahma on a round lotus pedestal, as at Phnom Krom and Phnom Bok, was found in the southern shrine. None of the carvings appeared to be *in situ* when the temple was visited in mid-1999.

Other monuments of the period
At Angkor: East Mebon, Pre Rup, Bat Chum
Best times to visit
Any time
Location and access
200m N of Banteay Kdei's N wall. On the road from Ta Prohm to Srah Srang, which follows the N outer wall of Banteay Kdei, pass this last temple's N *gopura*. After another 200m, stop and walk 200m to the left (N). The ruins are very difficult to find as vegetation has grown up around the site. Local villagers sometimes burn corpses near the ruins.

The W towers of the inner enclosure, from the SW corner of the second enclosure

BANTEAY KDEI ✢✢

Date: Late 12th to early 13th centuries
Style: Bayon
Reign: Jayavarman VII, enlarged by Indravarman II
Visit: 30 mins - 1 hr

In some respects a smaller version of Ta Prohm and Preah Khan, the contemporary temple of Banteay Kdei retains what Maurice Glaize called 'the spirit of confusion' which reigned over the works of Jayavarman VII. Its size, however, makes it easier to visit. Buddhist, with face-towers at the entrances, it was probably built over the site of another temple dating from the 10th-century reign of Rajendravarman,

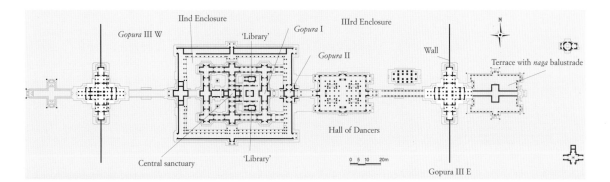

*The face-tower over the E entrance,
opposite Srah Srang*

and probably the work of the royal architect Kavindrari-mathana. Unlike Ta Prohm and Preah Khan, only small inscriptions of Jayavarman VII's time document the temple. The surrounding town was later enclosed by a wall, almost to the size of Ta Prohm.

Plan

The proportions are similar to those of Ta Prohm and Preah Khan: central sanctuary of no great prominence and compact galleried enclosures, all at the centre of a much larger outer enclosure. The entire area, bounded by a laterite wall and four entrance *gopuras* with face-towers, measures 700m x 500m. This is the town enclosure. Within this is the moat, which itself contains the third enclosure, measuring 320m x 300m and bounded by a laterite wall.

The temple proper consists of two galleried enclosures, preceded on the E, just as in Ta Prohm and Preah Khan, by a Hall of Dancers – an open-roofed building containing four courtyards. The second enclosure, 58m x 50m, has a main E *gopura*, a secondary one on the west, and simple doorways on the N and S. The inner enclosure, 36m x 31m, has corner towers and *gopuras* of similar size; the close grouping of towers is distinctive. Axial galleries join these to the central sanctuary, cutting the enclosure into four courtyards. Two 'libraries' occupy the E courtyards.

Visit

It is easy and practical to walk straight through the temple from E to W, or vice versa. Here, we begin at the E entrance, opposite the landing-stage of Srah Srang. In fact, we strongly recommend the

Gopura *III E, with its seated Buddha*

Devata, *second enclosure*

following triple visit, all on foot: Srah Srang; then walk through Banteay Kdei to its W entrance, turn N and follow its outer wall, continuing to the E entrance of Ta Prohm; cross Ta Prohm from E to W. The entire walk takes 2-3 hrs, depending on how much time you spend at each site, and your vehicle can pick you up at Ta Prohm's W entrance.

Enter through the E *gopura* with its face-tower; the view of this, the best preserved, with trees behind, is very attractive, particularly in the early morning. Follow the path for 200m to the cross-shaped terrace with *naga* balustrades, with the moat on either side. On the way, you pass the remains of two laterite-and-stone sanctuaries. In the *gopura* of the third enclosure, directly ahead, is a seated Buddha. The E lintel shows Rama and Sita. Inside small *garudas* support the roof, similar to those at Preah Khan.

Continue W over a *naga* causeway, with a lotus incised in the centre, into the third enclosure, and enter the Hall of Dancers, with its four courtyards surrounded by pillars that would have supported a

Dancing apsaras *on a column in the Hall of Dancers*

Left: Devata *on the wall of the SE corner tower*

Square columns of the second enclosure's W gallery

Right: The towers of the inner enclosure, from the NW

Balusters of a blind window on the extension of the SE corner tower

The moat and causeway leading to the W entrance of the temple

tiled or wooden roof. These pillars are decorated with *apsaras*, dancing singly and in pairs. Pass through *Gopura* II, which is only a few steps away from *Gopura* I. There is a small courtyard on either side, enclosed by the E gallery of the inner enclosure and two extensions from its NE and SE corner towers. Note the excellent *devatas* carved on the walls, and the multi-coloured stone, with shades of red and green.

Through *Gopura* I, there are two more small courtyards. These are the NE and SE corners of the inner enclosure, and each contains a 'library'. Continue past the central sanctuary to the two western courtyards, each of which has a single pillar with pedestal which would have carried a small wooden shrine for offerings. Out into the second enclosure once more, there is a reasonably clear view of the towers from either corner, among the remains of the double-columned gallery.

A causeway lined with *naga* balustrades leads W to the *gopura* of the third enclosure, and on the other side of this, a cruciform terrace. also with *nagas* and lions, crosses the moat. Another 200m takes you to the outer W entrance topped with another face-tower.

Other monuments of the period
At Angkor: Bayon, Ta Prohm, Preah Khan, Neak Pean, Ta Som, Srah Srang, Ta Nei, Ta Prohm Kel. Elsewhere in Cambodia: Banteay Chhmar
Best times to visit
Morning or afternoon
Location and access
Immediately southeast of Ta Prohm and immediately W of Srah Srang. From Siem Reap: Turn right at the T-junction opposite the S *gopura* of Angkor Wat. The road follows the moat almost until the E causeway, and then turns NE; from this point continue for 4 km (passing Prasat Kravan on your right after 2.8 km). The east entrance of Banteay Kdei with its face-tower is on your left, the landing-stage of Srah Srang on your right. From Angkor Thom: As for Ta Prohm, but continue on the road, keeping Ta Prohm's outer wall on your left until you reach Ta Prohm's SE corner. Directly opposite this, on your right, is the NW corner of Banteay Kdei. Turn right here; the W entrance of the temple is 250m further on.

SRAH SRANG ✣

Date: Mid 10th century, remodelled late 12th century, or beginning of 13th century
Style: Existing structures: Bayon
Reign: Rajendravarman, then Jayavarman VII
Visit: 15 mins, or longer for atmosphere

Other monuments of the period
At Angkor: Angkor Thom, Bayon, Ta Prohm, Banteay Kdei, Preah Khan, Neak Pean, Ta Som, Ta Nei, Ta Prohm Kel.
Best times to visit
Sunrise from the platform is spectacular. Late afternoon is also very attractive.
Location and access
1 km S of the East Baray; immediately E of Banteay Kdei; 1.5 km SW of Pre Rup, which is visible from the platform. From Siem Reap: Turn right at the T-junction opposite the S *gopura* of Angkor Wat. The road follows the moat almost until the E causeway, and then turns NE; from this point continue for 4 km (passing Prasat Kravan on your right after 2.8 km). The east entrance of Banteay Kdei with its face-tower is on your left, the landing-stage of Srah Srang on your right. From Angkor Thom: As for Ta Prohm, but continue on the road, keeping Ta Prohm's outer wall on your left, for another 750m beyond the SE corner of Ta Prom until the prominent milestone. Turn right and park; the landing-stage is on your left.

The small *baray* of Srah Srang has retained its water for more than nine centuries and offers a beautiful, tranquil resting place. The best access is from the stone landing-stage opposite the east entrance of Banteay Kdei. As the road is below the level of the *baray's* earth bank, the view from the terrace over the water comes as a pleasant surprise.

The landing-stage and the sandstone facing of the banks date to the reign of Jayavarman VII – contemporary with Banteay Kdei opposite –

but the original lake was built two centuries earlier, as the personal construction of the chief architect of King Rajendravarman, Kavindrarimathana. Although the *baray's* modern name, Srah Srang, means 'royal bath', the 10th century inscriptions state that here "water has been stored for the benefit of all creatures", except for the 'dyke breakers' – the elephants. In the distance to the east, may be seen one of Kavindrarimathana's other achievements – the towers of Pre Rup. In front of the staircase are visible traces of the original brick, covered over by Jayavarman VII when he built the terrace and lined the pond with sandstone, making it slightly smaller. Discovery of a few stones in the centre of the lake suggest that at one time there was a small Mebon-like sanctuary.

Plan
Measuring 700m x 350m, the lake is located immediately to the E of Banteay Kdei, and is aligned not quite exactly E-W (the axis is skewed very slightly S-E/N-W). The landing-stage is near the middle of its W side, on the axis of Banteay Kdei.

Aerial view of Srah Srang, from the NW

The landing stage with guardian lions and naga *balustrades*

Visit
Climb the steps up to the terrace from the road that runs by the eastern entrance of Banteay Kdei. The sandstone terrace of the landing-stage may have carried, at the time of Jayavarman VII, a wooden building. The steps that lead down to the water are flanked by two lions. Halfway down, more steps branch off to the left and right, these flanked by *naga* balustrades.

PRASAT KRAVAN ✤

Date: Early 10th century (consecrated 921)
Styles: Bakheng to Koh Ker
Reign: Harshavarman I
Visit: 30 mins

The row of sanctuaries facing E

On the road between Angkor Wat and Banteay Kdei, Srah Srang, the five brick sanctuaries of Prasat Kravan are not, at first glance, very prepossessing. However, they contain very fine interior brick bas-reliefs, the only known examples of their type in Khmer art. The temple, whose modern name means 'Cardamom Sanctuary' (named after a tree that stood there), was built in the early 10th century during the short reigns of either Harshavarman I or Isanavarman II by a group of high officials, and has a twin – Prasat Neang Khmau ('Sanctuary of the Black Lady') S of Phnom Penh near Ta Keo. The interior decoration at Prasat Neang Khmau, however, is in the form of frescoes. Both temples were dedicated to Vishnu, which is reflected in their decoration.

Plan

Within a small moat, the five sanctuaries are unusually arranged in one N-S row, facing E and all on the same platform. The low terrace facing this to the E is in fact the base of a *gopura*. Another base in the NE of the courtyard was possibly a 'library'. All five sanctuaries open to the E, but today only the central and S have a superstructure. This consists of receding tiers, each diminishing in height and proportions to enhance the impression of scale by means of false perspective; the tower of the central sanctuary is the most complete, with four tiers. The temple was completely restored in the 1960s based on what remained at that time.

Visit

The standard of bricklaying is particularly high, and is a good opportunity to examine the Khmer technique of the period. Note that no mortar was used, but a vegetable compound instead, so that the courses of the typically narrow bricks appear very precise. During the restoration it was necessary to add some new bricks and these are marked with a 'CA', representing Conservation Angkor. Flanking the door of the central sanctuary, guardian *dvarapalas* in niches are carved

Above: Vishnu on Garuda, *central sanctuary*

Left: Lakshmi and attendants, N sanctuary

154

Vishnu Crossing the Ocean, central sanctuary

into the brick, as are the pilasters. The lintels and octagonal colonettes of all five sanctuaries are in sandstone, although the lintels are in varying conditions. The lintel of the southern-most sanctuary is in the most complete state, and shows Vishnu on a *garuda* that is clutching the heads of *nagas* (although the central figures are not quite finished).

Only two of the sanctuary towers – the central and the N – contain interior bas-reliefs, indicating that work on the temple was incomplete. The motif on each of the three walls of the central sanctuary is Vishnu. As you enter, the wall to your left shows Vamana *avatara*, or Vishnu in the guise of a dwarf, stepping across the ocean, represented by three wavy lines below him. The god steps between a pedestal and an upturned lotus, symbolically taking possession of the world. His four arms carry the four attributes: discus, lotus, mace and conch shell. On the wall facing you, an eight-armed Vishnu stands between six rows of attendants, underneath the image of a crocodile, or lizard. The significance of the attendants and reptile remains to be discovered. It would seem to be associated with this particular Vishnuite sect. On the N wall, to your right, Vishnu rides his mount, *garuda*. In the middle of the cell is a large pedestal with a spout to carry away lustral water.

In the N sanctuary, the three interior walls are carved with representations of Vishnu's consort, Lakshmi. These were restored in the 1960s, a particularly difficult task. The wall at left as you enter shows a four-armed Lakshmi holding her attributes. Attendants kneel in prayer at the feet of the goddess.

Other monuments of the period
At Angkor: Baksei Chamkrong. Elsewhere: Koh Ker
Best times to visit
Sunrise for the most attractive view of the towers; any time during the morning for the bas-reliefs (those in the central tower are lit only by the single east-facing doorway). Around midday, some of the bas-reliefs in the N tower are lit directly by the sun through the open roof.
Location and access
3 km E of the E entrance of Angkor Wat and 700m south of the E entrance of Banteay Kdei, on the road connecting the two. From Siem Reap: Turn right at the T-junction opposite the S *gopura* of Angkor Wat. The road follows the moat almost until the E causeway, and then turns NE. From this point continue for 2.6 km, where the brick towers are clearly visible to the right of the road; turn off here. From Angkor Thom: As for Banteay Kdei and Srah Srang, but continue on the road SW for another 800m. Prasat Kravan is on your left.

BAT CHUM

Date: Middle of the 10th century
Style: Pre Rup
Reign: Rajendravarman
Visit: 30 mins

This small Buddhist temple was built by the same architect, Kavindrarimathana, who built King Rajendravarman's royal palace and the temple of East Mebon and probably began Pre Rup. He is the only Khmer architect whose name is known to us. On his own behalf, he also built Srah Srang and Bat Chum. The latter was dedicated in 960, shortly before the architect's death. There were houses around, and a Buddhist monastery nearby, but these have long since vanished.

Visit

Three brick towers (in poor condition), all facing E, on the same platform surrounded by an enclosure with a *gopura* to the E and a moat and with a pond in front of them.

   As is customary, the brick towers are finished with stone door frames, lintels and octagonal colonettes. There are also some fine stone guardian lions. There is an inscription in each of the three towers. Each poem, all praising the builder, is signed by a different person. The last verse of all three requests that elephant owners should prevent their animals from trampling on the dykes in the area, referring to the elephants as 'dyke breakers'.

One of the three inscriptions

Left: Octagonal colonette, entrance to the central sanctuary

Guardian lion on the east steps to the central sanctuary

Other monuments of the period
At Angkor: Pre Rup, East Mebon, Kutisvara
Best times to visit
Morning
Location and access
400m S of Srah Srang. From Banteay Kdei and Srah Srang: take the road S for 500m, and turn onto the small unmade road to the left. After 750m, Bat Chum is 250m to your left (N). From Angkor Wat: As for Prasat Kravan, then continue another 300m; the turn-off is on your right.

THE EAST BARAY

PRE RUP
EAST MEBON
BANTEAY SAMRÉ

PRE RUP ❖ ❖

Date: Middle of the 10th century (961)
Style: Pre Rup
Reign: Rajendravarman
Visit: 30 mins - 1 hr

Highlights
★ Imposing brick towers dominate the surrounding plain
★ Lintels of the towers
★ Views from the upper terrace
★ Harmony of colour between laterite, brick and sandstone

Pre Rup, some 500m S of the S bank of the East Baray, was the State Temple of King Rajendravarman's capital. After Jayavarman IV's reign, whose capital was away from Angkor, at Koh Ker, there was a struggle for succession and Harshavarman II, one of his sons, took power. But he died a few years later and his cousin succeeded him, re-establishing the capital at Angkor. The new king, Rajendravarman, chose the middle of the S bank of the East Baray as the site for his capital, and Pre Rup was built at its centre. In the previous century, Yasovarman I had constructed a line of four ashramas dedicated to Siva, Vishnu, Brahma and Buddha, spaced along the S bank of the *baray*. It is probable that Pre Rup occupies the site of the Sivaite *ashrama*. It is likely that Rajendravarman's architect Kavindrari-mathana had a hand in the building of Pre Rup, even though he had probably died by the time it was dedicated in 961 or early 962. Although its appearance may seem similar to East Mebon, Pre Rup is a temple-mountain while the former is not.

As so often, the temple's modern name is misleading and irrelevant, although its strangeness – Pre Rup means 'turning the body' – ensures that guides waste visitors' time explaining it. Turning the body of a corpse is a cremation rite, and the existence of a stone 'cistern' immediately E of the pyramid has prompted the legend of a king accidentally killed by 'the gardener of the sweet cucumber'. In fact, the name of the principal divinity, and so of the temple itself, was Rajendrabhadresvara.

Pages 156-57: The five central towers, Pre Rup

Plan
Like all the State Temples, Pre Rup was at the centre of a city, but nothing is left of the boundaries or the dwellings. The S bank of the East Baray was certainly the northern city limit, and as this is 500m N

The E approach to the temple

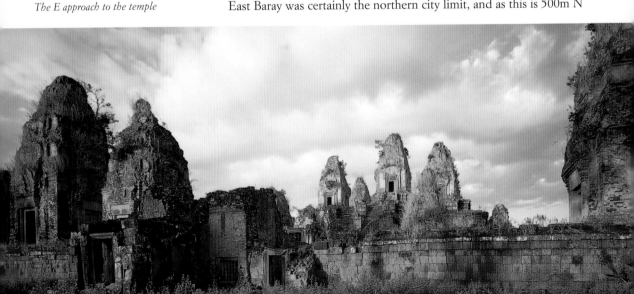

of Pre Rup, the city would have occupied a 1 km square around the temple. A laterite causeway lined with boundary stones ran E from Pre Rup for at least a few 100 metres, although little now remains.

The outer enclosure of the temple proper is a platform bounded by a laterite wall 127m E-W by 117m N-S, with substantial cross-shaped *gopuras* in each wall, each with three doorways. It contains some later buildings (perhaps built by Jayavarman V), notably one row of brick towers on the E, and long galleries on the other sides. The inner enclosure, measuring 87m E-W by 77m N-S, is also a platform bounded by a laterite wall, and it too has *gopuras* at the cardinal points, giving access to the pyramid. A number of buildings take up

The stone 'cistern' and adjacent N 'library'

the space surrounding the pyramid, including two 'libraries' on the E side, the 'cistern' that has provoked the legend of the temple's name, and a series of long galleries arranged around the walls.

The pyramid, square in plan and 50m on each side, rises steeply in three tiers to a 35m square platform, 12m above ground level. The lowest tier has 12 small shrines arranged symmmetrically around it, and the top carries the five principal sanctuary towers in a quincunx, the central one larger than the others.

Visit

Enter from the E, which is where vehicles park. The *gopura* has vestibules on either side that would have housed guardian images. As you pass through, the second enclosure is only several metres ahead, while to the left and right are platforms, each for three brick towers in a line. The central tower in each row is the largest, and the tower immediately to your right appears never to have been built. The most southerly tower has an E-facing lintel featuring Narasimha, the half-man half-lion *avatar* of Vishnu. These towers, which fit clumsily into the space between the two enclosures, are later additions, probably during the reign of Rajendravarman's son Jayavarman V. Other additions from this time are a group of long galleries on the S, W and N sides. Before this, the spaces were perhaps occupied by temple priests.

Continue through the next *gopura* into the inner enclosure. Directly in front of you is the legendary stone 'cistern' – almost certainly a base for a statue of Nandi, possibly in bronze. To your left and right are the two tall brick 'libraries', their

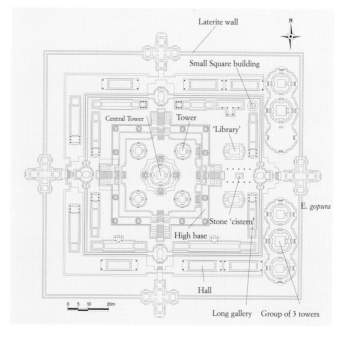

Lintel with Indra on a single-headed Airavata from the E door of the SE tower

Right: Devata *in lime mortar on one of the western towers*

entrances opening to the W, as usual. Their side walls have 'windows' in the form of narrow vertical gaps between the bricks. Beyond the 'libraries' and around the walls of the enclosure, is a series of long galleries. These were a distinctive feature of 10th century architecture, here making their last appearance at Angkor. In later temples they merged into a continuous gallery; here you can see that, even though they are separate buildings, they already make a near-continuous surround for the pyramid. An exception to the symmetry of the buildings in this enclosure is in the NE corner, on your far right; here, the long gallery is shorter than the others, and is preceded by a chamber that originally housed the temple's stele, and followed by a typical shelter that might have contained the stele of the earlier *ashrama.*

Climb the steep steps up the three tiers of the pyramid. Halfway up you pass small shrines on either side on the second tier; note how they almost fill the space on the ledge. Lions guard either side of the staircase. On top, the central tower sits on its own two-tiered platform, surrounded by the other four in each corner. The upper parts of the brick towers have crumbled, but still show the successively smaller four tiers. The lintels, doorways and colonettes are in stone, but the decoration over the brick was originally in lime mortar.

The SW tower originally housed a statue of Lakshmi, Vishnu's consort; the NW tower a statue of Uma, Siva's consort; SE tower a statue of Vishnu; the NE tower a statue of Siva. An inscription on the S side of the door of this last tower dates from Jayavarman VI, and is the only evidence at Angkor of his reign. In keeping with the dedication of the different towers, the guardian figures at the corners are male on the E towers and female on the W towers. Note on the walls of the SW tower a four-armed, four-headed Brahmi (consort of Brahma) and a similar boar-faced figure Varahi (the female principle of Varaha, Vishnu in the form of a wild boar).

EAST MEBON ✦✦

Date: Middle of the 10th century (953)
Style: Pre Rup
Reign: Rajendravarman
Visit: 30 - 45 mins

Highlights
★ Lintels of the towers
★ Elephant sculptures
★ Rural setting among ricefields

The huge East Baray that surrounds East Mebon was built about half a century earlier than the temple, by Yasovarman I. It was needed to guarantee a regular water supply for his new city, Yasodharapura, and was 7.5km long by 1830m wide. Now dry, it was capable of holding about 55 million cubic metres of water when the water level reached 4m, and was called Yasodharatataka, 'the reservoir of Yasodhara'. A stele was installed in each corner, engraved with Sanskrit poems that declared it under the protection of Ganga, the goddess of India's holy river Ganges. The *baray* was fed by water from the Roluos river, some of which was diverted to near its NE corner by a canal. It was King Rajendravarman who decided to build a temple on the island in the East Baray already prepared by Yasovarman. East Mebon, despite appearances, is not actually a 'temple-mountain'. Its impression of height comes from the fact that there is no longer any surrounding water, which on average would have come up some 5m. Built by the king's architect, Kavindrarimathana (in fact the only Khmer architect whose name has come down to us), the temple's divinity Rajendresvara was dedicated on Friday 28 January 953 at about 11 am.

Plan

Because of the 'island' setting of this three-tiered temple, there was no need for the customary succession of enclosures, moats and approach causeways. The laterite base of the temple, 126m by 121m, has four projecting landing-stages at the cardinal points. The outer enclosure,

Aerial of East Mebon

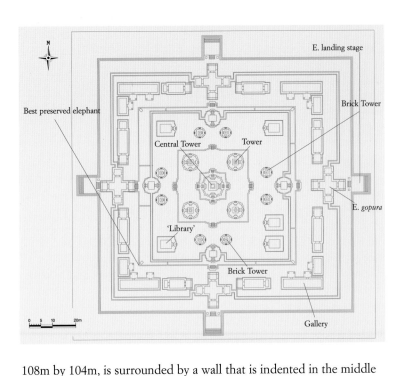

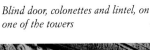

Blind door, colonettes and lintel, on one of the towers

108m by 104m, is surrounded by a wall that is indented in the middle of each side to allow sufficient space between the landing stages and the four *gopuras*. A series of long galleries ran around this enclosure. The next level is the inner enclosure, on a 2.4m laterite terrace. Its low wall is also indented to allow more space in front of the N, E and S *gopuras* (this was not needed for the W *gopura* because of the wider ledge outside the wall.

In the open space between the inner enclosure wall and the central platform are eight small brick towers in pairs at the cardinal points, and five laterite buildings of the 'library' type – three facing W on the E side and two facing E on the W side. The central platform, 3m high and faced with sandstone, supports the five brick sanctuary towers, all of them facing E. The central tower is, as usual, larger than the other four, and stands on a 1.9m platform.

Visit

Enter from the E landing stage (where the vehicles now park would have been water), and cross through the roofless E *gopura*, built of laterite and stone. The temple's stele which used to stand on the right has been moved to the Conservation Office. Once through the *gopura*, you can see on either side the remains of a succession of long galleries, of which those on the south side are in reasonable condition. All were built of laterite, with balustered windows and tiled roofs. From here you can see two monolithic stone elephants on the corners of the next terrace, facing outwards. In fact, there are eight similar elephants, at the corners of both enclosures, just outside the walls. To reach them, climb the steps leading to the *gopura* of the inner enclosure, but turn left along the ledge before the doorway and walk along to the elephant of the SE corner. In the early morning, this sculpture is very attractively lit. Walk along the ledge on the south side to the elephant at the SW corner; this is in the best condition of all.

Other monuments of the period
At Angkor: East Mebon, Bat Chum, Kutisvara
Best times to visit
Early morning, late afternoon
Location and access
In the centre of the now-dry East Baray, 1.3 km N of Pre Rup. From Siem Reap or
the main Angkor group: as for Pre Rup, then continue driving N for 1.3 km, 300m
past the turn-off to the right for Banteay Samré and Banteay Srei. From Ta Som:
follow the road S for 2.5 km; East Mebon is on your right.

Retrace your steps to the S *gopura*, enter and walk around the spacious inner enclosure. Here you can see that, far from being a 'temple-mountain', East Mebon culminates in quite a modest platform for its five towers. In pairs around the enclosure are eight small brick towers with foliate lintels and octagonal colonettes in stone. There are also five laterite windowless buildings: one each in the SW, NW and NE corners of the terrace, and two in the SE corner. These are a little unusual in that those on the east side have all the hallmarks of a 'library' – their position in the corners, W-facing, and dimensions – but the two on the W side face E. They seem to have been originally roofed with brick. The W lintel of the building in the NE corner shows two elephants sprinkling Lakshmi with water from their trunks. The E lintel of the W *gopura* shows Narasimha, Vishnu's man-lion *avatar*, clawing the king of the *asuras*.

Climb the central platform to the towers. Like those of Pre Rup, and indeed most brick Khmer towers, their superstructures recede in four tiers of diminishing size – an intentional effect of false perspective to give a greater appearance of height. Guardian figures on either side of the doors are lightly incised in the brick, and would have been filled out in detail in stucco. The many small circular holes were intended as an aid to binding the stucco to the brick, although no trace of it remains. The main interest of the towers is the stonework, in the form of the lintels and the blind doors on the N, W and S sides – all very

Elephant statue on the SE corner of the second level

similar in style to Pre Rup. On the central tower, the E lintel shows Indra on a three-headed Airavata, with small horsemen emerging from the garland. The W lintel shows Varuna, the Guardian of the West, on his *hamsa* mount, with figures holding lotuses. The S lintel has Yama on a bullock. On the SE tower (which, incidentally, contained a statue of Brahma), the N lintel shows a monster devouring an elephant. On the E face of the NW tower, Ganesha strangely rides his own trunk.

The views over the ricefields are also attractive.

BANTEAY SAMRÉ ✤✤

Date: First half of the 12th century
Style: Angkor Wat
Reign: Suryavarman II, continued by Yasovarman II
Visit: 45 mins - 1 1/2 hrs

Banteay Samré's present-day relative isolation, half a km E of the East Baray, ensures that it receives fewer visitors than most temples at Angkor, so that its completeness, thanks to a thorough restoration by Maurice Glaize, comes as a surprise. The design of its single ogival tower is immediately recognisable as that of Angkor Wat, though to anyone familiar with the monuments of NE Thailand, the temple has very much the appearance of a compacted Phimai. There are no inscriptions detailing its foundation, but it seems likely that it was built by a high official of the court of Suryavarman II during his reign.

Plan

The main elements of the temple follow a pattern that was consistent for many of the temples built at this time, including Thommanon, Chao Say Tevoda, Phimai and Phnom Rung. It has a single tower over the shrine, and this is connected by an *antarala* (a short corridor) to a *mandapa* (antechamber). All of this is flanked by two 'libraries', and concentric galleries surround the ensemble.

The S gopura of the inner enclosure, with the tower beyond, from the roof of the second enclosure's gallery

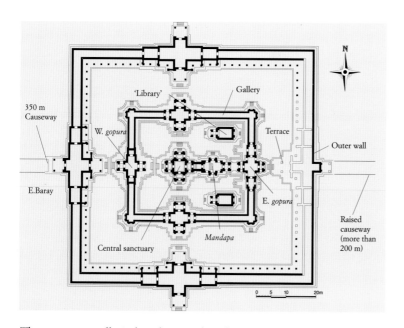

There are two galleried enclosures, but there are signs that the entire complex was much larger. Like Angkor Wat, Banteay Samré is approached by a long, raised causeway leading to a cruciform terrace, probably later. The causeway's length, more than 200m and unfinished to the E, suggests that Banteay Samré enclosed a reasonably sized town as well as the temple at its heart. To the W, an avenue of 350m leads from the East Baray, ending in another cruciform terrace. The outer enclosure, with its high laterite wall, measures 83m x 77m, and the inner enclosure 44m x 38m. Both have *gopuras* at the cardinal points.

Visit

The path from the road leads to the N side of the temple, and while most people enter through the *gopura* on this side, the experience is perhaps a little better if you turn left and follow the laterite wall of the outer enclosure to the corner, then turn right and continue to the E entrance. Before entering the enclosure, it is worth walking E a short distance to see the causeway and cruciform terrace. *Naga* balustrades and guardian lions on the steps recall the approach to Angkor Wat, while the cylindrical columns suggest that the terrace may have been added later, in the 13th century.

The outer wall of the enclosure is massive, 6m high and of laterite, giving it more the look of a fortification than of a gallery, hence the name '*banteay*'. The

The cruciform terrace on the E, with guardian lions

The Sun and Moon appear in roundels, on the E pediment of Gopura I W

entrance is relatively small, and as you pass through you can see the absence of both a proper *gopura* and a gallery on this E side. This may be because they were never finished or were at some point demolished. The gallery walls on the other sides of the enclosure, visible on your left and right, were completed; the roof was of tiles over wooden beams. Strangely, only the S wall of this enclosure has outward-facing windows. An inner platform extends from the base of the gallery, and this is lined with stone pillars, which would also have supported a tiled roof.

The three existing *gopuras*, in sandstone and laterite, are quite large. If you are interested in carving and iconography, make a circuit of these before entering the inner enclosure, to view the deep-relief pediments and half-pediments, many of them depicting scenes from the *Ramayana*. Clockwise: the N-facing pediment of the S *gopura* shows the building of the bridge to Lanka, while the half-pediment above has Vishnu battling an *asura*. On the S-facing pediment, the monkey general Sushena rescues Rama and Lakshmana, wounded by Indrajit. Continuing to the W *gopura*, the E-facing pediment shows Vishnu fighting with two *asuras*, and the half-pediment has a procession of gods on their mounts (Vishnu, Skanda and Yama). On the outside of this *gopura*, the W-facing pediment carries a battle between Hanuman's monkey troops and demons. On to the N *gopura*, where the S-facing pediment shows Rama riding on Hanuman and his brother Lakshmana on Angada, surrounded by the monkey army. The N-facing pediment has Rama on his chariot fighting Ravana on his.

The sanctuary tower, from the SW

Return to the E entrance, where a laterite terrace connects the two enclosures. Enter the inner enclosure through its E *gopura*. Immediately, the relatively small size of the buildings and the intact enclosure walls create an impression of compactness. The central unit of tower, *antarala* and *mandapa* is jammed into the enclosure, while the two 'libraries' to your left and right are pressed right into the corners. This sense is accentuated by the height of all the buildings above the ground.

Walk round the enclosure using the platform on the inner side of the gallery – indeed the only practical way. Another peculiarity is that the gallery is closed to the outside and open to the inner enclosure only via the windows with no continuous passage. Despite the over-crowding (on the W there is no space between the steps leading down from the W *gopura* and those leading up to the shrine), the architecture and decoration are impressive. Note the ogival form of the tower, the well-proportioned 'libraries', the tiered pediments, and the variety of carving. There are, however, no *apsaras* on the walls, which one might expect in a temple of the Angkor Wat period.

The many lintels, pediments and half pediments of the inner enclosure are unusually deeply carved and of considerable interest, and include the following, to mention only a few, clockwise from the E entrance. E *gopura*: Krishna fighting the serpent Kaliya (E-facing lintel), the Churning of the Sea of Milk (E-facing pediment), Vishnu Crossing the Ocean (S-facing pediment), Krishna lifting Mt. Govardhana (W-facing pediment). S *gopura*: various *Ramayana* scenes with monkeys. W *gopura*: the Sun and Moon, in circles (E-facing pediment). N *gopura*: dancing *apsaras* and musicians (S-facing pediment).

The pilasters also repay a close look: scenes and figures are included in the carvings at their base. Note, for example, a miniature version of Vishnu Reclining on the W face of the central sanctuary's S porch, and an *asura* assaulting a buffalo on the S face of the same porch.

Asura and buffalo, on a pilaster of the central sanctuary

Above: Dancing apsaras *and musicians, S pediment of Gopura I N*

Other monuments of the period
At Angkor: Angkor Wat, Thommanon, Chao Say Tevoda. Elsewhere: Beng Mealea (30km E); Phimai, Phnom Rung in Thailand; most of Wat Phu (Laos).
Best times to visit
Early morning, late afternoon, although its relatively isolated location means that allowance must be made for travelling time (see below). Combining it with a visit to Banteay Srei is convenient.
Location and access
500m E of the SE corner of the East Baray, and 4.2 km E of both East Mebon and Pre Rup. Follow the road E from just S of East Mebon for 1.9 km until it turns left for Banteay Srei at the village of Pradak; at this point continue E for 2.2 km. The entrance is to the right of the road.

NORTHEASTERN ANGKOR

PREAH KHAN
NEAK PEAN
KROL KÔ
TA SOM

PREAH KHAN ❖❖❖

Highlights
★ Atmosphere similar to Ta Prohm, on a larger scale
★ Buddhist university and city
★ Entrance causeways with boundary stones and *nagas* held by gods and *asuras*
★ Unique round-columned, two-storied building

Pages 168-69: Face tower, Ta Som

Fallen masonry

Date: Late 12th century (1191)
Style: Bayon
Reign: Jayavarman VII, alterations by Jayavarman VIII
Visit: At least 1 hr

One of Jayavarman VII's largest projects, Preah Khan was much more than a temple: with over 1,000 teachers it appears also to have been a Buddhist university, as well as a considerable city. As at Ta Prohm, the foundation stele was discovered *in situ*, and it gives a considerable amount of information about the temple, its foundation and its maintenance. It was probably the site of the previous palace of Yasovarman II and Tribhuvanadityavarman, while references to a 'lake of blood' indicate that Preah Khan was built on the site of a major battle in the recapture of Angkor from the Chams, and the Cham king died here. Just as Ta Prohm was dedicated to the king's mother as Prajñaparamita, so Preah Khan, five years later in 1191, was dedicated to the king's father, Dharanindravarman. In his likeness, a statue of the bodhisattva Lokesvara, Jayavarmesvara, was consecrated in this year. In other shrines in the city there were 430 secondary deities.

Plan

Preah Khan is located on the western edge of its own long *baray*, the Jayatataka, and a terraced landing-stage at the end of the temple's W-E axis gave access to the lake. A moat encloses the city, which covers 800m x 700m – 56 hectares. Within the outer wall, most of the space was occupied by the city dwellings.

The third enclosure, 200m x 175m, is bounded by another laterite wall, with four *gopuras*, of which the eastern one is the grandest. Inside, much of the space between the wall and the second enclosure is taken up with additional structures and ponds, including a Hall of Dancers on the E side, subsidiary galleried enclosures on the N, W and S, and ponds of different sizes in each of the four corners.

There is little space between the wall of the second enclosure, 85m x 76m, and the gallery of the inner enclosure, 62m x 55m, and on the east side it is filled with later small buildings. This is nothing, however, compared with the confusion that reigns in the inner enclosure, with small shrines and other structures crowding the four corners that are separated by the axial galleries leading from the central sanctuary.

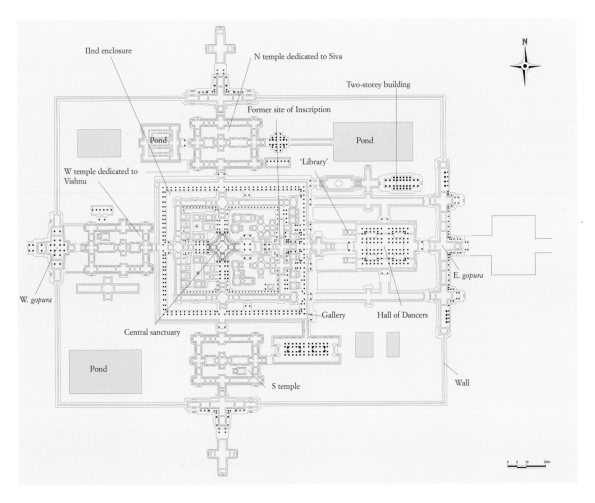

Visit

You can cross Preah Khan from E to W and vice versa (and so have your vehicle pick you up on the other side). Here we describe the approach from the E. From the main road that runs between Angkor Thom and Ta Som, turn south at the western end of the now-dry *baray* of Jayatataka. This small road ends at the eastern entrance, between the walkway lined with boundary stones and a terrace overlooking the Jayatataka – the elongated *baray* 3.5 km long by 900m with Neak Pean at its centre (see page 178). This terrace, with its guardian lions and *naga* balustrade, served as a landing stage similar to that at Srah Srang (see page 151). The walkway covers 200m to the *gopura* of the fourth enclosure, and the first part is lined with boundary stones. The faces of their square-sectioned pillars carry the carving of a monster with a human torso, the legs of a *garuda*,

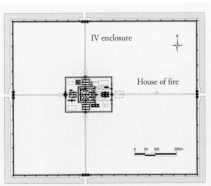

Plan of the city

Above: Plan of the temple

Lion-headed figure on boundary stone lining causeway

and a lion-like face. Niches in the caps of the boundary stones originally had a Buddha image, but these were disfigured in the return to Brahmanism in the second half of the 13th century.

The alley of boundary stones is followed by a *naga* 'bridge' similar to those crossing the moats of Angkor Thom – the bodies of two giant *nagas* on either side of the causeway, supported by rows of gods (on the left, S) and *asuras* (on the right, N). Here, however, the relatively isolated location has allowed the heads to be stolen. The stance of the giant figures recalls the well-known scene of the Churning of the Sea of Milk (as, for example, on the east wall of Angkor Wat's Gallery of Bas-Reliefs). Here, as at the gates to Angkor Thom, the *nagas* lead you across the moat, and it is likely that

Giant garuda *on the E wall of the fourth enclosure*

here, too, they function as a *naga* 'bridge' between the worlds of men and the gods (see the entry for Angkor Thom on p. 76). Note that in fact water cannot flow under the 'bridge' on the W and E which has no passageways. On the E and W *naga* 'bridges' are bas reliefs showing people but they are not often noticed, because you have to climb down the bank to see them. They are best preserved on the S side.

The E *Gopura* of the city ahead of you has three entrances, each with a tower, of which the central one through which a cart could pass is the largest. The walls on either side are of laterite, and carry magnificent stone sculptures of giant *garudas*, each one grasping the tail of a *naga*, its traditional enemy, in each hand. These 5m-tall figures are spaced at 50m intervals all the way around the fourth enclosure, with even larger *garudas* at the corners – 72 in all. Cross through the *gopura*; a beautiful statue of a kneeling princess, now in the Musée Guimet, was found here, although this was probably not her original location.

Continue W to the *gopura* of the third enclosure. This is preceded by a large cross-shaped terrace with *naga* balustrades and lions, and just before you reach it, you can see on your right a substantial 'house of fire', one of 121 such chapels built by Jayavarman VII along the main roads of the Empire. They are very specific in their construction, aligned E-W, with a tower at the W end and a windows on the S side only. From their name in the inscriptions, it is most probable that they were used in connection with the arks of the Sacred Flame, maybe as staging posts on a ritual journey. Similar in construction to those at Ta Prohm and at Banteay Chhmar in northwest Cambodia, this 'house of fire' features extremely thick walls and double-balustered windows. The *gopura*, through which you enter the laterite-walled third

The root of an old silk-cotton tree over Gopura III E

enclosure, is the most elaborate of all those at Preah Khan. Its three widely spaced towers and the small pavilions at either end are connected by galleries supported on this outer side by pillars. 100m in overall length, it has five entrances, and the gallery to your left, between the central and southern towers, bears two giant silk-cotton trees, their trunks at an angle to each other. While extremely beautiful, the trees are causing problems because they are old and likely to fall down damaging the temple in the process.

Cross through the *gopura*; on the side facing in towards the enclosure its gallery walls are solid, with false balustered windows. Immediately ahead, exactly as at Ta Prohm, is a large, building (now minus its roof) containing four small court-yards, each surrounded by 24 pillars that would have formed a small gallery. This, as indicated by the friezes of dancing *apsaras*, is the Hall of Dancers. In passing, note the empty niches above the frieze of dancers; these originally had carvings of Buddhas, but were systematically

Frieze of dancing apsaras, *the Hall of Dancers*

Above: The two-storey building with round columns, indicating perhaps a date from the second half of the 13th century

Left: Garuda *at cornice level within the E gopura of the second enclosures*

Below: Male and female divinity on the pediment of Gopura I E

destroyed during the reign of Jaya-varman VIII, along with thousands of others throughout Angkor. Walk through the doorway in the middle of its northern side. Across a *naga* walkway (that leads from the north tower of the *gopura* that you passed through a short while ago) is one of Angkor's most unusual buildings: two storied, with closely spaced columns and no trace of a stairway

Devata *in the NE angle*
of Gopura I E

Right: The stupa *in the central*
sanctuary can be seen in the
background

(undoubtedly wooden) or any means of access to the upper level. Possibly it once was a granary. In front of the building to the W is a laterite base for a shrine, probably of a later date.

Return to the main E-W axis of the temple. On the W side of the Hall of Dancers are two 'libraries', as usual with W-facing doorways. The *gopura* directly in front of you unusually projects E from the

Part of the crowded inner enclosure

gallery of the second enclosure, and from here to the *gopura* of the inner enclosure is a complicated arrangement of additional building work. Inside, if you allow your eyes to adjust to the darkness, you can admire above you the extremely well carved *garudas* at the corners. On the columns, the small Buddhas originally carved here have been transformed into hermits. Even higher, and difficult to make out without a torch, the E-facing pediment of the *gopura* of the first enclosure shows a male and female divinity (or a king and a queen) standing on pedestals. If you make your way around either side of the *gopura*, to your left or right, you can see clear evidence of successive building – truncated pediments and narrow spaces that are difficult to squeeze through. The *devatas* in their niches are hidden from normal view.

Return to the inner *gopura*. Looking W you can see all the way through the axis of the temple and its succession of doorways. In the western porch of the *gopura*, just in front of you, stood the famous stele of Preah Khan, 2m tall and 60cm square, with inscriptions on all four sides. It was recently removed to the Conservancy for safe-keeping.

Continue W, into the inner enclosure. If you look back you will see the pediment showing Rama returning to Ayodhaya. Unlike at any other temple, even Ta Prohm, this courtyard has seen the later additions of so many small buildings, most of them irregularly spaced, that its layout is obscured. The central sanctuary is, as usual, set back towards the W. At its centre is a small *stupa*, added around the 16th century. Originally a statue in the likeness of Jayavarman VII's father Jayavarmesvara stood here. It was probably smashed by Jayavarman VIII. The interior walls here are pierced with small holes, presumed to have been for attaching large bronze plates, as a covering. Similarly, the outside of the central sanctuary was not well finished, since it would

Vishnu Reclining on the W pediment of the N temple of the third enclosure

Dvarapala guarding the entrance to Gopura I S

Asura *on the west* 'naga *bridge*'

*The Battle of Lanka on the
W pediment of* Gopura *III W*

also have been covered with bronze. Indeed, the inscription mentioned that more than 1500 tonnes were used at this temple. There are four doorways, at the cardinal points, which give an unusually spacious and open feeling to the sanctuary, with long views along each axis.

Three small rectangular temples surround the Buddha temple: the N is dedicated to Siva; the S, to the deceased kings and queens; the W to Vishnu. If you have time, you can make a side-trip from this point, along the N axis (the S is blocked), to visit the N temple. The N temple W pediment shows Vishnu Reclining, and the E the Hindu Trinity: Siva flanked by Brahma and Vishnu. Continue through the substantial *Gopura* III, which gives out onto a cross-shaped terrace and, eventually, the remains of a *naga* 'bridge' with gods and *asuras*. The outer doorway of this *gopura* is guarded by two enormous *dvarapalas*. This will be quite a long walk and you should then return to the Central Sanctuary and exit by the W.

Return to the central sanctuary, and continue W. In the vestibule immediately to the W of the sanctuary is a *linga* and its *yoni* pedestal, placed here probably in the second half of the 13th century. On either side, filling the NW and SW corners of the inner enclosure, are more small chapels similar to those in the eastern courtyards.

As you leave *Gopura* II, you enter the small Vishnu temple, identical to the other two except that the opening is, of course, to the W and the 'library' is accordingly in a different position. In its eastern entrance is a long pedestal with holes for three statues (the inscription on the door jamb states that these were Rama, Lakshmana and Sita) and a spout for carrying off lustral water. The W pediment shows Krishna raising Mount Govardhana. A few steps beyond this small enclosure is *Gopura* III W, with its pillared vaults and half-vaults very similar in style to the galleries at Angkor Wat. Its pediment shows a game of chess in progress on a boat (there is a similar scene at Angkor Wat). The W pediment, facing out across a large cruciform terrace, shows fighting during the Battle of Lanka, from the *Ramayana*. Two large *dvarapalas* (now headless) guard the W entrance.

The route W, leaving Preah Khan, recapitulates the eastern approach, although it is a little shorter due to the offsetting of the temple to the W. Pass through *Gopura* IV and the laterite wall with giant *garudas*, then across the moat by means of the causeway flanked with gods and *asuras* holding the bodies of the two giant *nagas*, and finally along the walkway between the rows of boundary stones to the road.

A hermit in prayer, on the side of one of the inner enclosure's many small chapels

Other monuments of the period
At Angkor: Angkor Thom, Bayon, Ta Prohm, Banteay Kdei, Neak Pean, Ta Som, Srah Srang, Ta Nei, Ta Prohm Kel. Elsewhere in Cambodia: Banteay Chhmar.
Best times to visit
At any time because of the complex layout of buildings and passageways, but late afternoon is best for the W entrance causeway and for the round-columned building near the NE corner.
Location and access
Immediately N of the NE corner of Angkor Thom. The road leaving Angkor Thom's North Gate runs NE for 600m, E for 300m, then N — after 250m it passes the W entrance to Preah Khan. As the temple is large it is a good idea to ask your taxi to drop you at the E entrance and pick you up at the W entrance.

Below: Boundary stones along the western approach

NEAK PEAN ✦✦

Date: Late 12th century
Style: Bayon
Reign: Jayavarman VII
Visit: 30 - 45 mins

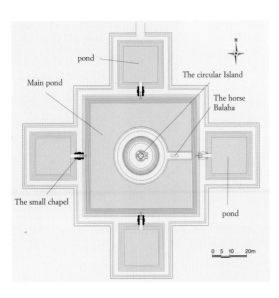

The central pond, sanctuary and horse, from the S

This unusual small monument (pronounced 'Neak Pouan'), a cruciform arrangement of ponds with a sanctuary tower on a circular island in the middle, is pure symbolism. Set in the middle of the Jayatataka *baray* on what was formerly an island, it may represent the sacred Himalayan lake of Anavatapta. This lake was famous for its miraculous healing properties and as the source of four great rivers issuing through the mouths of a lion, an elephant, a horse and an ox. However, this Buddhist symbolism only came later, during a period of rebuilding, and it was originally a royal Hindu site; the stele of Preah Khan gives its name as Rajyasri – 'the Fortune of the Kingdom'. In the 13th century, Zhou Daguan gave a description that is precise about the temple's location, but different in a number of other respects: *"The Northern Lake lies one and a quarter miles to the north of the Walled City. At its centre stands a square tower of gold with several dozen stone rooms. If you are looking for gold lions, bronze elephants, bronze oxen, bronze horses, here is where you will find them."*

Plan

Like West Baray and East Baray, each with their Mebon, the *baray* of
Preah Khan was also designed with an island temple in its middle.
Although the Jayatataka is now dry, the island was a substantial 300m
square. At its centre is the main pond, 70m square, with four smaller
ponds, each 25m square, joined to it at the cardinal points. In the
centre of the main pond, a tiny circular island 14m in diameter
supports a sanctuary tower. Surrounding these restored parts were
another eight ponds, now dry.

Visit

The path reaches Neak Pean from the N. Walk around the edges of
the small northern pond to the main pond. The circular island in the
middle is encircled at its base by two *naga* serpents, their heads on its
E side and their tails entwined on the W. They seem to represent the
naga kings Nanda and Upananda, linked in Hindu mythology with
Lake Anavatapta, and give the monument its modern name, which
means 'entwined sepents'. The top of the circular steps that form the
temple's platform is ringed by lotus leaves. Another set, inverted, forms
the base of the tower.

The sanctuary opens to the E, with blind doors on the other three
sides. Originally the temple was cruciform with doors on all four sides.
Later the doors were closed and elephants were placed at the corners
making the temple round. A standing Lokesvara is carved on each of
the blind doors. Above the one facing you on the N side, whose head
was recently stolen, the pediment shows the 'Great Departure'. On the
E pediment is the cutting of Siddartha's hair, on the W pediment the

*Statue of Lokesvara on the S side of the
sanctuary*

*Statue of the horse Balaha, in the pond
just E of the sanctuary*

Right: Fountainhead in the E chapel

Buddha in meditation under the *Bodhi* tree, while that on the S is unrecognisable. The tower itself is ogival and topped with a lotus bud.

Just to the E of the island, the statue of a flying horse rises from the water. Clinging to its tail and its flanks is a group of men. Although unfinished, the horse is clearly Balaha, one of the forms taken by the compassionate Bodhisattva Lokesvara, and in this instance he is helping seafaring merchants escape from an island inhabited by an ogress. Balaha also appears in the hidden part of the Terrace of the Elephants in Angkor Thom. Stone images were found on the other three sides of the island: a statue of Vishnu to the W, some *lingas* to the N, and an unrecogniseable image to the S.

Four small chapels link the main pond with the smaller ones; only their vaulted roofs appear above the level of the terrace surrounding the pond, and these are decorated with pediments and half-pediments. Enter from the side of each small pond. Inside, at the end, is a sculpted fountainhead. It seems that water would emerge when visitors poured water from the main pond into the small receptacle in the steps above. This then passes through a conduit to emerge from the mouth. That in the eastern chapel, in the form of a man's face, is the best carved; the others are a lion in the southern chapel, a horse in the W, and an elephant in the N. Apart from the replacement of an ox with a man, these correspond with the legend of Lake Anavatapta. The Buddha on the E pediment of the N chapel has been transformed into a *linga*, during the reign of King Jayavarman VIII.

Attendant of Lokesvara, upper W pediment of the N chapel

Other monuments of the period
At Angkor: Angkor Thom, Bayon, Ta Prohm, Preah Khan, Banteay Kdei, Ta Som, Srah Srang, Ta Nei, Ta Prohm Kel. Elsewhere in Cambodia: Banteay Chhmar.
Best times to visit
Early morning, late afternoon. In December and January there is water in the main pond.
Location and access
2.5 km due E of Preah Khan and 2 km W of Ta Som; enter from the road running W-E between these two monuments. The track and path lead S from the road for 300m to Neak Pean.

KROL KÔ

Date: Late 12th to early 13th centuries
Style: Bayon
Reign: Jayavarman VII
Visit: 10 mins

A small temple in the Bayon style of no special interest. It is close to Preah Khan and may have been linked with it.

A pediment showing Krishna lifting Mount Govardhana

Plan

Two concentric enclosures, walled in laterite, surround a simple sanctuary, facing E, and a 'library'. The outer wall is entered through a simple gap, while the inner enclosure, 35m x 25m, has a *gopura* on the E side.

Visit

Enter from the E, through the outer wall to the E *gopura*. There are pediments on the ground, including two showing Lokesvara and one carved with Krishna raising Mount Govardhana. The *gopura* is in stone, as is the central sanctuary, the tower of which has collapsed. On your left, as you enter the inner enclosure, is a single 'library' in laterite and stone, facing W as usual.

Best times to visit
Any time
Location and access
Close to Neak Pean. Enter from the road running W-E between Preah Khan and Ta Som, 100m E of the turn-off for Neak Pean. The track leads N for 100m to the E entrance of Krol Kô.

The central sanctuary from the SW

TA SOM ✤

Date: Late 12th century, 13th century
Style: Bayon (3rd Period)
Reign: Jayavarman VII, enlarged by Indravarman II
Visit: 30 - 45 mins

This small temple, like a miniature simplified version of Ta Prohm or Banteay Kdei, owes its charm to a combination of remoteness, semi-ruined state, and face-towers. It lies at the foot of the E dyke of the *baray* Jayatataka, slightly N of the axis formed by Neak Pean and Preah Khan to the W. It is perhaps the temple referred to in the Preah Khan inscription as Gaurasrigajaratna – 'the Jewel of the Propitious White Elephant', and it should then have housed 22 divinities.

Inner enclosure

The inner enclosure from the NW

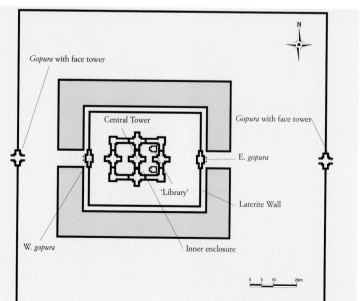

Gopura with face tower

Central Tower

Gopura with face tower

E. gopura

'Library'

Laterite Wall

W. gopura

Inner enclosure

N

0 5 10   20m

Fragment of an octagonal colonette

Plan

Unlike the larger constructions of Jayavarman VII, Ta Som's layout is extremely simple: three concentric enclosures and very little in the way of annex buildings. The outermost, third, enclosure measures 240m x 200m. The normal entrance was through the E, which would suppose some urbanisation on this side. It is walled in laterite, with *gopuras* on the E and W. Inside the third enclosure is a moat and, just inside that, the second enclosure, walled in laterite and also with two *gopuras*, E and W. The inner, first enclosure is bounded by a gallery measuring 30m x 20m, with four corner towers and four *gopuras*. The inner courtyard contains a straightforward central sanctuary with four porches, and two 'libraries' in the usual positions (the NE and SE corners). The inner enclosures are successively offset towards the W, indicating that the temple's main entrance was to the E.

Devata with stretched earlobes

Visit

The usual entry nowadays is from the W: the road between East Mebon and Neak Pean passes by the western *gopura* of the third enclosure. As at Banteay Kdei and Ta Prohm, this enclosure was added later and similarly the *gopuras* have face towers. In the past the temple was famous for a large strangler fig which enclosed the face of the W *gopura*, but the tree died in the 1970s. Enter here, passing under the face-tower. Continue, crossing over the moat, and through the *gopura* of the second enclosure. The fact that the moat is situated inside the third enclosure confirms the later date of the enclosure.

The gallery of the inner enclosure directly ahead of you is almost completely sealed by fallen blocks of stone crowding the entrances. Walk to your right around the gallery to the S side, and climb through the small door

to the right of the *gopura*. The semi-ruined state of the buildings inside the small enclosure and the jumble of masonry blocks makes an attractive scene, completely isolated from the outside. The sanctuary, with its collapsed tower, opens on all four sides, and in the NE and SE corners are two 'libraries', their stone roofs imitating a vault of tiles. In the NW and SW corners are isolated pillars for small wooden shrines, as at Preah Khan, Ta Prohm and Banteay Kdei.

The E *gopura* of the outer enclosure has three pediments with scenes of Lokesvara, the E pediment within the roots of a strangler fig.

Gopura *III E, with its face-tower and a strangler fig*

Other monuments of the period
At Angkor: Angkor Thom, Bayon, Ta Prohm, Preah Khan, Banteay Kdei, Neak Pean, Srah Srang, Ta Nei, Ta Prohm Kel. Elsewhere in Cambodia: Banteay Chhmar.
Best times to visit
Early morning, late afternoon
Location and access
2 km E of Neak Pean; 2 km N and slightly W of East Mebon. From East Mebon: follow the road N for 2.5 km — the entrance is on your right. From Neak Pean: follow the road E for 1.8 km, where it turns S at the corner of the now-dry Jayatataka baray — the entrance is 300m further, to the left of the road.

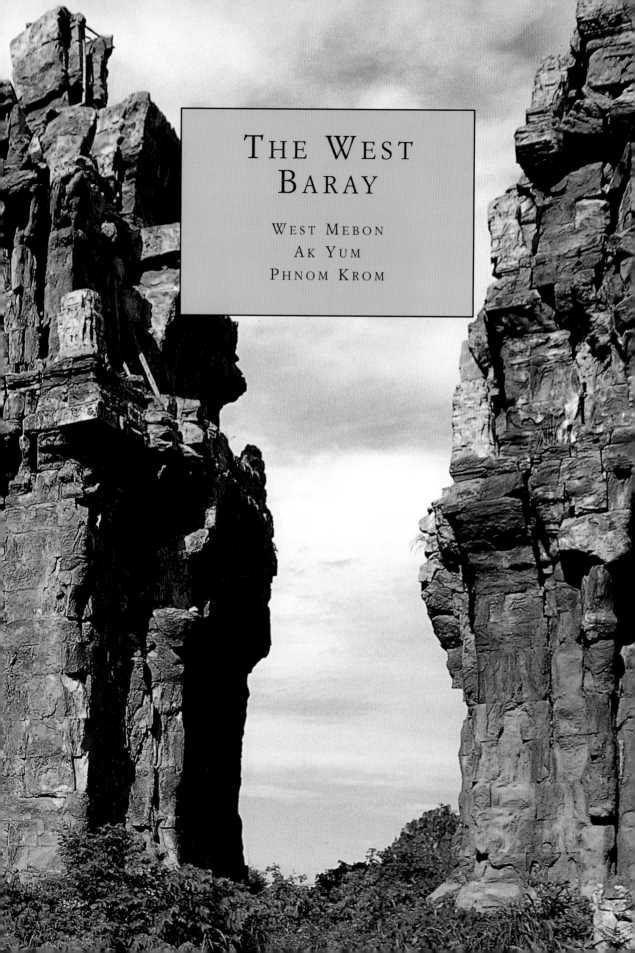

THE WEST BARAY

WEST MEBON
AK YUM
PHNOM KROM

WEST MEBON

Date: Middle of the 11th century
Style: Bapuon
Reign: Udayadityavarman II
Visit: 40 minutes including boat trip

Pages 186-187: Three towers at Phnom Krom

Other monuments of the period
At Angkor: Bapuon
Best times to visit Anytime
Location and access
In the centre of the West Baray, 6.3 km W and slightly S of the Bayon. You can take a boat from the American Lock which takes around 15 minutes.

The West Baray (8km x 2.2km) was constructed in the reign of Suryavarman I and covering an area of 1,760 hectares was the largest reservoir at Angkor. With an average depth of 7m it had a capacity of over 123 million cubic litres and has remained full of water to this day providing a rich source of fish and recreation to the Khmer people. Later in the 11th century, Udayadityavarman II (d.1066) ordered the building of the West Mebon constructed on an artifical island in the middle.

Originally the sanctuary comprised a large square pond some 100m square with a sandstone platofrm in the middle. Of the temple only the E and S *gopuras* are intact, while the beautiful bas-reliefs have been largely vandalised. The magnificent bronze Vishnu found here in 1936 may be the bronze Buddha referred to by Zhou Daguan. It was discovered by Glaize after a peasant told him he had dreamed of finding a statue.

AK YUM

Date: Second half of the 8th century
Style: Uncategorized
Reign: Unknown
Visit: 10 mins

Ak Yum is of great historical interest, being the earliest known temple mountain, but is probably only worth a visit if you have a lot of time and a particularly interested in early Angkor. It was built over during the construction of the West Baray, and as a result was not discovered until 1932. Unfortunately, there is no clear evidence of which Khmer king built it, or of which king modified it. Stones carrying inscriptions, including one with a date corresponding to Saturday 10 June 674 during the reign of King Jayavarman I, that is now in the main doorway of the sanctuary, were re-used. So, the remains that can now be seen are of a temple built over an earlier construction. One inscription dated to the very beginning of the 11th century, shows that the temple dedicated to Gambhiresvara, 'God of the Depths', or 'Hidden Knowledge', was still in use a few years before being covered by the dyke of the West Baray. This deity was particularly associated with the seventh century. Therefore the temple was in use for about three centuries.

A number of bronze statuettes have been found here, both Brahmanic and Buddhist (the latter including Lokesvara and Maitreya).

Location and access
900m E of the SW corner of the West Baray, and 12 km NW of Siem Reap. Leave Siem Reap on Route 6 in the direction of Battambang, and follow directions for West Baray. When you reach the Baray turn left (W) and drive along the edge of the lake for around 400m. Ak Yum is then on your left. It is quite difficult to find because of all the vegetation that has grown up.

Plan

Set in an enclosure which may have been as large as 2km square, Ak Yum has the elements of a temple-mountain. Built principally in brick, it was a three-tier pyramid surmounted by a quincunx of towers. The lowest tier is 100m square and built of earth, while the upper two terraces were of brick. The central tower was larger than the other four, and all were in brick, with only the door surrounds in stone. It is today very difficult to discern how the temple once was.

The colonettes are round in section and carved with leaf and pearl motifs. The lintels featured medallions, pendants and floral embellishments, and appear to have been re-used from the earlier temple. There were traces of *devatas* carved into the brick of the sanctuary, most clearly visible in the SE corner, but this is difficult to see today as the vegetation has taken over and no excavation or restoration work has been carried out.

If you visit this temple you may wish to combine it with a walk along the S bank of the West Baray, or have a swim.

The unrestored remains of Ak Yum

PHNOM KROM

Date: Late 9th to early 10th century
Style: Bakheng
Reign: Yasovarman I
Visit: 1 hr, including climb

Highlights
★ Three towers dedicated to Brahma, Vishnu and Siva
★ Views of the Tonlé Sap and West Baray from the summit

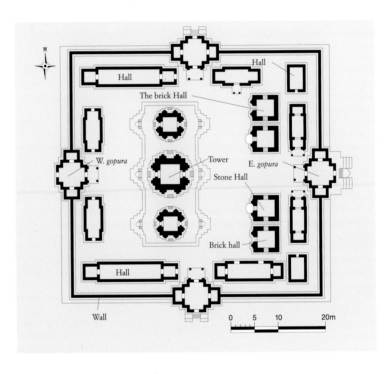

Hamsa on base of Brahma's pedestal in the S sanctuary

Built by Yasovarman I or perhaps his court officials, but with no known inscription to give the date or name.

Plan

Within a square enclosure 50m x 50m on the summit of this isolated 140m-high hill, three stone sanctuary towers stand aligned N-S on the same platform. The central tower, which is slightly larger than the others, was dedicated to Siva, while that on the N was dedicated to Vishnu, and the S tower to Brahma.

Other buildings in the enclosure are 10 halls, now in ruins, that make an almost-continuous surround, just 1m in from the outer wall. In front of the three sanctuary towers (to their E) is a line of four smaller buildings, also all facing W. The centre pair of these is in stone, the outer two in brick. A laterite wall, with a *gopura* in the middle of each side, surrounds the enclosure.

Unusually, the three sanctuaries open to both the E and W, with false doors on the other two sides. Its layout is identical to Phnom Bok, which must have been built at the same time.

The lintels, in very poor condition, feature garlands and inward-facing *makaras*. Octagonal colonettes decorate the doorways.

Visit

At the top of the path, you enter the enclosure through the E *gopura*. This, like the other three, is relatively deep, cross-shaped, and has a small chamber on either side. As you pass through, note the foundations of a series of long halls in laterite, lining the inside of the enclosure wall. There were 10 in all, originally roofed in wood and tiles.

Directly in front of these, in a N-S row, are four nearly-square small buildings, 3.5m x 3m, facing W towards the main sanctuary towers. The inner two are stone, the outer brick, and the walls are pierced with a pattern of holes, like the two 'libraries' of the same period at Bakheng. Continue between these to the central platform, laterite faced with sandstone. Three short staircases, each flanked by guardian lions, lead up to the three towers. These, in sandstone, had superstructures of four diminishing tiers capped with a round stone; miniature buildings served as antefixes at the corners, and some of these remain. The central tower, with a central shrine 4m x 4m, is a little larger than the other two (3.4m x 3.4m). The statues from these shrines – Siva in the central, Brahma in the S and Vishnu in the N, are now at the Musée Guimet, but the pedestals remain. Note, in particular, the *hamsa* birds and lotus petals carved on the circumference of Brahma's round pedestal in the S tower. This tower is in all respects the best preserved of the three, but the decorative work on all the exteriors, however, is in very poor condition due to the strong winds blowing off the Tonlé Sap.

One of the best features of the visit is the view, which covers 360° and great distances, including the West Baray, and the Tonlé Sap with its floating fishing villages.

Other monuments of the period
At Angkor: Bakheng, Phnom Bok. In Thailand: parts of Phnom Wan. In Laos: Huei Thamo.
Best times to visit
Early morning and late afternoon for the views from the summit
Location and access
On the summit of Phnom Krom (140m), 9.5 km SW of Siem Reap. Take the road S from Siem Reap to the Tonlé Sap for 10 km. The path up the hill starts from close to the road, where there is parking, and the climb takes about 15 mins. You can combine the visit with a boat trip on the lake.

Antefix on a tower in the form of a miniature temple

Roluos

PREAH KÔ

BAKONG

LOLEI

PREAH KÔ ✦ ✦

Date: Late 9th century (880)
Style: Preah Kô
Reign: Indravarman I
Visit: 30 mins

Highlights
★ First temple at Roluos
★ Lintels, colonettes and dvarapalas
★ Lime mortar mouldings on towers

This elegant small brick temple, with six towers and some fine lime mortar decoration, was the first temple built by Indravarman I in the capital city of Hariharalaya. Its surrounding moat is large in proportion to the temple buildings, and should have included the Royal Palace, of which no trace has so far been found.

Plan

The temple consists of six brick towers on a single base, surrounded by two concentric enclosures. The outermost of these is 500m x 400m, and a laterite causeway connects its largely collapsed E *gopura* to that of the second enclosure which is surrounded by a laterite wall measuring 97m x 94m.

Inside the second enclosure are the remains of eight long halls, symmetrically arranged in pairs on either side of the temple's E-W axis.

Pages 192-93: Stucco kala *disgorging a* naga *from one of the lintels of Preah kô*

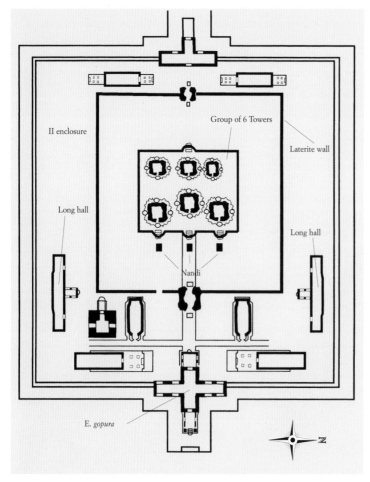

One pair is aligned N-S close to the E wall, another N-S pair are next to the W wall, and a third pair aligned E-W next to the N and S walls. The remains of another, shorter, E-W pair stand on either side of the main causeway, close to the E *gopura* of the inner enclosure. Finally, just outside the SE corner of the inner enclosure's brick wall (now very low) is a square brick building opening to the W and comparable with later 'libraries'.

The inner enclosure, 58m x 56m, is offset to the W, and has a *gopura* on the E and W. In its centre are the sanctuaries – six brick towers on the same sandstone base in two rows. Their arrangement is not quite symmetrical: the central tower of the front row is set back slightly, while the N tower of the row behind is displaced to the S so that it is right next to the central tower.

Visit

Enter through the ruined E *gopura* of the outer, 3rd enclosure, next to the access road. Built of laterite blocks, it was cross-shaped, with two second-ary aisles and heavily balustered

The three front towers

sandstone windows, and was probably originally roofed with tiles. Cross through this, and continue W along a laterite causeway to the remains of the next *gopura* of the second enclosure.

Almost all of the buildings and galleries surrounding the six central towers are in ruins, giving the approach a more open view than it would have had. As you cross through the second *gopura* (one of its balustered stone windows is completely free-standing), you can see the remains of the various long halls. An exception to this general state of collapse is the brick 'library' to your left, in the SE corner of the second enclosure. Its massive walls support an upper level with smaller dimensions, a pitched roof, and 'windows' in the form of a pattern of spaces between the bricks.

Ahead is the sandstone platform that supports the six towers, in two rows. The upper storey of each tower is recessed, and carries miniature false doors on the faces. Three sets of steps give access, each aligned with a door and guarded by a pair of lions. The statues of three kneeling bulls – Siva's Nandi – face these steps, and give the temple its modern name, 'The Sacred Bull'.

Indravarman I had this temple dedicated on 25 January 880 in honour of his predecessors. The door jambs of the three front towers have long inscriptions on all sides, whereas of the back row only the middle has an inscription. The middle tower of the front row, set back

One of the inscriptions from Preah Kô

The lintel of the SE sanctuary

slightly from the other two, was dedicated to Paramesvara, 'the supreme lord'. This was one of the names of Siva, and in this case also the posthumous title of the founder of the Khmer empire, Jayavarman II. The N tower, on your right, was dedicated to Rudresvara, the protecting divinity of King Rudravarman, Indravarman's maternal grandfather, while the S tower was dedicated to Prithivindresvara, representing the protecting divinity of his father, King Prithivindra-varman. These dedications show that Indravarman I was ruling over the lands held by these three kings. Another significant fact is that these three divinities, all with names which could be variants of that of the god Siva, were symbolised not as might be expected by a *linga* but in the form of statues. The three towers in the row behind are smaller and were dedicated to the principal queen of each king, as goddesses.

The stone lintels, with pronounced garlands from which minature horsemen are emerging, are notable, as are the octagonal colonettes. Stone *dvarapalas* standing in niches guard the corners of each tower, surrounded by the flaking remains of lime mortar that once covered the brick completely. On the towers behind, dedicated to the queens, the *dvarapalas* are appropriately replaced by female *devatas*.

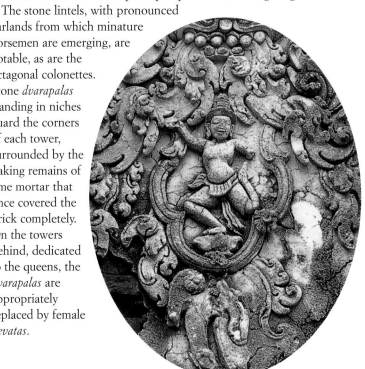

Detail of a lintel showing a dancer in lime mortar

Opposite: The SE corner of the NE sanctuary

Other monuments of the period
At Angkor: Phnom Bakong, Lolei
Best times to visit
Early morning – the towers face E.
Location and access
In Roluos, 13 km E of Siem Reap. Take Route 6 for 12.5 km; here, a signposted sandy road leads S for 400m to the temple, on the way to Bakong.

BAKONG ✤ ✤ ✤

Date: Late 9th century (881)
Style: Bakong
Reign: Indravarman I, central tower possibly added by Yasovarman II
Visit: 45 mins - 1 hr

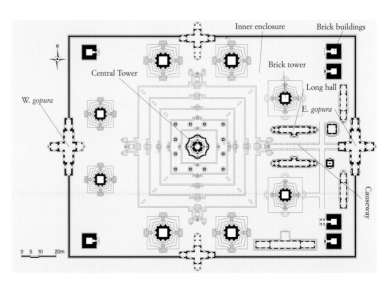

Opposite: The pyramid and its tower from the northern approach

The W brick tower of the southern pair

Bakong is the State Temple of Indravarman I at Hariharalya, the capital utilized by Jayavarman II at the end of the 8th century just before he moved down from the Kulen Mountains after 802. Bakong was the first significant temple-mountain; it appears that it was previously constructed in laterite possibly by Jayavarman III and simply finished in sandstone by Indravarman as his last work. The five tiers of its pyramid, and other elements, symbolised Mount Meru, and the temple was dedicated to Siva. The foundation stele describes the consecration of its *linga*, Sri Indresrava, in 881.

Plan

The size is considerable – 900m x 700m – and includes two moats and three concentric enclosures. The outer moat, on average 3m deep, had a surface area of 15 hectares. The moat is the boundary of the outer, third enclosure, which has no trace of a *gopura,* but there are the remains of two avenues, one leading E, the other N. Between the outer and inner moats are the remains of 22 regularly spaced brick towers, not all of them finished, and in each corner a pair of 60m-square towers (intended to flank a tower, of which only that in the E corner was completed).

The second enclosure, with the remains of its laterite wall, covers 400m x 300m, and most of the space between this and the inner enclosure is taken up with a broad moat, now dry but faced with stone steps. There are ruined *gopuras* at the cardinal points (the northern and southern ones much smaller).

The inner enclosure, containing the pyramid and surrounding brick towers, measures 160m x 120m, and is also bounded by laterite wall.

Miniature temple carved on the N entrance pavilion at the base of the steps

Other monuments of the period
At Angkor: Preah Kô, Lolei
Best times to visit
Sunrise and early morning are particularly attractive
Location and access
In Roluos, 13 km E of Siem Reap. Take Route 6 for 12.5 km; here, a signposted sandy road leads S for 1.2 km to the temple, passing Preah Kô on the way. When the road reaches the N wall, it turns E (left) and then S (right) to the E entrance.

This, too, has *gopuras* at the cardinal points, although only the laterite foundations remain; the east and west *gopuras* are larger than those on the north and south. Inside the enclosure, and surrounding the pyramid, are a number of buildings. Chief among these are eight brick towers, arranged in pairs along each side, in different conditions. In the corners of the enclosure are the remains of eight small square brick buildings: one each in the NW and SW corners (doors facing E), two each in the NE and SE corners (doors facing W). In addition, two distinctive, but later, long halls in stone flank the eastern approach to the pyramid, aligned E-W, and these are preceded by two small buildings, the northern one of which was built to house the stele. Finally, there are the remains of two other long halls aligned N-S in laterite just inside the east entrance, and the traces of another aligned E-W in the SE corner.

The pyramid itself, almost square in plan, has a clear, uncomplicated profile. It was painstakingly reconstructed by the end of the 1930s by Maurice Glaize. Before this time the sandstone blocks were scattered about and this explains why many corners are damaged. Symbolically, its five tiers perhaps represent, from bottom to top, the realms of the *nagas*, *garudas*, *rakshasas*, *yakshas*, and finally *Maharajas*. The base is 67m x 65m, the top 20m x 18m, with steps up each axis. Statues of elephants were placed on the corners of the three lower tiers as guardians (although on the lowest tier they are hardly recognisable as elephants), while the fourth tier has 12 small shrines regularly spaced around it. The pyramid is crowned with a tower of a much later period, in the style of Angkor Wat.

Visit
The access road from Route 6 crosses into the outer enclosure, so that by the time you reach the main E-W axis of the temple, you are at the edge of the second enclosure. A broad earthen causeway crosses the wide moat, and is flanked by monumental seven-headed *nagas* with their serpent bodies flat on the ground. Once you have crossed over this *naga* 'bridge', you pass the buildings of a modern monastery on either side and enter the inner enclosure through the ruins of the E *gopura*. To your left and right are the remains of the various buildings described above. There is a good overall view of the temple, particularly striking at sunrise, from the remains of the brick buildings in the NE corner, to your far right. From here, you look across the stone foundations of one of the brick towers towards the pyramid. The main door frame of this tower is free-standing, with excellent octagonal colonettes and a typical deep lintel. A fine statue of Vishnu and two consorts was originally here.

Returning to the main axis of the temple, the two long sandstone halls aligned on either side, just before the pyramid, are very distinctive. Their entrances, unusually, are in the middle of the long side, facing into the causeway, and the windows are balustered. These are later additions, from the 12th or 13th centuries. Pass between these buildings and enter the small but massive pavilion that precedes the first flight of steps. There are four of these unusual entrances around the pyramid, with pitched roofs and gable ends. In front of each is a statue of Nandi, Siva's bull, today almost unrecognisable as such.

Climb the steps to the first tier of the pyramid. Another four flights take you up the remaining tiers. Note how the dimensions of each set of steps diminishes from the lowest tier to the top: this was a deliberate device of false perspective to increase the apparent height of the pyramid when see from below.

Lions guard the stairways, while at the corners of the three lowest tiers, statues of elephants face outwards, as at East Mebon. On the fourth tier, the remains of 12 small shrines are arranged around the platform – one at each angle, two on each side. This level was entirely decorated with bas-reliefs but only traces remain. The best surviving panels is on the south, showing *asuras* losing a battle, at the moment when the figurine on top of their standard has just been sliced off.

Climb the last flight of steps to the top of the pyramid, 14m above ground level. The sanctuary tower, 15m high, with its mixture of styles of carving and its ogival tower, is much later than the pyramid – from the period of Angkor Wat. The original, sandstone tower, dating to the time of Indravarman, was probably destroyed, profaned, or both, during the war of succession. Angkor Wat is certainly the style of the worn pediments: on the E is Siva dancing; on the S the Churning of the Sea of Milk, very worn indeed; on the W Vishnu Reclining; and on the N the scene from the *Ramayana* in which Lakshmana has been caught in the serpent-arrows of Indrajit. Only the base of the sanctuary dates from the time of Indravarman. The shrine opens to the E, with false doors on the other three sides. Full-bodied *devatas* carved in stone decorate the corner angles.

From the top, you can see the eight surrounding brick towers, or their remains. The western pair are smaller than the others, and of the eastern pair the brick structure has collapsed, leaving only the base (this, uniquely, is in stone) and the stone door frame of the N tower. Guardian *dvarapalas* and *devatas* in lime mortar flank the doorways, and the stone lintels are among the finest in Khmer art. The history of these towers is very complicated and still not well established, representing the work of a succession of builders.

The remaining bas-relief fragment on the S side of the pyramid's fourth tier

The N long hall on the approach to the base of the pyramid

LOLEI ✤

Date: Late 9th century (893)
Style: Preah Kô to Bakheng
Reign: Yasovarman I
Visit: 15 mins

Highlights
★ Lime mortar mouldings on towers
★ Lintels and blind doors

Although hard to imagine as such nowadays, Lolei was an island temple, in the middle of the Indratataka *baray*, some 15 km SE of Angkor and nearby Bakong and Preah Ko. The site was, in fact, prepared during the previous reign. Indravarman I had built all but the N dyke of the *baray*, and had located the 'island' that would carry the temple. In the event, it was Indravarman's son, Yasovarman I, who completed the project. One peculiarity is that while Lolei is centred on the longer E-W axis of the *baray*, which measures 3800m x 800m, it is offset towards the N. The reason seems to be that Indravarman had originally intended the *baray* to be broader, but Yasovarman, in a hurry to move the entire capital to Angkor, simply closed off the N side where the other dykes stood. The Indratataka *baray* is distinctly elongated compared to others at Angkor. On Sunday 8 July 893, the temple was dedicated to its four gods. Its modern name, Lolei, is perhaps a corruption of the city's original name, Hariharalaya.

Plan

The artificial island on which the temple was built is today a large terrace, 90m x 80m. This originally supported an enclosing brick wall with four *gopuras*, but all of these have disappeared. There are four brick sanctuary towers, similar to those at Preah Kô, but asymmetrically placed – the temple's E-W axis runs through the two N towers – showing that another two towers were originally intended to the N. It would then have looked much as Preah Kô, with two rows of three towers. In fact, as the foundation stele mentions only four gods, the change of plan must have been made during the construction, and it may be because Yasovarman had not succeeded in conquering lands whose kings the N towers would have honoured.

The main E lintel of the NE tower showing Indra on Airavata

Visit

Enter from the E. Although this is the conventional direction, the inscription, visible on the door jambs of the E doors of the NE, SE and SW towers, states that the entrance was from the N through a gate 'facing four ways', of which no trace now remains. This is unusual, and it may be because Yasovarman built a causeway from the NW corner of the *baray* to his new capital at Angkor, centred on the Bakheng. Today, the site is more or less taken over by a modern monastery (the towers are on the left, beyond the *vihear*), but even in the 9th century there was an *ashrama* – a hermitage. At the beginning of his reign, around 889, Yasovarman had built about 100 of these all over the empire.

Of the four sanctuary towers, the E two are the most important, with four-tiered superstructures. The condition of the NE tower is rather poor while the SE collapsed in 1968. Square in plan, they measure 6m x 6m. The lintels, colonettes, blind doors and corner guardian figures are sandstone; of interest is the fact that the blind doors are carved from stone monoliths. The remaining brick surfaces were covered in lime mortar, although most of this has fallen off. As at Preah Ko, *dvarapalas* in niches guard the doors of the E towers, while female guardians occupy the same position on the W towers. Their style shows some touches of the Bakheng, which was just beginning.

The lintels are in mixed condition, some badly damaged, others missing. On the NE tower, the E lintel has Indra on Airavata and *nagas* emerging from *makaras*; the N and S lintels show a divinity over a *kala* head.

Lion in lime mortar, the SE corner of the SW tower

Other monuments of the period
At Angkor: Preah Ko, Bakong, Phnom Bakheng (some features).
Best times to visit
No particular time
Location and access
In Roluos, 13 km SE of Siem Reap. Drive along Route 6 for 13 km. 400m after the turning on your right to Bakong, take the turning on your left to Lolei, 600m to the NW.

The sanctuary towers from the NW

BANTEAY SREI

BANTEAY SREI ✢ ✢ ✢

Previous pages:
At left a devi *from on E face of the S tower and on the right, the central sanctuary*

Looking towards the inner enclosure from the outer E gopura

Date: 2nd half of 10th century (consecrated 22 April 967)
Style: Banteay Srei
Reign: Rajendravarman
Visit: At least 1 hr

A little more than 20 km north of Angkor, almost at the foot of the Kulen Mountains, sits the remarkable small temple of Banteay Srei. The name, relatively modern, means 'Citadel of the Women', or perhaps 'Citadel of Beauty', and presumably refers to its size and the delicacy of its decoration. The temple's actual name, taken from that of its central *linga*, was Tribhuvanamahesvara – 'Great Lord of the Threefold World'.

Unlike the major sites at Angkor, Banteay Srei was not a royal temple. It was built by one of Rajendravarman's counsellors, Yajñavaraha, who was also the *guru* of the future king Jayavarman V. Yajñavaraha was granted this land on the banks of the upper Siem Reap river by the king. He and his younger brother commissioned the temple, which was finished just a year before King Rajendravarman died. As usual, a settlement surrounded the temple; in this case, the name of the small city was Isvarapura.

Routinely described in gushing terms as the 'Jewel of Khmer Art', Banteay Srei is nevertheless a temple of great beauty, and compares with little else in Angkor. Its miniature scale almost always surprises visitors, and the near-total decoration of its surfaces is exceptional.

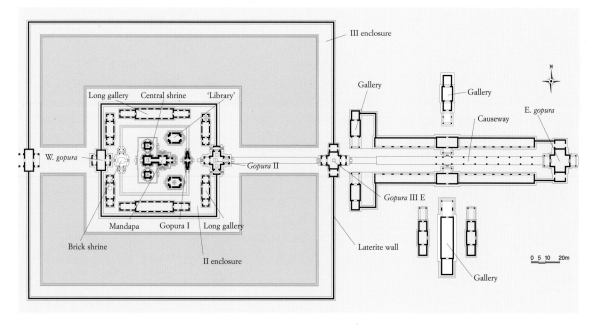

Discovered by the French only in 1914 (it escaped the attention of both Aymonier and Lunet de la Jonquière), it achieved an early notoriety when André Malraux, who later wrote *Man's Fate* and was Minister of Culture under the de Gaulle administration, removed four *apsaras* in 1923. He was caught almost immediately and the pieces recovered. The restoration of the temple between 1931 and 1936 by Marchal was notable for the first significant use at Angkor of the technique of anastylosis, adopted from the Dutch work in the East Indies.

Plan

Facing east, Banteay Srei is arranged in three concentric enclosures, each offset slightly towards the W. These are approached, from the E, by a 67m-long causeway, but there is no trace of the usual earth bank that would have marked the limits of the town around the temple – only one spacious outer *gopura* opening onto the causeway marks the the eastern boundary. Possibly, a wooden palisade formed the outer enclosure, which would probably have been about 500m square.

The outermost (third) enclosure measures 95 x 110m, with a laterite wall and *gopuras* on the E and W. Inside this is a moat divided by two causeways on the E and W. The two inner enclosures are much closer together, measuring 38 x 42m and 24 x 24m, and the space between them taken up almost completely by six 'long galleries', two longer ones on the N and S sides, four shorter flanking the *gopuras* on the E and W.

The innermost (first) enclosure had a brick wall, with a single *gopura* on the E and on the W. However, the central entrance of the latter was closed to create a shrine and entry was on either side. A raised terrace at its centre carries the three sanctuary towers, arranged in a N-S line, and a *mandapa* connected to the central tower by an *antarala*. Two 'libraries' in the NE and SE corners complete the ensemble.

*One of the 32 boundary stones lining
the causeway*

*Above right: Narasimha clawing
Hiranyakasipu, N 'long gallery'*

*Inscription on the door-frame of
Gopura III*

Visit

Enter through the town *gopura* (*Gopura* IV) with its E-facing pediment
in pink sandstone showing Indra on his three-headed elephant mount
Airavata; appropriately, as Indra is the guardian of this direction. This
gopura is the largest at the site – the others decrease in size towards the
central sanctuary. The *gopura* is cross-shaped in plan and it was here
that the main stele of the temple was discovered in 1936, enabling the
date of consecration to be worked out precisely from its information
about the position of the sun, moon and planets.

Walking through, you face the causeway that leads, almost 70m
distant, to the next enclosure. It is lined on either side with stone
boundary posts (32 in all), which are almost identical to those at the
cliff-top temple of Preah Vihear far to the N. To left and right, beyond
these posts, the causeway is flanked by the remains of galleries, with
stone pillars on the inner sides and laterite walls facing outwards.

Halfway along the causeway, stop to look at the two porches on the
left and right. Each of these leads to a 'long gallery' aligned N-S and
originally roofed with tiles. The 'long gallery' to the S has a pediment
facing you that shows Siva and his wife Uma riding the bull Nandi –
the motif known as *Umamahesvara* – and is flanked by two other,
slightly shorter galleries. On the other side of the causeway the 'long
gallery' has a pediment showing Vishnu in the form of the lion
Narasimha ripping the chest of the king of the *asuras* Hiranyakasipu.
The purpose of these 'long galleries' is unknown.

At the end of the causeway and just in front of the *gopura* of the
next enclosure (*Gopura* III) are two long galleries on either side. A
passage between these and the walls of the third enclosure allowed
access from the town. This *gopura* immediately in front of you is the
entrance to the temple proper; though smaller than the outer *gopura*, it
was flanked by lions, and contains the pedestal for a *linga*. There are

inscriptions on the inner door-frames. The E-facing pediment, which lies on the ground just N of the causeway, shows Sita being seized by the demon Viradha (from the *Ramayana*). The W-facing pediment is now in the Musée Guimet in Paris, and shows a scene from the *Mahabharata* in which two *asuras*, the brothers Sunda and Upasunda, fight over the possession of the *apsaras* Tilottama. Crossing through this *gopura*, you are inside the laterite-walled third enclosure, on a broad earth causeway with the moat on either side.

The next *gopura* (II), with its magnificent double-tiered pediments, takes you through another laterite wall into what at first glance appears to be an over-crowded central enclosure. However, this is only because the brick wall of the innermost enclosure has collapsed and was, in any case, only 9m away. The tiny, exquisite building directly ahead of you is, in fact, the innermost E *gopura* (*Gopura* I). On either side you can see laterite 'long galleries' in poor condition. These, continuing with four others round the walls, take up most of the space between the second and inner enclosures, and were originally roofed with tiles. Almost at your feet are the remains of a sculpture of the bull Nandi in a sitting position.

The most immediately striking feature of the central enclosure in front of you is its scale, more suited to small children than to normal adults. The doorway of the central shrine, for example, is only 108cm high. The slim east *gopura*, now free-standing, appears hardly to have been designed as a gateway. The three

Above: Gopura *II*

Below: The inner enclosure at sunrise

sanctuary towers stand in a row on a 90cm-high T-shaped platform, so close together that it is hardly possible to walk between them, let alone stand back to view their pediments and lintels. Each has an E-facing entrance, with the usual blind doors on the other three sides. The central sanctuary, taller than the other two, is fronted by an arrangement that became common much later elsewhere – a *mandapa*, or antechamber, connected to the sanctuary by a narrower corridor – the *antarala*. The central sanctuary was dedicated to Siva, as was the southern sanctuary, while the northern one was dedicated to Vishnu – a lopsided and unusual arrangement (contrast this with the three-tower layouts at Phnom Krom and Phnom Bok, dedicated to Siva in the centre, Vishnu to the N and Brahma to the S).

A fight probably between Arjuna and Siva. The boar underneath may refer to Yajñavaraha, founder of the temple

Below: Carved details from the central sanctuary

There are six short stairways leading up to the platform, and at the top of these there were originally a pair of kneeling guardian figures, sculpted in the round. The bodies were human, but the heads varied – monkey, lion, *garuda* and *yaksha*. Most of the surviving guardians are copies, and all are damaged – the standards of thievery apparently being too low to distinguish between 20th century cement and 10th century stone. Nevertheless, note the significance of the different heads: *garuda* guardians squat in front of Vishnu's tower to the N (the *garuda* is Vishnu's mount), while the lion guardians in front of the southern tower may indicate that there was also a statue of Durga, Siva's consort in her terrible aspect. The original statues are in the National Museum, Phnom Penh.

On either side of the towers, and a few metres to the E, are two 'libraries' in sandstone and laterite, typically aligned E-W. Behind the sanctuary towers, the W *gopura* has been somewhat modified to create is a shrine in brick. It contained a statue of Siva with Uma sitting on his left thigh dedicated to the parents of the builder of the temple, now in the National Museum, Phnom Penh. The W *gopura* of the second enclosure, in rather poor condition, is almost right next to this shrine. Its pediment, also now in the National Museum, Phnom Penh, has a scene from the *Mahabharata* in which Bhima leaps in the air with a stave to strike the Kaurava Duryodhana.

Lintels, pediments and decorations

The sandstone relief carvings of Banteay Srei are among the finest in all Khmer art, in invention, richness and execution. The pink sandstone, apart from being attractive in itself, is relatively hard, and has weathered only a little to retain the sharpness of the original work. What also contributes to the interest of the decoration is the depth of

View towards the W gopura *from the central sanctuary*

the relief – some of the foliage is sculpted virtually in three dimensions – and that it covers almost every square inch of stone surface. Moreover, the small scale of the buildings means that you can get as close as you like to most of the carving – some of the lintels and pediments are actually at eye-level.

Durga, W pediment of Gopura I E

Most of the lintels and pediments are within the inner enclosure, and we start the description from the E *gopura*. The E-facing pediment shows *Siva Nataraj* – the god, multi-armed, in the dance of the rhythm of life which culminates in destruction at the end of a *kalpa*, or world cycle. At his feet are a drummer and an emaciated Kareikkalammeyar, his disciple. Walk round to the other side of the small *gopura*; the W-facing pediment shows Siva's consort in her terrible form, Durga, dancing on a bound demon in the form of a lion. Underneath, the lintel shows Vishnu as a horse, Hayagriva, clutching the heads of demons he has just slain.

The two 'libraries' carry particularly fine pediments. On the southern 'library', the scene in the E-facing pediment is of the multi-headed demon Ravana shaking Mount Kailasa, where Siva and Uma are

seated. On the pediment of the other side, facing west, the God of Love, Kama, fires an arrow at Siva in an attempt to draw the god's attention to his wife Uma. On the northern 'library', the E-facing pediment shows Indra, God of the Sky, riding his three-headed elephant Airavata and creating rain to put out a fire in the Khandava forest, created by the god Agni in order to kill the *naga* Taksaka who lived in the forest. The god asked Krishna and his brother Balarama to help, and they positioned themselves on either side of the forest, to stop the animals from fleeing and to fire their arrows to stop the rain from falling. These arrows have often been misinterpreted as streaks of rain. On the W-facing pediment, in a scene that occurs later in the same epic, Krishna finally kills his uncle Kamsa, who has pursued and tormented him.

Turn to your right to begin a circuit around the central platform. Facing you is the N door of the *mandapa*, with a pediment with Kubera, God of Wealth, here appearing in his capacity as guardian of

Ravana shaking Mount Kailasa, on the E pediment of the S 'library'

Kama fires an arrow at Siva, on the W pediment of the S 'library'

the N, above Rahu devouring an elephant; the lintel has a more typical depiction of Rahu among foliage. Walk clockwise around the platform. Over the E entrance to the *mandapa* Indra rides a three-headed Airavata; the lintel below has three *simhas*. The pediment and lintel over the southern and northern doors of the *mandapa* are identical and show Kubera. To your left, the E-facing pediment of the S tower shows Siva and Uma on Nandi, while the lintel has Indra on a three-headed Airavata. On the S side of this tower, both the pediment and lintel show Yama, God of the South as well as of Judgement, on a buffalo. Here also, as on all the façades of the towers, are magnificent *devatas* and guardians standing in niches.

Devi *on the S sanctuary*

Continue round to the back of the tower, facing W. Both the pediment and lintel show Varuna, the guardian God of this direction, riding a *hamsa*. To see the N pediment and lintel, squeeze into the narrow space between the S and central towers. The pediment shows Kubera, God of the North, supported by *simhas*. On the lintel, the loss of the figure's head makes it difficult to identify but it is likely to have been Kubera; it is supported by a lotus and *simhas*.

Turn round to face the S blind entrance to the central sanctuary. The pediment, like that of the S tower in the same position, shows Yama on a buffalo. In fact, on either pediment or lintel, and sometimes on both, each of the three sanctuary towers carries an image of the appropriate guardian of direction (Indra to the E, Yama to the S, Varuna to the W and Kubera to the N). The scene on the lintel of two figures with arms around each other is uncertain but possibly of Rama fighting Tataka, or Arjuna and Siva; below them is a wild boar, and this could be the *avatar* of Vishnu, as well as representing the temple's builder Yajñavaraha, whose name means 'sacrificial boar'. Step round to the

214

W face of the central sanctuary. The pediment, like those of the other towers, shows Varuna on geese. The lintel depicts Ravana abducting Sita, wife of Rama, in a scene from the *Ramayana*. Around to the north face, the pediment again mirrors those of the other towers – Kubera on a throne supported by three *simhas*. The lintel also carries a scene from the *Ramayana*, in which the two monkey brothers Valin and Sugriva, battle for the crown. If you look over to your right, you can see the same scene carved on the pediment of the *gopura* of the second enclosure.

On the S face of the N tower, immediately behind you, the pediment has Yama on a buffalo,

Fire in the Khandava Forest, E pediment of the N 'library'

while the lintel shows Krishna killing a demon. On the W of this tower, Varuna is supported by geese on the pediment, and on the pediment Vishnu is seen riding his mount, *garuda* (this northern

Detail from the W pediment of the N 'library', showing Krishna killing Kamsa

sanctuary tower was dedicated to Vishnu, who is depicted on either pediment or lintel of each face, either as himself or as Krishna). On the N side, Kubera once again occupies the pediment, and on the lintel Krishna kills a double-torsoed demon. Finally, over the E entrance to the N tower, Krishna kills a demon on the pediment, tearing out an organ; on the lintel, Indra rides Airavata, but in an unusual version – the elephant has just one head.

Other monuments of the period
Parts of Preah Vihear, particularly the upsweeping gable ends and the richly detailed carving.
Best times to visit
Early-to-mid-morning and middle-to-late-afternoon have the most attractive light – the red sandstone glows richly when the sun is low. The surrounding trees cut off direct light at sunrise and (particularly) at sunset, although the atmosphere at these times is special. As the temple is isolated and quite far from Angkor, you must check on the security situation before venturing to the temple
Location and access
Some 25 km north of the main group of Angkor monuments, on the road that leaves Angkor near the East Mebon. Turn onto this road 300m S of East Mebon, and drive E for 1.8 km to the village of Phum Pradak, where the road turns N (an smaller unmade road continues E to Banteay Samré). Continue driving N, past Phnom Bok on the right, and at 17.5 km from Phum Padak take the left fork at a small intersection. 1 km beyond this, pass through the small village of Phum Banteay Srei, and 800m later cross the bridge over the Siem Reap River. The entrance to the the temple is 300m further on. The road has recently been improved, and is negotiable by ordinary cars, at least in the dry season.

Opposite: The fight between Valin and Sugriva on the W pediment of Gopura I W

PRACTICALITIES

SUGGESTED ITINERARIES

The order of visiting Angkor's temples is very much a matter of opinion – and the time available. Ideally, you should have at least three days, and a week is even better, but recognising that this is sometimes just not possible, we start by constructing some very limited itineraries. In any case, the guides and travel companies in Siem Reap have their own ideas, and for quick visits it may be as well to follow them.

There is usually a conflict between on the one hand spending enough time at a temple to be able to study it, absorb the atmosphere, examine details and explore, and on the other hand seeing as much as possible of Angkor's great variety. Necessarily, the following itineraries are a compromise, but we tend to favour taking more time over fewer temples – particularly in the case of those of greater interest.

SHORT VISITS
These itineraries depend on the flight schedules, and as these may vary, we suggest some differences in the order of visit. For example, a mid-afternoon arrival allows you to visit only one, or at the most two, temples satisfactorily. On the other hand, a mid-morning departure still allows enough time for a sunrise visit. The following itineraries are fairly energetic but allow for the need to take a reasonable amount of time at each place.

HALF-DAY *morning arrival, afternoon departure*
South Gate of Angkor Thom - Bayon - Elephant Terrace - Terrace of the Leper King - Ta Prohm - Angkor Wat

ONE OVERNIGHT *afternoon arrival, morning departure*
Day 1 South Gate of Angkor Thom - Terrace of the Leper King - Elephant Terrace - Bayon - Angkor Wat (sunset)
Day 2 Angkor Wat (sunrise) - Elephant Terrace - Ta Prohm

ONE OVERNIGHT *morning arrival, morning departure*
Day 1 morning: South Gate of Angkor Thom - Elephant Terrace - Terrace of the Leper King - Phimeanakas & the Royal Enclosure - Bayon
    afternoon: Ta Prohm - Angkor Wat
Day 2 Angkor Wat (sunrise) - Ta Prohm

ONE OVERNIGHT *morning arrival, afternoon departure*
Day 1 morning: South Gate of Angkor Thom - Elephant Terrace - Terrace of the Leper King - Phimeanakas & the Royal Enclosure - Bayon
    afternoon: Preah Khan - Angkor Wat (sunset)
Day 2 Angkor Wat (sunrise) - Prasat Kravan - Srah Srang - Ta Prohm - Ta Keo - Thommanon - Chao Say Tevoda

TWO OVERNIGHTS *morning arrival, afternoon departure*
Day 1 morning: South Gate of Angkor Thom - Elephant Terrace - Terrace of the Leper King - Phimeanakas & the Royal Enclosure - Bayon
    afternoon: Ta Prohm - Angkor Wat (sunset)
Day 2 morning: Angkor Wat (sunrise) - Prasat Kravan - Pre Rup - East Mebon - Ta Som - Neak Pean
    afternoon: Preah Khan - Bakheng (sunset)
Day 3 morning: Srah Srang (sunrise) - Banteay Kdei - Ta Prohm - Ta Keo - Thommanon - Chao Say Tevoda

LONGER VISITS
These itineraries allow further sites to be visited - in particular the important Roluos and Banteay Srei - as well as minor monuments en route.

THREE OVERNIGHTS *morning arrival, afternoon departure*
Day 1 morning: South Gate of

Angkor Thom - Elephant Terrace - Terrace of the Leper King - Phimeanakas & the Royal Enclosure - Bayon
    afternoon: Ta Prohm - Angkor Wat (sunset)
Day 2 morning: Angkor Wat (sunrise) - Prasat Kravan - Pre Rup - East Mebon - Ta Som - Neak Pean
    afternoon: Preah Khan - Bakheng (sunset)
Day 3 morning: Roluos
    afternoon: Banteay Srei - Banteay Samré
Day 4 morning: Bakheng - Baksei Chamkrong - Bapuon - Tep Pranam - Preah Palilay - Preah Pithu - Suor Prat Towers - the Khleangs

FOUR OVERNIGHTS *morning arrival, afternoon departure*
Day 1 morning: South Gate of Angkor Thom - Elephant Terrace - Terrace of the Leper King - Phimeanakas & the Royal Enclosure - Bayon
    afternoon: Ta Prohm - Angkor Wat (sunset)
Day 2 morning: Angkor Wat (sunrise) - Prasat Kravan - Pre Rup - East Mebon - Ta Som - Neak Pean
    afternoon: Preah Khan - Bakheng (sunset)
Day 3 morning: Roluos
    afternoon: Banteay Srei - Banteay Samré
Day 4 morning: Bakheng (sunrise) - Baksei Chamkrong - Thma Bay Kaek - Prasat Bei - Prasat Chrung (SE) - Bapuon - Tep Pranam - Preah Palilay - Preah Pithu - Suor Prat Towers - the Khleangs
    afternoon: Banteay Kdei - Ta Prohm - Ta Keo (sunset)
Day 5 morning: Ta Prohm Kel - Thommanon - Chao Say Tevoda - Spean Thma - Hospital Chapel - Ta Keo - Ta Nei

FIVE OVERNIGHTS *morning arrival, afternoon departure*
Day 1 morning: South Gate of Angkor Thom - Elephant Terrace - Terrace of the Leper King - Phimeanakas & the Royal Enclosure - Bayon
    afternoon: Ta Prohm - Angkor Wat (sunset)
Day 2 morning: Angkor Wat (sunrise) - Prasat Kravan - Pre Rup - East Mebon - Ta Som - Neak Pean
    afternoon: Preah Khan - Bakheng (sunset)

Day 3 morning: Roluos

afternoon: Ta Prohm Kel - Thommanon - Chao Say Tevoda - Spean Thma - Hospital Chapel - Ta Keo - Ta Nei

Day 4 morning: Bakheng (sunrise) - Baksei Chamkrong - Thma Bay Kaek - Prasat Bei - Prasat Chrung (SE) - Bapuon - Tep Pranam - Preah Palilay - Preah Pithu - Suor Prat Towers - the Khleangs

afternoon: Banteay Kdei - Ta Prohm - Ta Keo (sunset)

Day 5 morning: East Mebon (sunrise) Banteay Srei

afternoon: the Kulen mountains - Banteay Samré

Day 6 morning: Phnom Krom, West Mebon

THEMATIC VISITS

These itineraries are less concerned with accommodating the maximum number of sites conveniently, than with following a specialist interest. The chronological tour, for example, is not at all efficient in making use of time, but it gives an unfolding view of evolving styles of art and architecture.

SHORT CHRONOLOGICAL TOUR

Day 1 morning: *9th century, at* Roluos: Preah Kô (880) - Bakong (881) - Lolei (893)

afternoon: *10th century:* Bakheng (about 907) - Prasat Kravan (921) - East Mebon (952) - Pre Rup (961)

Day 2 morning: Banteay Srei (967) - Srah Srang (originally)

afternoon: *Late 10th to early 11th century:* Phimeanakas. *11th century:* Bapuon (1060). *Early 12th century:* Preah Pithu - Thommanon - Chao Say Tevoda

Day 3 morning: Angkor Wat (1113-1150) - South Gate of Angkor Thom

afternoon: *Late 12th century:* Ta Prohm (1186) - Preah Khan (1191)

Day 4 morning: Neak Pean - Ta Som - Terrace of the Leper King - Elephant Terrace - *Late 12th to early 13th century:* Banteay Kdei

afternoon: *13th century:* the Suor Prat Towers - Preah Palilay - Bayon

FULL CHRONOLOGICAL TOUR

Day 1 morning: *Late 8th century:* Ak Yum

afternoon: *9th century, at*

Roluos: Preah Kô (880) - Bakong (881) - Lolei (893)

Day 2 morning: *Late 9th to early 10th century:* Phnom Krom - Kutisvara

afternoon: *10th century:* Bakheng (about 907) - Prasat Kravan (921) - Baksei Chamkrong (948) - Bat Chum

Day 3 morning: East Mebon (952) - Pre Rup (961) - Banteay Srei (967)

afternoon: Thma Bay Kaek - Prasat Bei - Srah Srang (originally)

Day 4 morning: *Late 10th to early 11th century:* Phimeanakas - the Khleangs - Ta Keo - *11th century:* Bapuon (1060)

afternoon: *Mid 11th century:* West Mebon - West Baray

Day 5 morning: *Early 12th century:* Preah Pithu - Thommanon - Chao Say Tevoda - Banteay Samré

afternoon: Angkor Wat (1113-1150) - Angkor Thom (gates, Prasat Chrung)

Day 6 morning: *Late 12th century:* Ta Prohm (1186) - Preah Khan (1191)

afternoon: Neak Pean - Ta Som - Srah Srang (remodelling) - Ta Nei - Terrace of the Leper King - Elephant Terrace - Ta Prohm Kel - Hospital Chapel

Day 7 morning: *Late 12th to early 13th century:* Banteay Kdei - Krol Kô. *13th century:* the Suor Prat Towers - Preah Palilay

afternoon: Bayon - Mangalartha (1295). *16th century:* Spean Thma - Tep Pranam - late bas-reliefs at Angkor Wat

BEST OF THE BAS-RELIEFS *In approximately chronological order*

Day 1 morning: Lintels and guardians at Roluos (Preah Kô - Bakong - Lolei), including the surviving fragment on the fourth tier of Bakong

afternoon: Prasat Kravan (interior brick reliefs) - East Mebon (lintels) - Pre Rup (lintels) - Bapuon (individually designed panels on walls)

Day 2 morning: Banteay Srei (lintels, pediments, guardians, *devatas* and colonettes)

afternoon: Thommanon and Chao Say Tevoda (*devatas*) - Banteay Samré

Day 3 morning: Angkor Wat (*apsaras, devatas* and the bas-relief galleries)

afternoon: Ta Prohm and

Banteay Kdei (lintels and pediments) - Terrace of the Leper King - Elephant Terrace

Day 4 morning: Preah Khan (lintels, pediments, friezes, guardians) - Neak Pean (the central sanctuary and four chapels)

afternoon: Bayon (historical bas-reliefs) - Preah Palilay (pediments)

ROMANTIC ANGKOR

Day 1 morning: Sunrise at Angkor Wat from the west entrance - Ta Prohm

afternoon: Late afternoon on the upper terrace of the Bayon - sunset from the summit of Bakheng

Day 2 morning: Sunrise at Srah Srang - Ta Som - Preah Khan

afternoon: Late afternoon at Ta Prohm - sunset from the summit of Ta Keo

. . . and depending on the date, full moon at Angkor Wat.

ARCHITECTURAL HIGHLIGHTS *In approximately chronological order*

Day 1 morning: Roluos (Preah Kô - Bakong) - Prasat Kravan

afternoon: Pre Rup - East Mebon - Banteay Srei

Day 2 morning: Phimeanakas and the Royal enclosure - Bapuon - Ta Keo - Thommanon - Chao Say Tevoda

afternoon: Banteay Samré - Angkor Wat

Day 3 morning: South and North Gates of Angkor Thom - Preah Khan - Neak Pean

afternoon: Banteay Kdei - Bayon

TRADITIONAL 'PETIT CIRCUIT'

additional to the basic group of Angkor Wat, Bakheng and surrounding small monuments, and Angkor Thom Thommanon - Chao Say Tevoda - Spean Thma - Hospital Chapel - Ta Keo - Ta Nei - Ta Prohm - Kutisvara - Banteay Kdei - Srah Srang - Prasat Kravan

Traditional 'Grand Circuit' *additional to the basic group of Angkor Wat, Bakheng and surrounding small monuments, and Angkor Thom* Pre Rup - East Mebon - Ta Som - Krol Kô - Neak Pean - Preah Khan.

WHERE TO SEE

ARCHITECTURE. . .

Angkor Wat-style towers
Angkor Wat, Thommanon, Banteay Samré

Arogayasalas (chapels of hospitals)
Ta Prohm Kel, the Hospital Chapel

Dharmasalas (chapels of resting-places)
Preah Khan, Ta Prohm

Face towers
Bayon, outer gate towers of Angkor Thom, Ta Prohm, Banteay Kdei, Ta Som

Island temples
East Mebon, Neak Pean, Lolei, West Mebon

Naga 'bridges'
The five causeways entering Angkor Thom, the W and E causeways entering Preah Khan, and the E causeway of Bakong.

State Temples
Bakong (of Hariharalaya), Bakheng (of Yasodharapura), Pre Rup (of ??), Bapuon (of Yasodharapura), Angkor Wat, Bayon (of Angkor Thom)

Temple mountains
Angkor Wat, Bakheng, Ta Keo, Bapuon, Pre Rup, Bakong, Ak Yum (the forerunner)

Trees growing out of ruins
Ta Prohm, Preah Khan

SCENES FROM MYTHOLOGY. . .

Apsaras
Strictly speaking, *apsaras* are celestial dancers, but the description is usually stretched to include any semi-naked celestial maidens. They can be seen emerging from the Churning of the Sea of Milk at Angkor Wat (S section, E Gallery; SW corner pavilion, Gallery of Bas-Reliefs) and the Bayon (N section, W Inner Gallery); flying in attendance to various deities at the Bayon (Inner Gallery); dancing at the Bayon (pillars around the Outer Gallery), Angkor Wat, Preah Khan (Hall of Dancers), Ta Prohm (Hall of Dancers), Banteay Kdei (Hall of Dancers). When not dancing or flying, they can be seen at their most provocative at Angkor Wat (throughout).

Balaha saving the shipwrecked sailors
Neak Pean

Valin and Surgriva fighting
Angkor Wat (SW corner pavilion, Gallery of Bas-Reliefs)
Banteay Srei (E pediment, *Gopura* II W); N lintel, central sanctuary tower)
Preah Pithu (pediment, fifth temple (Y))

Battle of Kurukshetra
Angkor Wat (S section, W Gallery)
Bapuon (*Gopura* II E)

Battle of Lanka
From the Ramayana
Angkor Wat (N section, W Gallery)
Preah Khan (W pediment, *Gopura* III W)
Banteay Samré (W pediment, *Gopura* II W; N pediment, *Gopura* II N)
Bapuon (*Gopura* II W)

Buddha subduing the elephant Nalagiri
Preah Palilay (N pediment, *gopura*)

Building the Bridge to Lanka
Banteay Samré (N pediment, *Gopura* II S)

Churning of the Sea of Milk
From the Bhagavad Purana
Angkor Wat (S section, E Gallery; SW corner pavilion, Gallery of Bas-Reliefs; pediment, 'cruciform cloister')
Causeways entering Angkor Thom (possibly)
Bayon (N section, W Inner Gallery)

Preah Pithu (lintel, sanctuary of first temple (T); N lintel, sanctuary of second temple(U))
Kutisvara (lintel, N tower)
W and E causeways entering Preah Khan (possibly)
Banteay Samré (E pediment, *Gopura* I E)
Bakong (S pediment, sanctuary tower)

Death of Valin
Angkor Wat (SW corner pavilion, Gallery of Bas-Reliefs)
Thommanon (interior pediment of *mandapa*)
Bapuon (*Gopura* II W)

Hindu Trinity (Siva, Brahma and Vishnu)
Preah Khan (subsidiary enclosure N of the second enclosure)
Preah Pithu (W lintel, sanctuary of second temple)

Indra on Airavata
Baksei Chamkrong (lintel)
Prasat Bei (lintels, central & S towers)
Preah Palilay (pediment, sanctuary)
East Mebon (E lintel, central tower)
Lolei (E lintel, NE tower)
Banteay Srei (E pediment, *Gopura* IV; E pediment, *mandapa*; E lintels, N and S sanctuary towers)

Kama fires an arrow at Siva
Angkor Wat (SW corner pavilion, Gallery of Bas-Reliefs)
Bayon (W section, N Inner Gallery)
Banteay Srei (W Pediment, S 'library')

Krishna killing demons
From the Harivamsha
Angkor Wat (E section, N Gallery)
Banteay Srei (E pediment, N and S lintels, N sanctuary tower)
Preah Pithu (pediment, fifth temple (Y))

Krishna killing Kamsa
From the Bhagavad Purana and the Harivamsha
Banteay Srei (W pediment, N 'library')
Angkor Wat (pediment, central tower)

Krishna killing the serpent Kaliya
Banteay Samré (E lintel, *Gopura* I E)
Bapuon (*Gopura* II S)

Krishna raising Mount Govardhana
Angkor Wat (SW corner pavilion, Gallery of Bas-Reliefs)
Banteay Srei (E pediment, N 'library')
Preah Khan (E pediment, *Gopura* III E)
Banteay Samré (E pediment, *Gopura* I E)

Kubera on simhas
Banteay Srei (N pediments, all three sanctuary towers)

Rama shoots the golden deer
Angkor Wat (SW corner pavilion, Gallery of Bas-Reliefs)

Rama's Return to Ayodhya
Angkor Wat (NW corner pavilion, Gallery of Bas-Reliefs)
Bapuon (*Gopura* II E)

Ravana abducts Sita
Banteay Srei (W lintel, central sanctuary tower)

Ravana shaking Mount Kailasa
From the Ramayana
Angkor Wat (SW corner pavilion, Gallery of Bas-Reliefs)
Bayon (E section, N Inner Gallery)
Thommanon (S pediment, *mandapa*)
Banteay Srei (E pediment, S 'library')

Sacred Fire
Angkor Wat (W section, S Gallery)
Bayon (N section, W Outer Gallery; S section, E Inner Gallery; N section E Inner Gallery)

Siddhartha leaves his father's city (the Great Departure)
Ta Prohm (W pediment, E *gopura*, subsidiary enclosure S of the second enclosure)
Neak Pean (N pediment of sanctuary tower)

Sita's Trial
Angkor Wat (NW corner pavilion, Gallery of Bas-Reliefs)

Siva as an ascetic
Angkor Wat (SW corner pavilion, Gallery of Bas-Reliefs)
Bayon (S section, W Inner Gallery; Thommanon (S pediment, W *gopura*)

Siva Dancing
Banteay Srei (E pediment, *Gopura I*)
Bakong (E pediment, sanctuary tower)
Bayon (W section, N Inner Gallery)

Siva pardons Arjuna
Bayon (E section, N Inner Gallery)

Siva with Uma on Nandin
East Mebon (S lintel, central tower)
Banteay Srei (S 'long gallery' between *Gopuras IV* and *III*; E pediment, S sanctuary tower)

Varuna on geese
Banteay Srei (W pediments, all three sanctuary towers)

Vishnu on garuda
Angkor Wat (E & W sections, N Gallery)
Bayon (S section, W Inner Gallery)
Thommanon (E lintel of sanctuary; W pediment, W *gopura*)
Prasat Kravan (N face, interior, central sanctuary; E lintel, S sanctuary)
Lolei (E lintel, SE tower)
Banteay Samré (E pediment, *Gopura* I E)
Banteay Srei (W lintel, N sanctuary tower)

Vishnu crossing the ocean
Prasat Kravan (S face, interior, central sanctuary)
Angkor Wat (pediment, 'cruciform cloister')
Banteay Samré (E pediment, *Gopura* I E)
Preah Pithu (pediment, fifth temple (Y))

Vishnu Reclining
Angkor Wat (NW corner pavilion, Gallery of Bas-Reliefs; pediment, 'cruciform cloister')
Preah Khan (subsidiary enclosure N of the second enclosure)
Bakong (W pediment, sanctuary tower)

Yama on buffalo
Angkor Wat (E section, S wall, Gallery of Bas-Reliefs)
Banteay Srei (S pediments, all three sanctuary towers)

TEMPLES RANKED BY INTEREST

❖ ❖ ❖
Angkor Wat
Angkor Thom
Bakong
Banteay Srei
Bayon
Preah Khan
Ta Prohm

❖ ❖
Banteay Kdei
Banteay Samré
East Mebon
Neak Pean
Pre Rup
Ta Keo
Ta Nei
Thommanon

❖
Bakheng
Bapuon
Chao Say Tevoda
Elephant Terrace
Lolei
Phimeanakas & the Royal Enclosure
Prasat Kravan
Preah Kô
Preah Palilay
Srah Srang
Ta Som

Ak Yum
Baksei Chamkrong
Bat Chum
Krol Kô
Kutisvara (only worth a visit if you are really keen)
Mangalartha
Phnom Krom
Prasat Bei
Prasat Chrung
Preah Pithu
Spean Thma
Suor Prat Towers
Ta Prohm Kel
Tep Pranam
Thma Bay Kaek
West Mebon

THE GREAT VIEWS AT ANGKOR

1. The towers of Angkor Wat at first light, from the western entrance

2. The towers of Angkor Wat reflected in one of the two basins, just before sunrise

3. The *apsaras* on the east-facing wall of Angkor Wat's western entrance, at sunrise

4. The towers and central sanctuary of Angkor Wat from the NW corner of the second terrace, late afternoon

5. Angkor Wat from Phnom Bakheng, mid-morning and late afternoon

6. The South Gate of Angkor Thom from the middle of the road on the other side of the moat, shortly after sunrise

7. The cluster of face-towers in the SE corner of the Bayon's upper terrace, seen from the SW corner in late afternoon

8. The central sanctuary of the Bayon under the full moon, shortly after dark

9. The ruins of the central sanctuary of Ta Prohm, seen from the rooftops of its NE corner in late afternoon and early morning

10. Banteay Kdei's eastern entrance, with its face-tower, seen from the road running between it and Srah Srang, early morning

11. Sunrise over Srah Srang from its platform

12. Sunrise over the Bakong, seen from the top of the northeast

13. The unwalled inner enclosure of Banteay Srei from the SE corner, early morning

Because of the preponderance of sunrise views in this list, it takes at least three days to see all of them at prime time. A suggested order, which can be combined with another itinerary, is:—

Day 1
Pre-dawn to sunrise at Angkor Wat (1), (2), (3), followed by the South Gate of Angkor Thom (6) and the summit of Phnom Bakheng (5). Late afternoon at the Bayon (7)

Day 2
Sunrise at Srah Srang (11), then Banteay Kdei (10) and drive to Banteay Srei while the light is still good (13). Late afternoon to sunset at Angkor Wat (4). If a full moon, the Bayon at night (8)

Day 3
Sunrise at Roluos (12) followed by early morning at Ta Prohm (9)

ACCOMODATION & TRAVEL

The only place to stay when visiting Angkor is in Siem Reap which is about 15 minutes drive from the temples. In the last two-three years hotels have begun to spring up in response to increased tourism and the visitor now has, on paper at least, a wide choice of possible accomodation from the ultra expensive, newly-renovated Grand Hotel d'Angkor to simple guest houses. In between are a number of large hotels, very similar in appearance (rather ugly blocks with a Khmer-style roof line) and standard. One hotel that stands out as different from the rest is the Angkor Village (see below) but apart from that it may be best to choose a simple guest house, most of which are very clean, have hot water, air conditioning, television and fridge from $20-30 per night.

Below we list merely a brief selection of hotels as a starting point:

Grand Hotel d'Angkor ***
1 Vithei Charles de Gaulle
Khum Svay Dang Kum, Siem Reap,
Tel: 855-63-963 888,
Fax: 855-63-963 168.
E-mail: ghda@worldmail.com.kh.
Owned by the Raffles group this international-standard hotel is very much in their style which is immaculate and with a period feel, if somewhat sterile. The 35m swimming pool is magnificent, there are 8 different restaurants, a tennis park and cultural performances. Currently 131 rooms including suites, more will open later in the year to give 310 in total. Doubles from $360-510 for a suite including breakfast and dinner.

Angkor Village**
Tel: 855-63-963-563,
Fax: 855-63-380-104.
E-mail: angkor.village@worldmail.com.kh
This small, privately owned hotel consists of Khmer-style teak bungalows set in a lush, tropical garden creating an intimate tranquil atmosphere. There is a small but very pleasant pool surrounded by banana trees and cultural performances take place twice a week in an elegant building opposite. There are 24 rooms

all with shower and most with air-conditioning. $60 per room including breakfast and a set menu Khmer dinner in the open-sided dining area.

Angkor Hotel*
St. 6, Phum Sala Kanseng, Sangkat Svay Dong Kom, Siem Reap
Tel: 855-63-964-301,
Fax: 855-63-964-302.
This newly-opened hotel is situated on the road to the airport and is typical of the latest batch of hotels to appear, namely clean and adequate but with no atmosphere. 62 rooms from $125-200 for a suite.

Nokor Phnom Hotel*
Airport Road, Siemreap
Tel: 855-63-380106-12
Typically anodyne hotel. Facilities include swimming pool, air conditioning, minibar, television, and bathtubs. 92 rooms from $90-130 for a suite.

Angkoriana Villa**
297 Phum Boeng, Siem Reap
Tel: 855-15 630 096,
Fax: 855-63-380-065.
This quiet and pleasant villa run by Mrs Sou Ny is situated on the road to the temples. The 5 rooms have air-conditioning, TV, mini-bar, and hot showers. $25.

Travel to Siem Reap

From Phnom Penh
Royal Air Cambodge has flights a day. The flight lasts 40 minutes.

You can travel by fast boat across the Tonlé Sap during most of the year. The trip takes between 3-4 hours and costs around $50.

From Bangkok
Bangkok Airways has three daily flights from Bangkok to Siem Reap, departing Bangkok at 0800, 1240 and 1430. The flight lasts one hour. Flights from Siem Reap to Bangkok depart at 0930, 1420 and 1610. These flight times may change. Offices: Head Office in Bangkok
Tel: 02-229-3456,
Fax: 02-229-3454,
e-mail: pg@bangkokair.co.th
Donmuang Airport office
Tel: 02 535 2497-8
Siem Reap Office
Tel: 855-63-380-191 to 2,
Fax: 855-63-380 191.

ARCHITECTURAL TERMS & BUILDING TYPES

Anastylosis Integral restoration in which all the elements of a structure are analysed and numbered, following which the building is made structurally sound and rebuilt using original materials as much as possible. Additional materials are used only where structurally necessary. Dutch archaeologists originated the technique in Java, where it was studied by the French, who then used it extensively at Angkor (first at Banteay Srei).

Antarala Corridor connecting the *garbhagrha* (shrine) to the *mandapa* (antechamber).

Antefix Pinnacle or other ornament that stands on a parapet. Upper levels of Khmer sanctuary towers were often decorated in this way.

Arogayasala A hospital, or possibly a dispensary. Part of a building programme undertaken by Jayavarman VII.

Ashrama A hermitage (Sanskrit).

Baluster Circular-sectioned post or pillar, as in a barred window or the uprights of a balustrade.

Balustrade Railing or similar in which balusters are the uprights surmounted by a beam or coping.

Banteay Khmer for 'citadel'.

Baray An artificial reservoir which has not been excavated but in which the water is contained by dykes.

Colonette Small column, usually decorative in Khmer architecture, standing at either side of a doorway.

Corbel Deeply embedded load-bearing stone projecting from a wall.

Corbel arch False arch built from corbels projecting from opposite walls in tiers so that the topmost stones meet in the centre.

Cornice Decorated projection that crowns or protects an architectural feature such as a doorway. The cornice level is that immediately above the lintels.

Decorative lintel Rectangular stone slab carrying a carved design with important iconographical features. Attached above any doorway in a Khmer temple; Not used as a structural support.

Gopura Entrance pavilion, sometimes surmounted by a tower.

'Houses of Fire' As described in inscriptions, these buildings have an as yet unknown religious function. Part of a building programme undertaken by Jayavarman VII, usually in stone or laterite, and sited along the main roads leading from Angkor. One theory is that it was the chapel of a resting-house, but it may well have been a way-station for journeys involving the Sacred Flame.

Kalasa A pot filled with water and plants, symbolising prosperity - a kind of cornucopia. A stone representation frequently crowns sanctuary towers.

Laterite Red, porous, iron-bearing rock; easy to quarry but extremely hard when dried.

'Library' Isolated annexes usually found in pairs on either side and in front of the main entrance to a temple, or the entrance to an enclosure. This is a traditional name for them, and they were more likely to have been a kind of shrine than a repositiry of sacred texts. They nearly always open to the west except at Angkor Wat where they open to the east and the west. They generally have high openings and could have been used to store the sacred fire.

Lintel Block spanning an entrance, across the two door pillars. May be load-bearing or decorative. Also see structural lintel, decorative lintel.

Mandapa Antechamber: a pavilion or porch in front of the main sanctuary.

Pediment The triangular vertical face above the lintel, over a portico or other entrance. Used decoratively.

Pilaster Square- or rectangular-sectioned pillar that is actually engaged in the wall, so that it becomes a projection.

Portico Entrance porch.

Prasat From the Indian 'prasada', a terraced pyramid temple typical of South India.

Quincunx Arrangement of five objects in which four occupy the corners and the fifth the centre.

Redenting Architectural treatmrent of a structure in plan whereby the corners are indented (cut back) into successive right angles.

Sema Buddhist boundary stone.

Somasutra Stone pipe or channel through which the lustral waters used to wash the image inside the sanctuary are drained, projecting outside the temple. Often terminates with a carved *makara* head at the spout. Indicative of a Saivite temple.

Srah Artficial pond, which has normally been excavated as opposed to a *baray,* which is also larger (*see above*).

Stele Upright slab bearing inscriptions.

Structural lintel The load-bearing upper member of a stone door-frame. Normally concealed for the most part.

Stucco Plaster used for covering walls or for decorative purposes. In Khmer architecture, it was used to cover brick and laterite.

Vault Arch extended in depth.

Vihara Temple building, rectangular in plan, designed to house a Buddha image (Sanskrit).

Vihear Khmer name for *vihara.*

Wat Modern Buddhist temple, from the Sanskrit '*vatthu*'.

GLOSSARY

Airavata The elephant, mount or vehicle of Indra, usually portrayed with three heads, but occasionally with one only.

Agni The Vedic god of fire, and one of the three principal gods in the Rig Veda (with Indra and Surya). Agni grants immortality and cleanses sin, and mediates between the gods and men.

Amitabha The Bodhisattva of infinite light, who helps those who falter and are weak.

Amrita The elixir of life, or ambrosia, produced by the Churning of the Sea of Milk, and over which the gods and demons fought. Literally, 'non-dead'. May also be the same as 'soma'.

Ananta The endless World Serpent floating in the cosmic sea, and supporting Vishnu as he sleeps through the night of Brahma before the rebirth of the world. Also known as Sesha.

Anantasayin Term used to descibe Vishnu reclining on the back of the Naga Ananta.

Angada The monkey warrior son of Bali.

Angkor City (*see* Nagara).

Apsaras Celestial dancers who entertain the gods and are the sensual rewards of kings and heroes who die bravely. In Hindu mythology they always performed with the celestial musicians, *gandharvas*, but in Khmer mythology they were elevated alone to special importance in temple decoration.

Arishta Demon in the form of an ox, sent to kill Krishna by his uncle Kansa.

Arjuna A Pandava king.

Asura Demon, and enemy of the gods. *Asuras* and gods are locked in perpetual conflict, although in the Churning of the Sea of Milk they act, albeit temporarily, in concert. *Asura* originally meant something quite different in the Rig Veda - a divine being.

Avalokitesvara The Compassionate Bodhisattva, also known as Lokesvara. He is the Mahayana Buddhist ideal of compassion, choosing not to pass into Nirvana but to help instead to bring enlightenment to humans. Often represented as a young man holding a lotus in his left hand, and wearing an image of the Bodhisattva Amitabha on his head.

Avatar The 'descent' or incarnation of a god, in the form of a human or animal. Rama, for instance, is one of the *avatars* of Vishnu.

Balaha Lokesvara in the form of a horse.

Balarama Half-brother of Rama - the serpent Ananta in human form.

Beng Pond.

Bhadresvara Alternative name for Siva.

Bhaisajyaguru A Mahayana Buddha considered the master of medicine, worshipped in the arogayasalas.

Bhumidevi Goddess of the Earth and one of Vishnu's two consorts.

Bodhisattva In Mahayana Buddhism, a being who voluntarily stops short of reaching Buddha-hood in order to help humanity. The stage in the development of a Buddha before Enlightenment.

Bhumisparsa-mudra The *mudra*, or gesture, of touching the Earth. With this *mudra*, Buddha called the Earth-goddess to witness. From 'bhumi' meaning Earth.

Brahma The Creator of all things, originally conceived as the deification of Brahma, becoming the principal deity of the Trimurti (with Vishnu and Shiva). Brahma has four heads and four arms, holding sceptre, rosary, bow and alms-bowl. Brahma is born from Vishnu's navel at the beginning of each world cycle. His vehicle is the *hamsa*, or goose.

Brahman The transcendent absolute.

Brahmani *See* Brahmi.

Brahmi One of the Sapta Matrikis (Seven Divine Mothers); also called Brahmani.

Brahmin Hindu priest.

Buddha 'The Enlightened One'. Gautama Siddartha, born in 543 BC.

Chakra The wheel, emblem of Buddhist law and of the sun.

Chakravartin Universal ruler.

Cham Inhabitant of Champa, a kingdom contemporary with Angkor located in what is now central Vietnam.

Chedei Funerary tomb.

Chenla The Chinese name for Cambodia before the Khmer era.

Dasaratha Rama's father and king of Kosala.

Deva Deity, one of 33 in the Vedic system.

Devaki Krishna's mother.

Devaraja Meaning 'god who is king', a cult deriving from Siva-worship in which the king had divine associations.

Devata Female deity.

Devi Consort of Siva in her benevolent form. Also known as Uma, Gauri, Parvati, Jaganmata. *See also Durga.*

Dharma The doctrine of Hindu moral duty. Also, an ancient hermit.

Dharmachakra The Buddhist Wheel of the Law, representing the dominon of the Buddha's Law over everything.

Dikpala (*also* dikpalaka) One of the gods of direction.

Durga Consort of Siva in her terrible form. Also called Kali, Chandi, Bhairavi.

Dvarapala Temple guardian, normally sculpted as a door watchman.

Funan The oldest Indianised state of Indochina and precursor of Chenla.

Gaja Elephant.

Gajasimha Mythical creature - part elephant, part lion.

Gandharva Celestial musician, normally associated with *apsaras*.

Ganesha Elephant-headed son of Siva. According to legend, Siva decapitated his son in a moment of anger, and in remorse replaced the head with the first that came to hand - that of an elephant.

Garuda Mythical bird-man; the vehicle of Vishnu. Mortal enemy of *nagas*.

Gopala Alternative name for Krishna; also, the name of a cow-herd (Krishna lived as one when a youth to escape his uncle Kamsa).

Govardhana The mountain that Krishna lifts in order to protect the cow-herds and their cattle from Indra's rain.

Guru Brahmin. Spiritual instructor.

Hamsa Sacred goose; vehicle of Brahma. In Buddhism, represents the flight of the doctrine.

Hanuman Monkey general and ally of Rama in the *Ramayana*.

Hayagriva Vishnu in the form of a horse.

Himavatta Mythical forest srrounding Mount Meru.

Hinayana 'Lesser Vehicle,' referring to the traditional, conservative form of Buddhism which concentrates on the doctrine rather than on the worship of the Buddha or Bodhisattvas. Its adherents use the term 'Theravada' instead.

Hiranyakasipu Demon killed by Vishnu in his *avatar* Narasimha (man-lion).

Indra The Vedic god of the sky, clouds and monsoon; guardian of the East. The principal god in the Rig Veda.

Indrajit Son of Ravana.

Janaka Father of Sita and king of Mithila.

Jatamukuta Hairstyle in the form of a tall chignon, worn by Siva and Shivaite hermits; also worn by Bodhisattvas in Mahayana Buddhism.

Jayabuddhamahanatha Statue of the Buddha made by royal command of Jayavarman VII to be sent to his vassal cities.

Kailasa, Mount Abode of Siva, named after the actual mountain Kailasa in western Tibet.

Kala Adopted Indian motif; demon commanded to devour itself. Commonly sculpted over a temple entrance as guardian. Name from the Sanskrit for 'blue-black'.

Kalanemi An *asura*.

Kaliya Name of the naga with multiple heads killed by Krishna.

Kalkin Future and last *avatar* of Vishnu, with the head of a horse.

Kalpa A cycle of time, at the end of which Siva destroys the world; following this, a new *kalpa* is initiated by the recreation of the world when Brahma is reborn from the navel of Vishnu. Each *kalpa* is a day and a night of Brahma, but 8,640 million human years, and contains 2,000 *mahayugas*, or 'great ages'. *See also yuga.*

Kama God of Love.

Kamsa Uncle of Krishna.

Kareikalammeyar Female disciple of Siva.

Kesin Horse-like demon sent to kill Krishna by his uncle Kamsa.

Kompong Village.

Krishna One of the *avatars*, or incarnations of Vishnu, and hero of

the *Mahabharata* epic.

Kubera God of wealth and guardian of the North.

Kurma One of the *avatars*, or incarnations, of Vishnu, as a giant turtle. Kurma appears supporting Mount Mandara in the Churning of the Sea of Milk.

Kuvalayapida Demon in the form of an elephant sent by Kamsa to kill his nephew Krishna.

Lakshmi Wife of Vishnu, goddess of fortune and symbol of Vishnu's creative energy. Her emblem is the lotus.

Lakshmana Brother of Rama.

Lanka Capital city of the demon Ravana, in the *Ramayana*.

Linga Stylised image of a phallus representing the essence of the god Siva. In Sanskrit, the word means 'sign' and 'distinguishing symbol'.

Lokesvara *See* Avalokitesvara.

Mahabharata Major Hindu epic written between about 400 BC and 200 AD with a central narrative of the feud between the Kaurava and Pandava dynasties

Mahakala One of the Siva's guardians (distinguishable by a pair of fangs), standing in a pair at an entrance with Nandikesvara.

Mahayana 'Great Vehicle', referring to the later form of Buddhism in which the Buddha and Bodhisattvas are worshipped as deities.

Mahesvara Alternative name for Siva.

Makara Sea monster with scales, claws and a large head, often in the form of a crocodile, sometimes with the trunk of an elephant. In Khmer sculpture, acquired from Java.

Mandara, Mount Mythical mountain used as a pivot for Churning the Sea of Milk.

Maricha Cousin of Ravana who disguises himself as the Golden Deer to lure Rama away from Sita, from the *Ramayana*.

Matsya (or *matsya-avatara*) The incarnation of Vishnu as a fish.

Meru, Mount The cosmic or world mountain of Hindu cosmology which lies at the centre of the universe. Its summit is the home of the gods. Also called Sumeru.

Mudra The ritual gesture of the hands of a deity or Buddha.

Mukhalinga *Linga* bearing the face of Siva.

Naga Multi-headed serpent with many mythological connections, associated with water, fertility, rainbows, and creation. Five-and seven-headed *nagas* are common motifs, usually with the basic form of a cobra.

Nagapasa A noose in the form of a *naga* that mutates from an arrow fired by Indrajit, from the *Ramayana*.

Nagara Hindu city or capital, the origin of the Khmer word 'Angkor'.

Nagini Serpent goddess.

Nandikesvara One of Siva's guardians, standing in a pair at an entrance with Mahakala.

Nandi Sacred bull; the mount, or vehicle, of Siva.

Narasimha The *avatar*, or incarnation, of Vishnu as part-man, part-lion.

Padmanabha Literally 'lotus from the navel', referring to Vishnu reclining on the Naga Ananta; a lotus springs from his navel and Brahma appears from its flower.

Pala Indian art style from the eastern Indian dynasty of the same name.

Parvati Goddess and consort of Siva. Also known as Devi, Uma, etc.

Phnom Khmer for 'hill' or 'mount'.

Preah Khmer word for 'sacred', from the Sanskrit 'brah'.

Puranas The sacred Hindu texts, including the *Ramayana* and *Mahabharata*.

Rahu Demon whose body was cut by Vishnu's discus; responsible for eclipses by his attempts to eat the sun and the moon.

Rakshasa Demon.

Rakshini Female demon.

Rama One of the earthly incarnations of Vishnu and eponymous hero of the *Ramayana*.

Ramayana Major Hindu romantic epic tracing the efforts and adventures of Rama to recover his wife Sita, who was kidnapped by the demon Ravana. The Khmer version is the Ramker.

Ravana Multi-armed and -headed demon; the ruler of Lanka in the *Ramayana* epic.

Rig Veda The earliest Vedic sacred text, meaning 'Wisdom of the Verses', written about 1400 BC. Its principal myth is the struggle between the major Vedic god Indra and the dragon Vritra.

Rishi Hindu seer, ascetic or sage. Forerunners of the brahmins.

Saivite Pertaining to Siva.

Sampot Traditional Khmer garment: a cloth worn around the waist.

Sanskrit Ancient Indian language and script.

Sapta Matrikis 'Seven Divine Mothers'. They comprise Brahmi, Maheswari, Vaishnavi, Kaumari, Indrani, Varahi, Chamundi.

Sarasvati Female form of Brahma.

Sema Buddhist boundary stone.

Sesha *See* Ananta.

Siva One of the Hindu Trinity of gods; the God of Destruction, but also of rebirth.

Simha Lion.

Simhamukha literally 'lion face'. Similar to a *kala*, but with a lower jaw.

Sita Wife of Rama.

Skanda God of war.

Spean Bridge.

Srah Pond, basin.

Srei Khmer for 'woman' and 'women'.

Sri Alternative name for Lakshmi, wife of Vishnu. its general meaning is 'auspicious'.

Stele Upright slab bearing inscriptions.

Stung River.

Sugriva Monkey-king ally of Rama in the *Ramayana*.

Surya God of the sun, and one of the three principal gods in the *Rig Veda* (with Indra and Agni).

Tantric Developed form of Hinduism and Mahayana Buddhism in which magic features strongly.

Tara Monkey wife of Valin.

Theravada The traditional form of Buddhism (*see* Hinayana).

Thom Khmer for 'large', 'grand'.

Tilottama An *apsaras*.

Trailokyavijaya Literally 'victory of the three worlds'; name given to one of the major Mahayana Bodhisattvas.

Trijata Wife of Ravana's brother, Vibeksha.

Trimurti The Hindu trinity of gods: Brahma the Creator, Vishnu the Preserver and Siva the Destroyer.

Trivikrama Vishnu making the three steps.

Ucchaisaravas Magical horse that emerges from the Churning of the Sea of Milk; later appropriated by Indra.

Uma Siva's consort.

Umamahesvara Term describing the image of Siva and Uma together.

Ushnisha Protuberance on the head of Buddha, symbolising his all-encompassing knowledge.
Vahana Mount or vehicle of a god, such as Siva on Nandi, the bull.

Vajra Diamond, thunderbolt.

Vajrasattva One of the six 'meditation-Buddhas'.

Valmiki Composer of the *Ramayana*.

Vamana The *avatar*, or incarnation, of Vishnu as a dwarf.

Vara–mudra Gesture signifying benediction, in which the right hand is extended palm outwards.

Varaha The *avatar*, or incarnation, of Vishnu as a boar.

Varman, –varman Literallly 'chest-armour', and by extension 'protégé', 'protected by'.

Varuna Originally a universal deity, encompassing the sky, later to become a god of the ocean and rivers, riding the *makara*. The guardian of the West.

Vasudeva Father of Krishna.

Vasuki Name of the giant *naga* used by the gods and demons to churn the Sea of Milk.

Vayu God of air and wind, linked with Indra.

Vedas The four religious books that instruct Brahmanic ritual. The most famous is the *Rig Veda*, composed in the first millennium BC.

Vibishana Ravana's brother.

Vihara Temple building housing a Buddha image. 'Vihear' in Khmer.

Viradha A *rakshasa* who attempts to abduct Sita in the *Ramayana*.

Vishnu Member of the Hindu Trinity; the Preserver and Protector. A popular deity among worshippers, he manifests himself on earth in a variety of incarnations, or *avatars*.

Vishnuite Pertaining to Vishnu.

Vitarka–mudra Gesture of preaching and giving a sermon, performed with one hand or both by joining thumb and forefinger, palm held outwards.

Yaksha General term for demon.

Yakshi Female demon.

Yama God of Death and guardian of the South. Son of Surya. His mount is a water buffalo.

Yogini Mahayanic goddess associated with Vajrasattva.

Yuga One of the four ages in the world cycle according to Hinduism.

FURTHER READING

Briggs, L. P.
The Ancient Khmer Empire
Philadelphia, 1951

Chandler, D. P.
A History of Cambodia
Boulder, 1992

Chandler, D. P & Mabbett, I.
The Khmers
Oxford (UK) and
Cambridge (USA), 1995

Coedes, G.
The Indianized States of Southeast Asia
(trans. Cowing)
Honolulu, 1968

Dagens, B.
Angkor, Heart of an Asian Empire
London, 1995

Dumarcy, J.
Le Bayon. Histoire architecturale du temple
Paris, 1967

Freeman, M.
A Guide to Khmer Temples in Thailand and Laos
Bangkok, 1996

Glaize, M.
Les Monuments du groupe d'Angkor
Paris, 1993

Groslier, B-Ph. & Arthaud, J.
Angkor, Art and Civilisation
London, 1966

Jacques, C.
Angkor: Cities and Temples
Bangkok, 1997

Jessup, H. & Zephir, T. (eds)
Angkor et dix siecles d'art khmer
(Exhibition catalogue)
Paris, 1997

Moore, E. & Siribhaddra, S.
Palaces of the Gods: Khmer Art and Architecture in Thailand
Bangkok, 1992

Mouhot, H.
Travels in the Central Parts of Indochina
London, 1864, rep. Bangkok, 1986

Roveda, V
Khmer Mythology: Secret of Angkor
Bangkok, 1997

Zhou Daguan
The Customs of Cambodia
Bangkok, 1992

INDEX

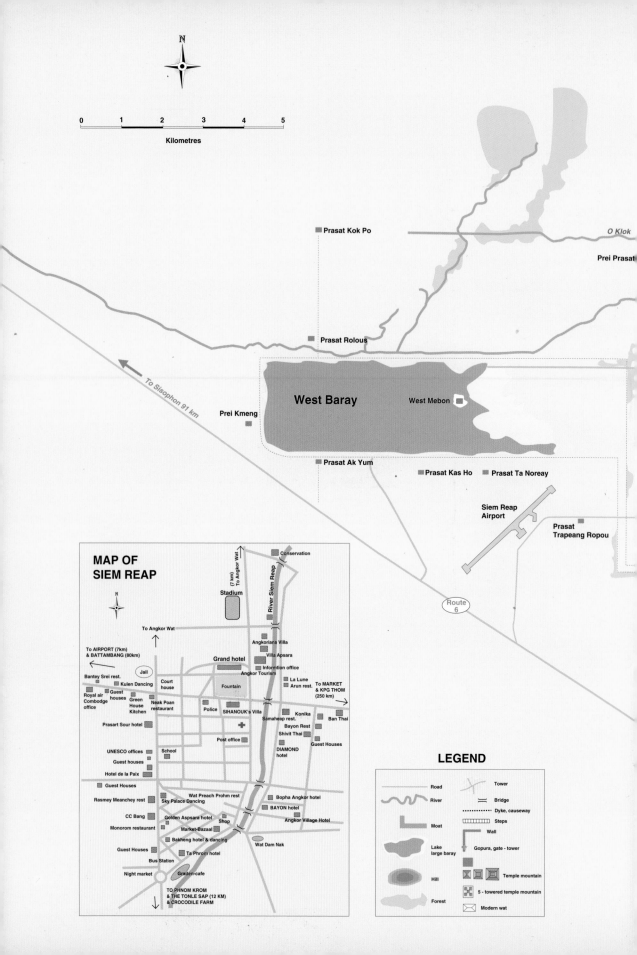

N

| 0 | 1 | 2 | 3 | 4 | 5 |

Kilometres

Prasat Kok Po

O Klok

Prei Prasat

To Sisophon 91 km

Prasat Rolous

West Baray

West Mebon

Prei Kmeng

Prasat Ak Yum

Prasat Kas Ho   Prasat Ta Noreay

Siem Reap
Airport

Prasat
Trapeang Ropou

Route
6

MAP OF
SIEM REAP

N

(7 km)
To Angkor Wat

Conservation

River Siem Reap

Stadium

To Angkor Wat

To AIRPORT (7km)
& BATTAMBANG (80km)

Angkoriana Villa

Villa Apsara

Grand hotel

Informtion office

Angkor Tourism

Jail

La Lune

Arun rest.

To MARKET
& KPG THOM
(250 km)

Bantey Srei rest.

Kulen Dancing

Court
house

Royal air
Combodge
office

Guest
houses

Green
House
Kitchen

Neak Poan
restaurant

Fountain

Police

SIHANOUK's Villa

Samaheap rest.

Konika

Ban Thai

Bayon Rest

Prasart Sour hotel

Shivit Thai

Guest Houses

Post office

DIAMOND
hotel

UNESCO offices

School

Guest houses

Hotel de la Paix

Guest Houses

Rasmey Meanchey rest.

Wat Preach Prohm rest

Sky Palace Dancing

Bopha Angkor hotel

BAYON hotel

CC Bang

Golden Aspsara hotel

Shop

Angkor Village Hotel

Monorom restaurant

Market-Bazaal

Bakheng hotel & dancing

Wat Dam Nak

Guest Houses

Ta Phrom hotel

Bus Station

Night market

Graden-cafe

TO PHNOM KROM
& THE TONLE SAP (12 KM)
& CROCODILE FARM

LEGEND

Road		Tower	
River		Bridge	
		Dyke, causeway	
Moat		Steps	
		Wall	
Lake
large baray		Gopura, gate - tower	
Hill		Temple mountain	
Forest		5 - towered temple mountain	
		Modern wat	